T0368184

The VROOMS of the FOOTHILLS

ADVENTURES OF MY CHILDHOOD

Other titles in the series
The VROOMS of the FOOTHILLS:

Pioneer Adventurers

The VROOMS of the FOOTHILLS

Volume 1

ADVENTURES OF MY CHILDHOOD

Bessie Vroom Ellis

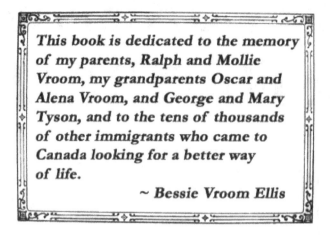

This book is dedicated to the memory
of my parents, Ralph and Mollie
Vroom, my grandparents Oscar and
Alena Vroom, and George and Mary
Tyson, and to the tens of thousands
of other immigrants who came to
Canada looking for a better way
of life.

~ Bessie Vroom Ellis

Order this book online at www.trafford.com
or email orders@trafford.com

Most Trafford titles are also available at major online book retailers.

Print information available on the last page.

ISBN: 978-1-5536-9840-1 (sc)

Trafford rev. 05/01/2019

 www.trafford.com

North America & international
toll-free: 1 888 232 4444 (USA & Canada)
fax: 812 355 4082

Evening, after the storm, southwest Alberta foothills.

CONTENTS

Acknowledgements   iv

Prologue   1
1   Riding When Very Young   5
2   Starting School, a Rough Ride   27
3   Daily Dangers of Ranch Life   47
4   My Four-Legged Playmates, the Sheep and Goats   67
5   Adventures with the Horses   89
6   Forty Miles on a Load of Poles, and Other Memorable Outings   107
7   Eating Minnows, and Other Childhood Adventures   137
8   A Savage Forest Fire, and Building a Cart   161
9   Killing a Grizzly Bear   179

Epilogue   197

Maps   199

References and Sources of Information   201

Appendix I   Glossary   203

Appendix II Index   227

About the Author   243

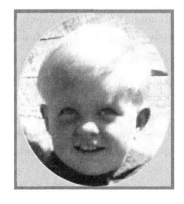

Acknowledgements

I wrote these stories down at the urging of and with the encouragement of my children over a period of several years. They had heard my remembrances many times and wanted to be able to pass the stories on to their children — my grandchildren. Writing these stories was also a way of keeping in touch with my grandchildren and passing on to them a written record of my childhood days spent on our family ranch in southwestern Alberta.

Every few months I would write a brief letter telling of the current news and activities in my life. Then I would write another story about when I was a child on my parents' ranch in the foothills southwest of Pincher Creek, Alberta, and enclose it with my letter. I made duplicate copies and mailed each successive letter and story to my four children and my sister Marion Vroom Grechman, who was younger than I was.

I would like to thank my children Edith Annand Smithies, Evelyn Annand Lailey, David Annand, and Jim Annand for their ongoing encouragement and support. I thank my brother, Donald Vroom, his first wife, Jacquie Rusch Vroom, and his second wife, Doreen Lund Vroom, for their help. I also thank my brother, the late Bill Vroom, his first wife, the late Joan White Vroom, and his second wife, Moe Swainger Vroom, for their help and advice.

I thank my brother-in-law, Mike Grechman, my cousins Adeline Cyr Robbins, Vera Cyr Gingras and Eugene Cyr, Robert and Isabel Vroom, and Ruby Peters Jaggernath, for their assistance. In addition, I thank Betty Annand Baker, Katherine Bruce, Heather Bruce Grace, George & Kay Kettles Hagglund, Alma "Jo" Ballantyne Johnson, Robin LaGrandeur, Elva Ballantyne McClelland, Frances Riviere McWhirter, Lorraine Riviere Pommier, Floyd & Evie Olson Riviere, John Russell, Adam "Dutch" and Hazel Truitt, and my good friend Joe Meade.

Thanks to so many friends for sharing their personal photos with me, and graciously allowing their use to illustrate my stories. Their contributions are greatly appreciated, and acknowledged individually in each photo caption.

If there are other friends and colleagues I have missed with my thanks, it is an omission of the head, not the heart. Readers who would like to contact me are invited to do so in care of Trafford Publishing.

PROLOGUE

This book tells my remembrances of how my parents, Ralph Vroom and Mollie Tyson Vroom, and we four children lived and thrived on our remote ranch in southwestern Alberta. We ranched in the foothills of the Rocky Mountains during the 1920s and the "Depression Years, the ten years of the 1930s up until the beginning of the Second World War.

My parents were very remarkable people. Ralph Vroom was the son of pioneers Oscar Vroom and Alena Munro Vroom of Beaver Mines. My mother, Mollie Tyson Vroom, was the daughter of early settlers in western Canada, George W. Tyson and Elizabeth Mary Brotherston Tyson of Fishburn, Alberta.

This book vividly recounts what life was like for us. We had no modern conveniences; we had to ride two and one-half miles to Beaver Mines to use a telephone. These stories are about various incidents and occasions that I remember from my childhood. Most of the experiences described are my own, though some of the material was also part of the oral lore of our family. Old neighbours and friends also helped with some of the details.

Ralph Vroom

In the beginning, because I first wrote the stories in the order in which I remembered them, the more exciting incidents were in the initial several chapters. After I had told my most thrilling experiences, I began to record everyday family activities on our ranch. I told how my parents and grandparents came west to settle in Alberta in the early 1900s, and explained the work we did on a pioneer ranch a day's journey from the nearest town.

Eventually, the chapters expanded to become my childhood memoirs, and then to a remembrance of a segment of social history. This book tells about the era during which I was a child. Most of the chapters can be read as stories in themselves, independent of the other chapters.

I have tried to express how I felt as a small, female child when certain events happened in

1

my life, and how proud I felt of my everyday achievements.

My hope, now, is that many other people and their grandchildren will have the opportunity to read my story and find out how a lifelong habit of positive thinking can be fostered during childhood years.

Mollie Tyson Vroom

My parents' families were immigrants to Canada, who, like other immigrants, came to Canada for various reasons. Some people wanted farm or ranchland of their own. Some were looking for adventure. Some just wanted a job where they would earn a decent wage. All immigrants wanted more personal freedom and better opportunities for their children. Most immigrants to Canada achieved their goals.

My mother, her parents and brother emigrated from Ambleside in the Lake District of England in 1914, just prior to the so-called Great War. Grandpa Tyson had driven a mail coach in Ambleside. They found work on a farm in the Fishburn District - a farming area east of Pincher Creek. A few years later they purchased their own land. While my mother's family came to Canada as part of the mass migration from Europe to Canada in the early part of the twentieth century, my dad's family had a much more adventurous history. About 1970, Winnifred MacFarlane, a career civil servant in Ottawa, ON, compiled an unpublished document entitled "Vroom, Holland: An incomplete genealogy of the first known Vrooms in Holland."

My dad's ancestors, who were mostly Dutch, moved from Holland to the Dutch colony in New Amsterdam on the southern tip of Manhattan Island, USA, in 1638. Some of my early Vroom ancestors lived in Ireland for a period of time hundreds of years ago.

The Vroom family descendants lived and thrived in the New England area until the American Revolution. In 1786, however, two sons, Peter and John Vroom, emigrated from the United States. They were accompanied by a number of other families, and settled in Clementsport and Annapolis Royal in the Annapolis Valley area of Nova Scotia in eastern Canada.

These settlers were called United Empire Loyalists (UEL) because they remained loyal to the British king, George III, after the American Revolution which lasted from 1763 until after the Revolutionary War (1775–83). As a reward for their loyalty, the English gave these settlers tracts of land. Although many descendants of Peter and John Vroom - UEL all - still live in Nova Scotia, not all of the Vroom family remained in Nova Scotia.

My Grandfather Oscar came west in 1902, and worked for various ranchers west of Pincher Creek. In 1904, my Grandmother Alena Vroom uprooted the family, my dad and his two brothers and one sister, and travelled west by train to join Oscar. The Vroom family homestead was in the foothills southwest of Pincher Creek.

My dad attended a one-room country school with children of all ages and grade levels until he was old enough to go out to work.

My dad, then a dashing young cowboy, met my mother at a dance at Utopia School, a one-roomed country school near my mother's home at Fishburn, Alberta. Dad had heard of my mother's beauty, and, when they met, he immediately fell in love with my mother, and she with him. They were married about four years later and started an adventurous marriage that spanned the Great Depression, the Second World War and a generation beyond.

My parents had four children. My brother Donald Vroom is two and one-half years older I am, my brother Bill Vroom was three and one-half years younger, my sister, Marion Vroom Grechman, was nearly eleven years younger than I was. It is with loving memories of, and deep appreciation for, my parents that I write these memoirs. I understand full well that many other families had similar experiences. I hope they enjoy these remembrances, too.

Alena Munro Vroom

For easier reading, I have divided my childhood memoirs into more than one volume. This is volume 1.

Chapter 1 tells how and why I learned to ride horseback by myself when I was less than three years old. It also tells how, when I was as young as four and one-half years of age, my riding ability enabled me to help my parents. This chapter also talks about the neighbourliness of people in those days.

Chapter 2 tells about some early school days experiences of my older brother, Don, and me. I started school on my sixth birthday in early January and, along with Don, rode horseback four and one-half miles to a country school in southwestern Alberta.

Chapter 3 points out some of the everyday dangers of living on a ranch.

Chapter 4 tells about some of the fun that I had, as a young child, playing with the sheep and goats on our ranch.

Chapter 5 tells some of the everyday-type of adventures, and some special adventures, that I had involving the horses.

Chapter 6 tells about the time that I travelled forty miles to my grandparents' farm sitting on a load of poles, and some of the memorable horseback-riding outings. Chapter 7 tells about some of the adventures my brother Bill and I had the summer that Mom was Down East. Bill stayed with Cy and Phyllis Truitt, and I stayed with various neighbours. I ran away from Mr. and Mrs. Frank Holmes and then went to stay with Alfie and Alice Primeau north of the Spread Eagle Stampede Grounds.

I spent the last part of the summer with Mrs. Nellie Gladstone Riviere and her family. While there, I became friendly with *Nichemoos* the widow of Kootenai Brown.

Chapter 8 tells how Don and I made a cart, and I trained a team of our ponies to pull it, during the summer of 1936. At the time, our dad was away helping to fight a savage forest fire in the Castle River Forest Reserve.

Chapter 9 is my grizzly bear story. It tells about the time, when I was only nine years old, I rode my pony along with my dad to a spot deep in the Rocky Mountains. There my dad had trapped a marauding grizzly bear. Dad shot and killed the bear from close range, as I stood mesmerized close behind him, my hands resting on his hips.

There are detailed descriptions of some of the physical features of our ranch, and of the surrounding countryside. I also have described certain areas that had designated uses.

In addition, several hand-drawn maps help the reader form a mental image of the layout of our ranch, and of the general area where we lived. These maps will help the reader to follow my written accounts of various events in my childhood. The maps also show the location of the homes of some of the ranchers who lived in the Beaver Mines and Gladstone Valley districts when I was a child.

Elizabeth Mary and George Tyson

Oscar Vroom

A number of snapshots, which show us children engaged in various everyday activities, are included in this book. The snapshots show the appearance of some of the physical features described in this document and shown on the various maps. To aid the reader, a Glossary and an Index, are included at the end of Volume 1.

RIDING WHEN VERY YOUNG

My first experience around horses was as a fetus in my mother's womb. My parents lived on their isolated ranch in southwestern Alberta at that time. Travel by horseback or by wagon in summertime, or by horse drawn sled in winter, was the only choice for several months each year.

There was rain, sleet and mud in the "spring," the growing season of the year, and in the "fall," or harvest time. From late fall to springtime there were often deep snowdrifts. This made riding a saddle horse[1] the most practical mode of transportation.

My mother was an able horsewoman, and often rode her saddle horse about two and one-half miles to Beaver Mines and back for the mail and a few groceries. Beaver Mines, is a small hamlet southwest of Pincher Creek, Alberta, that serves the ranch and farm families of that area.

My older brother, Donald, who was a lively two and one-half year old child when I was born, would "double-deck" with Mom, happily riding behind her saddle.

Bessie Is Born

Angels were with my mother and me when I was born on a frigid day, January 8, 1927. It so happened that the road up to our place was not totally blocked with snow at the time. Mr. Madorski, a wool and hide buyer from Calgary, Alberta and a long time friend of the family's, knew that my mother was expecting a second baby some time in January. He had come to our ranch almost once a month since September - no doubt at the urging of his kindly wife.

"Thank Heaven you have come," my mother greeted Mr. Madorski that day. "I think my baby is due very soon."

"Pack some things, Mrs. Vroom, and I'll take you into Pincher Creek to the hospital," Mr. Madorski volunteered. (That was the old St. Vincent's Hospital).

"I have arranged with my parents at Fishburn to look after Don while I am in hospital having my new baby," said my mother. "Could he come along with us to stay with me at Mrs. Halton's until my father, George Tyson, can come into Pincher Creek and pick him up?"

"Certainly," answered Mr. Madorski. "He's a fine young lad, too."

"I'll be fine, Ralph," Mom assured my dad, who was beginning to worry about how he would get Mom to the hospital if the roads became impassable.

Mom and Don drove with Mr. Madorski to Pincher Creek and then Mr. Madorski went on about his business. Next day my Grandfather Tyson came to pick Don up.

"You be a good boy, Don," Mom said to my older brother as he left for my grandparents' farm with Grandpa. "Granny and Grandpa will take good care of you; maybe I'll bring you home a baby sister."

And so it was that I was safely born that lucky January day. And sure enough, too, Mom did bring home a baby sister. I thrived and grew with my parents' loving care.

Until my birth, my mother had ridden many miles with me in her womb. Right after I was born, my mother could not get out very much because of the cold, snowy weather. As soon as the weather warmed up in the spring Mom was out on her saddle horse carrying me in a sack hung on the saddle horn with Don riding double-deck.

This is my brother Don over at Uncle Harold and Aunt Ruby Vroom's ranch in 1927. Don, nearly three years old, is wearing his straw hat.

Don loved me dearly. When one of the neighbours asked him, 'How do you like your baby sister, Don?' he replied wistfully, "She's tiny and toot!"

Nearly 80 years later Don and I are still "best friends." I cannot remember us ever having a serious quarrel. When we were children on the ranch we trusted each other implicitly. In adulthood we have always been supportive and nonjudgmental of one another. We visit each other's homes only occasionally but keep in touch regularly by telephone, email and regular mail. Author's collection.

A Saddle Horse for the Chase

When she was in her early twenties, my mother developed "rheumatoid arthritis," a disease of the joints in which they become inflamed and swollen. During the initial swelling period the joints are very painful and sensitive to the lightest touch.

Eventually, the joints calcify and become immovable, severely restricting the sufferer's limb movements. The affected fingers and toes become gnarled and twisted, the knees and hips become permanently bent at right angles; and the person's backbone is no longer flexible.

Nowadays, strong medication helps alleviate the pain and swelling of rheumatoid arthritis, but there are serious side effects, not the least of which are stomach ulcers. Modern surgical practices enable surgeons to replace arthritic joints with artificial joints made of space-age materials; pain is relieved and joints are straightened to restore a degree of movement.

None of these treatments were available to my mother. Even if treatment had been available we could not have afforded the medical costs. There was no social safety net and no medicare or pharmacare. Those were tough times, financially and physically.

Despite her physical afflictions my mother maintained a cheerful disposition and a positive attitude throughout her life; moreover, she was a very practical woman. Thus, Mom made whatever adaptations she had to make in order to carry out her daily tasks in our ranch house, which had no modern conveniences. My mother faced life with great courage. She was ingenious at figuring out ways to do things in spite of her pain and limited movements.

In addition, Mom never complained about her physical pain, and she never used her situation to control us children, like using guilt to coerce us into doing things. Truly, my mother was a remarkable woman.

Don and I in 1927 as we sat beside a small bush over at Uncle Harold and Aunt Ruby Vroom's ranch. I am about six months old. In the background are the hills north east of Uncle Harold's. Also shown are parts of some of their early ranch buildings. Author's collection.

In the spring and summer of 1927, my mother was faced with the reality of a nearly three-year-old child, Don, who had motorized feet. We had a large house yard with luxurious grass growing in it. The yard was enclosed with wire fence, which hardly even slowed Don down. Mom was busy with me as a baby, and with the many tasks that had to be done in running a ranch home - baking bread, hand washing clothes, mending socks and torn clothes, and making new clothes.

During the good weather of spring and summer and into early fall, when Don could play outside frequently, Mom kept a watchful eye on him. She would look out the kitchen door every few minutes to make sure Don was still within eyesight.

Sometimes, however, Don would have scrambled over the fence and "high-tailed it," as fast as he could until he was often out of sight.

"Yoo-hoo, Don!" Mom called. "Where are you? Yoo-hoo!" If she got no response, Mom had to go looking for Don on foot.

Mom's feet were already painfully swollen from her arthritis, so she could not walk very well under the best conditions. Walking over rough pastureland was almost impossible for her.

"Ralph," Mom remarked in a problem solving tone of voice to my dad one day, "something has to be done about Don; I just can't keep up with him. He gets over that fence so quickly and runs so fast that I can't catch him, and my feet are really too sore to go chasing him; I'm afraid he'll get away on me altogether one of these days."

"I'll tell you what," Dad, equally ingenious, replied, "I'll keep a horse in the yard for you, saddled and ready to go, and you'll always be able to catch Don if he does get away on you."

"All right, Ralph," agreed Mom, hoping for the best; she was always a very plucky person. Thus, there was almost always a saddle horse grazing in our house yard.

The saddle horse ready and waiting idea was a great success. Whenever Don did get away on Mom, she got on her trusty horse and rode after him.

My First Playground - the Ranch Yard

The "little creek", one of the enduring landmarks of my ranch home, played a significant role in my childhood. It was an unnamed stream, which started from a fresh water spring that gurgled to the surface in the northeast corner of the little pasture. The little creek ran west along the bottom of the side hill, which was located just northeast of the barn, then under a culvert and through a rocked-up channel underneath the root cellar.

The little creek then ran along the north side of the house yard for a ways then went out into the barnyard, where it filled the barnyard water trough. Located shortly after the creek passed under the root cellar, this water trough was just outside the house yard fence. Dad had fashioned it by hewing out a large log.

Dad used that part of the house yard fence as a frame to make a small dam in the little creek. Water from this dam ran into the water trough through a two-inch iron pipe.

Making an elongated S curve, the little creek wound outside the house yard fence, passed the barnyard water trough, and flowed underneath a little culvert between the house and the barn. It completed the S curve by looping back through the northwest corner of our house yard, and then out to run underneath a culvert under the road allowance.

The little creek then went on down through our west quarter section meandering through thick willows and through the Gus Gamache, A. Wojtyla, and M. Prozak quarter sections.

After flowing a mile and one-half, the little creek emptied into Beaver Mines Creek which flowed into the Castle River, and thence into the Oldman River, the South Saskatchewan River, and finally into the mighty Saskatchewan River, joining waters which eventually flowed into Hudson Bay through the Churchill River system.

The "household well" was located just inside the house yard fence, about 100 feet from the kitchen door. We pumped water from it by pumping the handle of an iron water pump up and down.

When I was about eight years, our Dad built the little dam. We packed buckets of water from the little dam for plants in the vegetable garden that was beside the house.

The little dam was a small dam that Dad built in the little creek in the northwest corner of the house yard. A small pond formed behind this obstruction of boards, rocks and soil.

As children, we also played in and on the little dam. We called the small, semi-circle patch of grass between the fence and the water "the island." To get to that patch of grass, we had to cross over the little creek on tiny bridge made with a short piece of a 2-inch x 12-inch plank. We sometimes had a picnic lunch on the island, pretending to be at some faraway place.

When the little creek dried up in the summer time, we had to pump water from the household well into the barnyard water trough. Alternately, we had to take our saddle horses and workhorses[2] about one-quarter mile to another water trough "down at the spring." The spring had a good year round flow.

The "barnyard" was a U-shaped grassy area that was rimmed by the little corral, the barn and the gate to the big corral, the blacksmith shop, the carpenter shop and the north side of the house yard.

The "little corral" was a pole enclosure that was located west of the back of the barn. It was large enough to hold a small herd of horses, and small enough that a cowboy, or cowgirl, could lasso a bronco in it.

The "big corral" was a large-sized pole enclosure located outside the house yard. Another smaller corral that was located right behind the barn, and between the barn and the big garden, separated the little corral from the big corral.

The "big garden" was a plot of land fenced off from the little pasture. It was directly north of the corrals behind the barn. We called the garden on the side hill behind the barn the "big garden" to distinguish it from the "little garden," which was beside the house.

In the big garden, we grew larger vegetables for winter storage, like turnips, parsnips, carrots, beets and horseradish. We also grew vegetables for summer use, like green peas, green beans, broad beans, spinach, Swiss chard, and other vegetables. There was a rhubarb patch in one corner of the big garden.

The "little pasture" figured prominently in my happiness as a child. I spent many happy hours chasing goats and horses there. It was an eighty-acre parcel of land located in the east quarter of my parents' ranch. A page wire fence[3] separated the little pasture from the rest of the quarter, on which hay was grown for winter-feed for our livestock. After haying season, the milk cows and the horses we were using every day grazed on the land not in the little pasture.

The little pasture contained a couple of grassy hillsides that were strewn with many small and medium-sized rocks. The rest of the little pasture was covered with "woodland" that included saskatoon and chokecherry bushes, willows and small poplar trees.

There were animal trails throughout the woodland. A couple of dozen scraggly fir trees grew in the northeast corner of the little pasture, on a rocky hillside that was really part of the big hill. The house yard, barnyard, and corrals were small areas cut out of the little pasture and separated from the pasture by pole fences. The sheep and goats and a few horses grazed in the little pasture during the spring, summer, and fall months.

The "side hill", on which we often played or chased the goats, was a south-sloping, rock-strewn, grassy hillside located in the little pasture. It was northeast of the barn and extended from north to northeast of the big corral. It was adjacent to and east of the big garden.

The "big hill", where our horses and goats often ranged, was a high hill that was situated about one-half mile north of our ranch buildings. It was located in a fenced-in area of about a half section of leased pastureland that was fairly rocky. Small poplar trees covered the big hill with a few firs here and there. The big hill was also known as "Bear Mountain.

We often chased horses on "trails over the big hill," that is, on paths that the horses followed that ran either around to the east or west end of the highest part of the big hill. To get the horses into the little corral we had to make sure they headed down the lane. I often rode at break-neck speed across the rocky patch of hillside at the top of the lane so that the herd I was chasing did not take the alternate trail that lead back over the big hill.

The goats, too, ranged up on the big hill, from early summer until fall. One of my summer jobs was to chase the goats in daily so we could milk them. They, however, had to be chased in on foot, an arduous task that required a good deal of stamina.

"The lane" was crucial to all our horse-hunting forays. It was a narrow strip of land about 400 yards long with a wire fence on either side. The lane ran along the west side of the big garden, which was behind the barn at the west end of the side hill. The trail, which ran down the lane, and connected the big hill area with the corrals by the barn, was located on Mom and Dad's "home quarter", or "the east quarter," the land on which our house was located.

Riding Alone - My First Saddle Horse

Dad and Mom kept me amused the summer I learned to walk by making house yard pets out of a couple of "kids," that is, baby goats. I played happily with my baby goats all summer long.

When I had a baby goat to play with, Mom knew I was safe. Eventually, however, I tired of just sitting with a baby goat, or following it around the yard. I wanted to ride a goat. The ones we had were too small to ride, so I had to wait, but not for very long.

One day, Dad came home leading a tall, placid smoky buckskin goat with a white stripe, a "blaze," on his nose. "Smoky buckskin" is a yellowish-gray colour with a tinge of grey-blue in it, so we named the new goat "Smokey."

"I think Bess will be able to ride this fellow," Dad explained to Mom when she looked at him enquiringly. We can lead him around to get her used to riding Smokey. Then she can ride him herself."

At first Mom would lead Smokey along at a slow walk with a strap around his neck while I balanced precariously on his back. Don would walk on the other side to help make sure I didn't fall off and hurt myself. It wasn't long before I could ride Smokey all by myself.

By the next summer, when I was two and one-half years old, I was no longer satisfied to ride around on Smokey. I could almost keep up to Don who was nearly five by then. If Don went somewhere without me, I went to look for him. Then Mom had to look for me.

My favourite toy when I was little was a wooden rocking horse, but I tired of it. "I want to ride a real horse," I declared one day when I was three.

Finally my mother could take it no longer. "Ralph," she said determinedly, "you'll have to do something about Bess. I just can't keep track of her. She wants to be out with the horses all the time."

"How about if we got her a horse of her own to ride?" my dad queried, suddenly struck with an inspiration.

"Well," agreed Mom, "it's worth a try. If we got a tame horse and put Bess on him and then tied the horse up at least I'd know where she was."

MAP 1 *The map, "House yard, barnyard and corrals, 1936" shows details of the Ralph and Mollie Vroom Ranch near Beaver Mines. Shown are: our ranch house, shack, outhouse, coal shed and woodpile, root cellar, house yard garden, little creek, little dam, barn, barnyard water trough, little corral, big corral, big garden, side hill, goat house, blacksmith shop and carpenter shop. Map hand drawn by the author.*

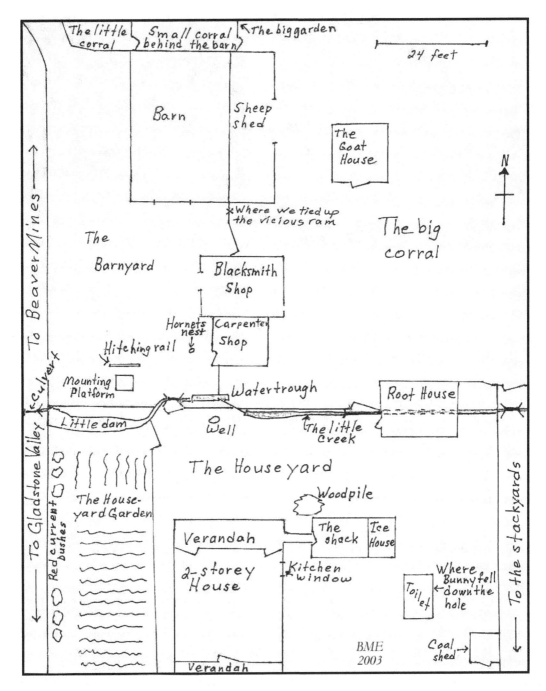

MAP 1   HOUSE YARD, BARNYARD AND CORRALS, 1936

In this 1928 picture of Don and me, we are standing in a wagon box with "Smokey." I am 1 ½ years old and am yelling with excitement. Author's collection.

"I think old 'Paddy' (a full-sized saddle horse about 15 hands tall) would be just fine for her. He's well broken and is a very steady horse," Dad stated. "Once we put Bess on top of him, she couldn't get off by herself. And she wouldn't be getting under any of the other horses' feet. And I'll be out there working in the blacksmith shop or carpenter shop, or somewhere around the barnyard, if she gets into trouble." I would be in plain view if Mom looked out the kitchen door, too.

Riding to Beaver Mines by Myself

Even when I was a little child, I was a "wheedler". I tried to persuade my parents to let me do rather adventurous things that may have involved some or quite a bit of danger. I was full of energy and did not like to be fenced in. It wasn't long before I was thinking up another scheme to get further from home.

My mother, who was a very wise woman, and somewhat of an adventurer herself, tried to stifle neither my energy nor my creativity. Sometimes she redirected me, but only in an indirect way. Mom once told me, long after I was grown up: "I used to try to figure out what you wanted to do, and then ask you to do that to get you in the habit of obeying me."

Because of the remoteness of our ranch, a lot of the work on and travelling out from the ranch was done either by saddle horse or by team and wagon. My dad was one of the best horsemen in the country. He was a real old-time cowboy, having got his first experience with horses looking after his mother's horses when they first moved west from Nova Scotia to southwestern Alberta in the early 1900s. At first I was content to sit on Paddy out in the barnyard. Soon, however, I was riding Paddy around in the barnyard with someone leading him. When Mom or Dad rode to Beaver Mines for the mail I begged to go until they gave in.

When I started riding Paddy he would go basically wherever he wanted to go or where he was used to going because I was not strong enough to make him do anything else.

This 1928 picture shows 1½ year old me, sitting on "Smokey." Mom is steadying me while Don looks on. Goats are affectionate animals - Smokey is nuzzling Mom.

The swelling in Mom's wrists and knuckles, a symptom of the early stage of rheumatoid arthritis, was already showing at this time.

I often rode my saddle horse hunting for horses along the rocky trails that ran along the "big hill", upper mid-left in the photo. Once I'd found the herd, I rode quietly around them, then let out a "whoop" to head them toward the home corral. Sometimes the horses detoured through thick brush and I had to follow them.

Once I got the horses on the trail I kept them on the run. The horses came over the crest of the big hill and down the south side on the gallop. In order to prevent the horses from circling back, I had to keep right on their tails - and be prepared to ride my horse on the full gallop across the rocky area at the top of the side hill should the herd decide they did not want to be corralled that day. Mrs. Mabel (Edward) Bruce photo, Author's collection.

However, by the time I was four and one-half years old I felt confident that I could ride Paddy to the store and post office at Beaver Mines all by myself. I was just waiting for a chance to prove myself.

One week we had some extra people for lunch and I overheard my mother remark, "We're out of bread, Ralph, I don't have any for lunch tomorrow." Usually Mom made her own bread; seldom did we have the treat of a loaf of "baker's bread," or store-bought bread.

That summer I was four and one-half years old, Mom was pregnant - with my brother Bill, as it turned out. She was not as able to get around by saddle horse as well as she had been able to on previous summers. Besides, she had both Don and me to look after and keep track of!

"I can't get away right now, Mollie," Dad stated.

Eagerly I piped up, full of self-importance, "I'll go, Mom."

My dad offered me support. To my delight, he stated, "I think you could go to Beaver on

Paddy for a few groceries, Bess."

"Well, I don't know, Ralph…." Mom hesitated, considering the possibilities.

"Pshaw, Mommy!" Dad interjected using his pet name for my mother. "Bess'll be all right. She's been to Beaver lots of times with both of us. Besides, Paddy knows the way."

"Well, all right," my mother agreed, "if you think she'll be all right, Ralph."

To me Dad remarked, "Make sure you give Paddy his head all the way to Beaver, Bess. But don't let him stop and turn around for home half way there. We don't want Paddy to get 'spoiled.'"

In this 1928 snapshot I am on our rocking horse, my favourite toy as a toddler. Mom is steadying me, while Don sits beside Mom, looking angelic.

I inherited my dad's love of horses and both my parents' spirit of adventure and persistence in doing a task, however hard it was. Whenever Dad was going riding, which usually meant hunting down a herd of horses that had strayed off our leased range land onto the property of one of our neighbours, I begged to go with him.

The spring that I was four years old I regularly went riding with my Dad. Sometimes we came home well after dark and I was so tired that my whole body ached, but I dared not complain, lest he not take me on the next outing. Mrs. Mabel (Edward) Bruce photo, Author's collection.

My mother watched with a certain amount of concern as I headed off on my mission; I was sure that I would have no trouble making the trip. And I was right. Paddy was so used to making the trip that he went quite willingly; I hardly had to steer him at all. He knew exactly where he was going.

My only problem arose when I had to get back onto Paddy after having dismounted to go into the store and post office to get my few groceries and the mail. At that time Dad had only regular-sized "saddle horses," which stood 14 or 15 hands tall and were used to go places on horseback. I was so small, and Paddy was so tall, that I could not get onto him from the ground. At home I would get on Paddy from the barn-step.

At Beaver Mines the only place high enough for me to get onto Paddy was the platform that ran along the front of the store. At first Paddy shied away from this new mounting station, but after a few times he became accustomed to the store platform. When I was ready to leave the store, I would untie Paddy from the hitching rail[4] and lead him over to the store platform.

Then I would go up onto the store platform using the four steps at either end, and get Paddy positioned parallel to the platform. Making sure he was standing still, I placed my foot in one stirrup. Then holding onto the saddle horn I clambered into the saddle.

I am on "Paddy" in this 1930 picture of 3½ year-old me. In the background is the tall gate into the big corral, the goat house, the side hill, and the big hill. Author's collection.

One of the first saddles that I rode was an old army saddle with adult length stirrups. When I rode Paddy my feet did not reach the stirrups. I just used them to help me get onto Paddy and then rode with my feet dangling down. A few years later, when my legs got longer, Dad used his saddle making skills to shorten the stirrup leathers of a full sized saddle so that I could put my feet in the stirrups as I sat in the saddle.

The Beaver Mines Store and Post Office

After my first successful solo ride to Beaver Mines, I regularly went for the mail and a few things from the small Beaver Mines General Store, which also housed the post office. George Ballantyne was the postmaster. Mrs. Ballantyne and their daughters, Elva and Alma, helped with both the store and the post office.

The mail was brought out from Pincher Creek on what we called the "stage." Mr. Melvin

Cain was our mailman all during my childhood.

In the summer time Mr. Cain drove a team and buggy. To break his 15-mile trip, according to information in the book *"prairie grass to mountain pass": History of the Pioneers of Pincher Creek and District,* Mr. Cain changed teams about halfway, at the home Fred Link, then came on to Beaver Mines. On the way back to Pincher Creek he changed back to his original team and continued on.

In the wintertime, Mr. Cain had a novel arrangement. He drove a team and sleigh, but he had a sort of wooden "shack" built to fit on top of the sleigh to protect him during the coldest weather. There was an oblong peep hole in the front of the shack, through which Mr. Cain threaded the team's lines. The horses knew the route by heart, so needed very little guidance.

People could "catch the mail stage" and, for a small fare, ride into Pincher Creek and back when they had a doctor's appointment, for instance. They would have to stay in Pincher Creek at least two nights before the next stage came again. Kindly people there rented rooms at a reasonable rate.

When I was a little child, Mr. and Mrs. George Ballantyne operated the post office. Mr. Ballantyne always looked stern to me and I was a little afraid of him. But Mrs. Ballantyne was a very kindly lady and always treated me respectfully.

On mail days people, mostly men, from a radius of about eight miles from the store would meet at the post office and discuss the local news, visiting while the mail was being sorted. As a child I got to know all these people, many of who were immigrants from central Europe. When I was out riding with Dad, often looking for a small herd of horses that had strayed from our regular range, I met most of the women and children, too. Later, I went to school with some of those children.

The Beaver Mines dances, put on two or three times a year by the "Women's Institute", an organization for farm women, were also great community gathering places, and were lots of fun for "us kids." The Women's Institute, to which my mother belonged, met once a month at Beaver Mines.

One of the men who were generally in the group at the post office visiting and waiting for the mail to be sorted was Billy Eddy. He had a "bay window," that is, a large stomach.

Mr. Eddy's big stomach fascinated me. Every mail day I would examine it, trying not to stare too hard. One day I could resist the temptation no longer. I walked up to Mr. Eddy, put my arms as far around his middle as I could and remarked in an awe-struck voice, "My! Your mommy must feed you well!"

My remark, heard by everyone in the small room, "brought down the house". The assembled crowd of people broke into gales of laughter.

I was embarrassed by the sudden attention, but jovial Mr. Eddy was not the least bit offended. He smiled down at small me, and stated in a firm voice, "Yes, she does, Bessie." His kindness ended my embarrassment.

The next time Dad and I called on Mr. and Mrs. Eddy, he recounted the story, and everyone had another good laugh about it.

Calling on Mrs. Ted Bruce, an Artist

One of my mother's close friends was Mrs. Mabel (Edward) Bruce, an artist who lived near the Beaver Mines Store and Post Office. Mrs. Bruce was a genteel English woman, and a very kind soul. Some years earlier she had moved to Canada with her husband and three sons, and had settled near Beaver Mines. Mr. and Mrs. Bruce always had fat, well-groomed saddle horses and a well-kept team of workhorses for farm work. They also kept geese.

I didn't like the geese very much because they would "hiss-s-s" at me and chase me if I was walking through the Bruces' barnyard, which I often did while Mom was visiting Mrs. Bruce.

Because I often went there with Mom, Paddy would go to Mrs. Bruce's when I wanted him to. So sometimes Mom had me take a note to Mrs. Bruce. I didn't know what was in the note, but, as we had no telephone on our ranch at that time, it was my mother's only way to get a message to Mrs. Bruce.

To get to Mrs. Bruce's I had to open a barbed wire fence gate and get back on Paddy again. There was no barn-step or platform, so I had to lead him up beside the fence, climb carefully onto the fence, put one foot in the saddle stirrup, and clamber back on. Looking back, that was a very dangerous maneuver. It was lucky Paddy was well broken or I could not have managed.

Mrs. Bruce was a gifted artist. She was especially talented with watercolours and used to let me watch her paint. Mrs. Bruce hand-painted all her Christmas cards. They were lovely. And she always gave me tea and cookies whenever I visited her.

Mrs. Bruce's painting intrigued me. I loved to stand and watch her paint delicate pictures on her small cards. Mrs. Bruce would dip the very tip of her extra-fine paintbrush gently into a tiny pot of liquid gold paint. Then she would carefully highlight the edges of some parts of the pictures. The cards on the following page are charming examples of Mrs. Bruce's artwork.

One time I went on my own to visit Mrs. Bruce. After Mrs. Bruce had given me tea she kept waiting for me to produce my usual note. Of course, I had no note. Finally she asked, "Do you have a note from your mother, Bessie?"

"No," I replied, "I just came to visit you, Mrs. Bruce."

Mrs. Bruce looked a little surprised, but did not scold me. After we finished our tea, she had one of her sons let me out the lower gate, and I was on my way home. The "lower gate," was a gate located straight down the hill from Mrs. Bruce's house — not the gate by the store and post office.

"Where have you been, Bessie," inquired my mother anxiously when I finally arrived home.

"I visited Mrs. Bruce," I declared, "and she gave me tea and some cookies."

"Did you remember your manners and thank her, Bess?" my mother checked.

"Yes, I did," I replied happily, hoping that I was "off the hook," that is, that I was not going to get a scolding for not coming straight home. I knew that I was supposed to go straight home after I had gone to the store or post office and not to dawdle along the way, unless Mom specifically asked me to see Mrs. Bruce.

"Bess," my mother explained to make sure I knew the seriousness of my actions, "you

These are cards hand-painted by Mrs. Ted Bruce of Beaver Mines in the 1930s. I loved to stand and watch Mrs. Bruce while she painted. She used real gold leaf paint to highlight her pictures. Photos by Edith Annand Smithies of Author's collection.

know that when I send you to the store for something you are supposed to come straight home. I know how long it should take to get to Beaver and back; if you don't get home when I expect you, I start to worry that something might have happened to you."

"I'm sorry, Mommy," I said contritely. "I won't do it again." I knew in my heart that if I did pull that stunt again my mother would send me over to the blacksmith shop, or to wherever my dad was working at the time, and my dad would give me "a talking to," a stern scolding. If my offence were serious enough to warrant sterner action my dad would turn me over his knee and give me a hand spanking.

Mom was a skilled amateur artist. She shared Mrs. Bruce's interest in painting and liked to use pastels or watercolours when she was young.

This Indian chief in full headdress is one of the many pictures that my mother painted while she was a patient in the Perley Rehabilitation Centre, Ottawa, ON, from about 1964 to her death on November 6, 1966. She did them so skillfully that there was no ridge between the colours. Mom's paintings looked as if she had done them free hand. The Perley Rehabilitation Centre is now called the Perley and Rideau Veterans' Health Centre. Courtesy Evelyn Annand Lailey, E. Lailey collection.

Years later, while she was a patient in the Perley Rehabilitation Centre in Ottawa, Ontario, my mother painted a number of paint-by-number pictures using oil paints. Upon my mother's death, my brothers, sister and I sadly divided up Mom's paintings. They arc lovingly and proudly displayed in our homes.

Visiting Mrs. Frank Holmes and Mrs. Elsie Belle Crosbie Joyce

I also liked to visit two other friends of my mother's from time to time, Mrs. Holmes and Mrs. Joyce. They knew my mother from " Women's Institute meetings and other community events.

Mr. and Mrs. Holmes owned what we referred to as the "Number One Coal Mine." It was located about one mile from Beaver Mines. They also ran a grocery store at Beaver Mines.

Mrs. Joyce was the daughter of early settlers in the Beaver Mines area, the Crosbies. My dad always referred to the buildings located next to the Gilles Curray buildings as "the Crosbie place."

When I was six or seven, Mrs. Joyce lived at Beaver Mines in a house behind the Holmes' store. I often visited her when I visited Mrs. Holmes, either on a weekend when I went to Beaver Mines for the mail, or when I was staying with Mrs. Holmes on a weekend or during the summer holidays.

I liked to ride the little trail that ran from the Beaver Mines Store and Post Office to Mrs. Holmes' cheerful home. The trail ran through a grove of trees and across a little stream, where there was water only in the springtime. I often visited Mrs. Holmes, who was my Godmother, and her neighbour Mrs. Joyce, a long-time family friend. They always seemed glad to see me and gave me milk and cookies.

Mr. and Mrs. Holmes had a small selection of groceries in one end of the building. Their living quarters, a kitchen, dining room, and two bedrooms were in the back, or west, end of the Holmes Grocery Store. Their large living room and the store were in the front, or east, end of the large, oblong building.

The front end was divided into two separate areas, each with big windows facing the road, and with separate entrances, and a connecting door between them. A few stair steps connected the east and west ends of the building. It was in this large living room that I remember Betty Holmes, and Elva and Alma Ballantyne trying to run on all fours like I could when I was a child.

Years later, Ken and Ina McDowall owned this store. They used only the back end for living quarters, and used one side of the front one for supply storage.

Mother, an Expert Horsewoman

My mother had been a fearless rider in her late teens and early twenties, good enough to accompany my dad, a master horseman, on his horse hunting forays. For their honeymoon, in the summer following their marriage in January 1921, Mom and Dad took a saddle horse trip in the mountains. They carried their camping equipment and food on "packhorses." Packhorses are sturdy horses that are used to carry heavy loads of supplies, camping equipment, food, and sometimes fire-fighting equipment, which are needed to survive for as long as a person or group of persons is in an isolated area where conventional vehicles cannot go.

Mom used a "lady's saddle" which had originally belonged to Grandmother Alena Vroom. A lady's saddle is an adult-sized saddle that is smaller than a man's saddle and that has a padded seat.

On our ranch in those days, being able to travel by saddle horse was critical. Even after she was debilitated by her rheumatoid arthritis, Mom was a very good rider.

But, getting Mom onto a horse became increasingly difficult. If Dad were at home he could boost Mom onto her horse. If he were not home, we kids had to help her. We could get Mom's lady's saddle onto her own quiet saddle horse, but we could not boost Mom onto the horse, and she could not step up by herself, using the stirrup.

Firstly, Mom's legs were too painful and stiff to stand on one leg while reaching up to the stirrup with the other one. Secondly, her hands were so swollen and painful that she did not have the strength to pull herself up onto the horse. Finally, because Mom was so disabled, she was afraid that the horse might move while she was getting on. Even a horse that is very tame and well trained sometimes moves while a rider is mounting it. If the horse had moved, Mom would have fallen and broken some bones, adding to her already very trying pain and misery.

My dad was really quite inventive and skilled in many ways. He could turn his hand to harness making, blacksmith work, carpentry, pole fence building, horse shoeing, horse handling, mountaineering, and many other tasks which early ranchers had to do from time to time. When Dad saw Mom's painful predicament in mounting her saddle horse, he got the bright idea of building a mounting platform for her.

The "mounting platform" was a special structure, built of boards, which enabled Mom to mount her saddle horse without a man to help her. The mounting platform had a top about 36 inches square.

We already had a hitching rail in the barnyard near the house yard. Dad built the mounting platform between the hitching rail and the house yard fence, leaving just enough room to lead a horse in between the rail and the platform. This meant the horse could not possibly step to one side as Mom was mounting it. The platform had three steps up one side so that Mom could clamber up to the top.

It was just the height of Mom's saddle stirrup when her saddle was on a medium sized saddle horse. Mom would stand on the platform and lean over to grab the saddle horn to steady herself. Then she would put one foot into the stirrup, slowly swing the other leg over the cantle,[5] and mount her horse safely.

Dad or one of us children would saddle up Mom's horse, always a "well-trained saddle horse," that is, a very gentle, easy to handle horse, but one which was not stubborn or lazy.

"The railing on the other side will keep your horse from moving," Dad reassured Mom as she clambered up the steps for the first time.

Dad knew he would not always be around to hold Mom's horse as she mounted it, so he showed Don and me how to do it.

"One of you fellows make sure that the horse doesn't move," Dad said to us as we led the horse in between the railing and the platform.

Having the mounting platform gave Mom a lot more freedom. When she rode to a Women's Institute meeting at Beaver Mines, or went to visit her friend Mrs. Bruce, she needed a man's help to dismount and remount. There was generally a helpful man working somewhere around at Mom's destination who helped her to remount, which removed the worry of getting off and on her horse when away from home.

But, having the platform at home meant, that with help from us kids, Mom could mount and dismount at the home buildings. This was especially important since Dad was often away working at another part of our ranch, or herding/hunting horses anywhere within a 30- to 40-mile radius. Once on the road, Mom was all right.

But Mom still preferred to have Dad help her mount her horse. When Dad was home, Mom insisted on his standing at the horse's head and holding it very securely so that it would stand still and not step forward. When Dad was not home, or was working in some other part of our ranch, however, Mom was forced to rely on Don and me to hold her horse steady by the mounting platform.

As further evidence of how brave my mother was, Don and I were probably only about five and three years old, respectively, when we started helping Mom to mount her horse. We took turns holding Mom's horse's head securely.

Though Mom rode a regular sized horse for many years, her favourite mount in the mid-1930s was a smaller-sized, half-Shetland black mare, a female horse, with a white blaze on her nose, named "Babe."

This 1930 picture shows three teenage chums, Betty Holmes, Jack Joyce, and Mae Vroom, who were living in the Beaver Mines, Alberta district when I was a child. Mae was fourteen at the time and was just finishing grade nine at Coalfields School. She is wearing fringed leather riding gloves.

Background: The store owned by Mr. and Mrs. Frank Holmes. This building, with its classic faux front, was one of the few-remaining original buildings at Beaver Mines. It was built when the Number One Coal Mine, and other mines, were going full blast.

The building on the right-hand side of the picture was another of the few remaining buildings after Beaver Mines town site was abandoned when the coal in the area went soft, and was no longer useful as fuel for steam engines. It looks like a shoe repair shop or a lady's shoe shop. It later became the Beaver Mines Women's Institute Hall. The building opposite the Holmes Grocery Store, mostly hidden by the three teens, was the old movie theatre, which was still standing when I was a child. Don and I, whenever we got the chance, used to climb up the narrow, dark, rickety stairs to the projection room and peer down on the dimly lit, empty theatre below.

The Kootenay and Alberta Railway line ran just east of this road, off to the right of the photo. The Beaver Mines Store and Post Office, where George and Mrs. Ballantyne lived, was about 300 yards south of the Holmes Grocery Store. The concrete foundation of a tipple, which had served a coal mine located in the hillside behind Mr. and Mrs. Ted Bruce, was located about ½ mile south of the Holmes. Courtesy Ruby Peters Jaggernath (daughter of Miles and Mae Vroom Peters), Author's collection.

With a little help, Mom could get on and off Babe by herself, as long as someone held Babe's head. To help keep Babe calm I would stroke her nose gently and talk quietly and lovingly to her, while Mom mounted slowly and carefully.

Brother Bill Is Born

My younger brother, Bill, was born in September 1931, the year that I was four and one-half years old; Don was seven. The weather in the foothills of southern Alberta is often quite beautiful in the autumn - warm, sunny days under a clear, blue sky. And so it was the year that Bill was born. For the event, Don and I went out to stay with Granny and Grandpa Tyson at Fishburn. Mom elected to go straight back out to our ranch after Bill was born. She had the help of a hired girl, Noemi Chiesa, for a short time.

Dad taught Mom how to tie a diamond hitch while they were on their honeymoon. In this picture, taken during the summer following their marriage on January 4, 1921, my mother is tightening a rope to hold the horse's pack steady for that day's travel. Author's collection.

Don and I were anxious to get home; we returned home as soon as Mom got settled in with her new baby. However, having a new baby meant that Mom did not have so much time to keep an eye on us. We were able to go further and further afield on adventures of our own. Dad was anxious for Bill to learn to ride at an early age, too. By the time he was six months old, Bill was sitting on one of our tamer goats.

By the next summer, before he was a year old, Mom had taught Bill to hang on tight so that he could ride double deck with her on her saddle horse, sitting behind her saddle and holding onto her as she rode along.

They could travel on a walk or a slow jog on Mom's quiet, but not a lazy nor a sluggish, saddle horse. Bill rode many a happy mile behind Mom's saddle when he was a small child. With this early experience, Bill rode the goats when he was only three or four years old.

Often Mom and we kids rode to pick wild saskatoons or chokecherries, or Mom went to one of her Women's Institute meetings. When we were all going out riding, Don and I would help Mom to mount her horse first. Then I would hold the horse's head while Don helped Bill up behind Mom. My mother steadied her mount with the bridle reins[6] and spoke gently to her horse during the procedure. Then Don and I would mount our own horses and off our little cavalcade would go. I thought that was the way the whole world operated. It wasn't, of course, but I was unaware of that!

In this picture, we are ready to go riding in early spring 1935. Don is on "Babe," I am on "Ribbons," Bill is on "Rex" (just a colt), and Dad is on "Scout."

I am standing up, practicing my "Annie Oakley" stunts. Annie Oakley was a trick rider in a Wild West show travelling across the continent at the time.

This picture gives a good idea of what our barnyard and house yard looked like, as viewed toward the northwest. In the background are the three big poplar trees beside the little dam area. Also, you can see the field across the road west of the barnyard and part of the road to Beaver Mines.

Further back is the oat field, the lane, the little corral, and part of the big garden. The front and back doors of the barn are open to air the barn air out. The blacksmith shop and the carpenter shop are to the right of the barn. Author's collection.

This 1934 photo is Ballantyne's Store & Post Office in Beaver Mines. Harry Truitt is second from the left; Alma "Jo" and George Ballatyne are on the right.

The Ballantyne's store was the social centre of the community. On Monday, Wednesday and Friday mornings, which were mail days all the year through, people who lived up Gladstone Valley like the Bill Barclays and John Truitts and others rode horse back more than eight miles one way to get their mail. In this picture there are several horses tied up at the two hitching rails.

There is one lonely car parked in front of the store. Very few people had cars in the 1930s. Ballantynes sold gasoline, which had to be pumped from an underground tank up into the top of the gasoline dispensing machine, seen at the left hand end of the store platform in this picture. The gasoline then ran down a flexible pipe into a can with a spout on it. The can was then emptied by hand into the car's gas tank. I have seen Elva using all her strength to push that pump handle back and forth.

Often 15 to 20 people at a time, coming from Gladstone Valley, Beaver Mines Valley, Coalfields School district, and over on Screwdriver Creek, congregated in the small store waiting for Mr. and Mrs. (Sarah McJanet) George Ballantyne to finish sorting the mail. When Elva and Alma "Jo" Ballantyne were old enough and were at home they pitched in and helped their parents with the mail sorting and served customers wanting to buy items from the general store. Sometimes Jack Frankish, the Castle River Forest Reserve warden stationed at Elk Lodge about 8 miles up the Beaver Mines Creek Valley, added interest to the scene by driving his dog team in to get his mail.

At Christmastime there was often an extra-long wait, it always seemed to me. Not only was there more mail, but often the mail was late arriving from Pincher Creek. Mr. Mel Cain, who brought the mail the 15 miles from Pincher Creek by team and sleigh in winter, was sometimes delayed because of deep snow drifts on the road.

Waiting time was put to good use by the neighbours, though. They caught up on all the news from each others' families and discussed upcoming community events. People generally bought a few groceries on mail days. Sometimes, however, the arrival of unexpected guests necessitated an extra trip to the store on other days as well. Mabel (Mrs. Edward) Bruce photo, courtesy Katherine Bruce, Author's collection.

This 1935 photo is my dad on one of his fine Morgan horses. Dad is dressed in his regular working cowboy clothes with plain leather chaps over his blue jeans. Good-sized saddle bags with woolly angora flaps are fastened behind the cantle of his saddle. Saddle bags were like portable suitcases and were very handy for carrying various things.

One day dad brought a tiny piglet home in his saddle bag. The piglet had been given to him by "W.D." McDowall. She was the runt of the litter; the McDowalls thought for sure she would die. However, Mom could work marvels with weak and ailing animals and nursed "Grunty," as we called the piglet, back to health. Grunty became a real family pet. It was a sad day for me when she had to be slaughtered for food.

This picture is taken looking east from the Bruces' home at Beaver Mines. The hill in the background is the north slope of the "big hill", which was straight north of my childhood home on my dad's ranch at Beaver Mines. A couple of small herds of our horses grazed on the quarter section of land on this north slope. Some of my cherished memories of very exciting times involve chasing horses on and over the "big hill." Michael Bruce photo, courtesy Katherine Bruce, Author's collection.

---

[1] A saddle horse is a full-sized riding horse that stands about 14 or 15 hands tall at the shoulders.

[2] Workhorses, sometimes called draft horses, were used to pull wagons and farm implements.

[3] In a page wire fence the wire is divided into rectangles so animals like sheep and goats cannot crawl through it.

[4] A hitching rail is a horizontal pole on top of two posts to which saddle horses and teams are tied temporarily.

[5] The cantle is the raised back part of a saddle against which a rider's buttocks rest.

[6] Bridle reins are the long, thin leather straps attached to either side of the horse's bridle bit, the metal bar in the horse's mouth used to control the horse.

STARTING SCHOOL, A ROUGH RIDE

A Big Disappointment

By the time Don started school, I was five and one-half years old, and could ride almost as well as Don. Thus, I was prepared to start school on September 1, too. "Bess, you can't go to school," Dad informed me.

"Why not?" I cried, with tears in my eyes, not understanding why I was suddenly cut out of my beloved, nearly worshipped, older brother's life, and relegated to staying home with the baby, as I saw it.

"Because you are not old enough to go to school," Dad explained. Mom gave me the same answer when I went to her for support.

"When will I be old enough to start school?" I queried further, not happy with their answer. "When you are six you can start school," Dad promised me.

I had been used to having Don to play with all the time and missed him terribly when he started school. Gradually, a plan formed in my mind, but I had to wait until just the right moment to spring it on my dad.

First thing every morning I would ask plaintively, "Am I six yet?"

"No, Bess," Dad would say, "not yet."

I kept asking, "Am I six yet?" for the first couple of weeks in September, but seemed to get nowhere with my questioning. The days seemed very long when playing by myself; to me, Bill was just a baby, so he was no fun.

"When will I be six?" I finally asked.

"On your birthday," Dad replied with finality.

Then I got a bright idea. I changed my strategy so that my daily question became, "Can I go to meet Don coming home from school today?"

"Well, all right, Bess, but go and see what your mother says," Dad finally said, giving in to my pleading.

Like a shot I ran over to the house and used my line that proved to be a very effective tactic for several years. "Mom!" I said breathlessly, "Dad says I can go meet Don if you say I can go. Can I?"

"Well, all right Bess, if your dad says so," Mom replied. She, too, was getting tired of my daily attempts at persuasion.

So back to the barn I raced. "Mom says I can go, if you say I can," I reported.

"Oh, all right then, Bess, but not 'til after you've eaten your dinner," Dad replied, to which I heaved a sigh of relief. Things were working out okay.

Right after dinner,[1] very happy with myself, I saddled my horse and headed down the road to meet Don. "Now don't you get to the school before Don gets out and bother the teacher," Dad admonished, as I left the barnyard.

"I won't," I called back blithely as I purposefully started out with my horse at a walk. I knew that school did not get out until half-past three, so I had to figure out some way to judge the time. Being small, I could not open the gates through the short cut past Harry Zurowski's land, and had to take the long way around past Beaver Mines.

So I got the "brain wave," a bright idea, of stopping to visit one of my mother's good friends, Mrs. Frank Holmes, at Beaver Mines.

The first day, Mrs. Holmes was sort of surprised to see me. "Did you bring me a note from your mother, Bessie?" she asked me after I had accepted her gracious offer of milk and cookies and had visited awhile.

"No, I'm going to meet Don at school," I replied.

"It's just about time you were leaving then, dear," Mrs. Holmes said, glancing at the clock. I took note of the time. "Come back and see me again, Bessie," Mrs. Holmes said as I bade her good-bye and mounted my horse, which I had tied up in her back yard.

I took her at her word. Every day thereafter I showed up on Mrs. Holmes's doorstep in the early afternoon. The dear, kind soul visited with me and gave me tea and cookies, heading me off down the road so that I would arrive at Coalfields School just at 3:30 p.m., or shortly thereafter. Then, very happy with the situation, I would ride home with Don.

Miss Marjorie Clements - A Kindly Teacher

I liked Miss Marjorie Clements right off. She would talk with me while I waited for Don to get his horse ready. Since Miss Clements was so friendly and kind, I thought it would probably be all right if I got to school before Don got out. Hence, after a few more days I did not stop at Mrs. Holmes's and just kept riding right on to the school arriving, at first, just after afternoon recess.

I had judged correctly. Miss Clements did not have the heart to turn this little waif away, and let me sit with the grade ones in their double-occupant type desks. The classroom was crowded already; there were about 40 children in that one-room school.

To further complicate the teacher's task, many of the children in Coalfields School could speak very little, or no, English. Their parents had emigrated from central European countries to the Crows Nest Pass[2] area, first to work in the coalmines, and then to take up farmland.[3] Their fathers had a very limited English vocabulary, and some of their mothers spoke no English at all. So the teacher had the double task of teaching the children English, as well as teaching them "readin' and writin' and 'rithmetic."

Perhaps Miss Clements thought that a child who could speak English very well would be a help to the non-English-speaking children, and hence to herself. Years later, I taught at the East Cardston Hutterite Colony School, a one-room school near Cardston, Alberta. I found one of my own children, Jim Annand, then only four years old, to be a great help to me in teaching the Hutterite children, for whom English was a second language.

For whatever reasons, Miss Clements allowed me to sit in the classroom until dismissal time. "I thought Bessie would get tired of it in a few days," Miss Clements recounted, some time later, to my parents.

But I did not "get tired of it." Furthermore, I got in the habit of arriving at school earlier and earlier, first just before afternoon recess, and then just after lunch, so that I was in school nearly half a day. Mom and Dad probably thought that I was still following their initial instruction "not to bother the teacher" and spending most of the afternoon with Mrs. Holmes.

To my mother's very great credit she never said to me "Bess, stay home and be a little mother and help me with Bill." Little girls are not little mothers, and should not have to feel guilty if they do not act like little mothers. Some parents mistakenly make their children take on adult roles often with disastrous results, especially for little girls.

Mom probably thought that I would get tired of going to meet Don each day and stop of my own accord; I did not. There was some advantage to her in having me doing something specific for a whole afternoon; at least she had a general idea what I was doing and where I was. Without me around to disturb him, Bill probably slept all afternoon, too, so Mom could get some of her work done without having to constantly check on my whereabouts.

Around the beginning of December, I got more anxious about the birthday business. "How long until my birthday now, Daddy?" I queried one day.

"Oh, about a month, Bess," he answered, almost absent-mindedly.

Having no concept of that length of time, I pursued the idea further. I asked plaintively, "How long is a month, Daddy?"

Anticipating My Birthday

"Oh, it's after Christmas, Bess," Dad answered, thinking that would put me off asking more questions. He was right - Christmas, I understood. I also knew that if children were not very, very good for quite awhile before Christmas, Santa Claus might not find them with toys and other presents.

So I was very careful not to annoy Mom and Dad with a bunch more questions about my birthday.

Mom and Dad probably thought that surely I would forget all about my birthday and the whole school idea by the time Christmas was over and the really cold, dark, heavy-snowfall days had set in.

Finally, the Christmas holidays came, allowing Don to be home all the time, and not just on weekends as when school was on. I was in seventh heaven, thinking/hoping that the situation (of having Don home) would continue indefinitely.

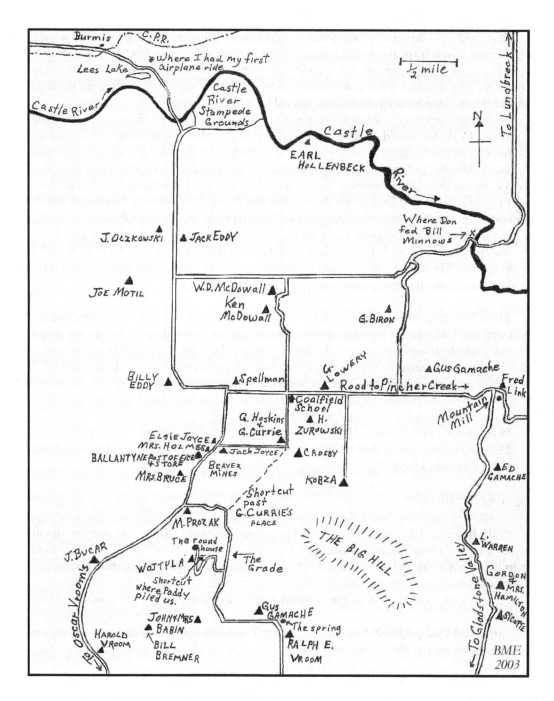

MAP 2 BEAVER MINES – CASTLE RIVER, circa 1935

MAP 2 *The map "Beaver Mines – Castle River, circa 1935" shows:*

- *Our ranch in relation to neighbours who lived north, west, and east of us. It also shows the road to Beaver Mines, as far east as Mountain Mill, north to the Castle River Stampede Grounds and where Don fed Bill minnows, and the road to Grandpa Oscar Vroom's.*

- *The road to Beaver Mines, the big hill, the roundhouse, Beaver Mines Creek, the hamlet of Beaver Mines, Burmis, Coalfields School, the CPR line, Lees Lake, Mountain Mill, the shortcut where "Paddy" piled Don and me — he threw us off, the shortcut to Coalfields School and the Castle River Stampede ground.*

- *Neighbours' homes, including those of: John Babin, George and Mrs. Ballantyne, G. Biron, Bill Bremner, Mr. and Mrs. Ted Bruce J. Bucar, the Crosbies, Gilles Currie and his sister, Billy Eddy, Jack Eddy, Grace Hoskins, Ed Gamache, Gus Gamache, Gordon and Mrs. Hamilton, Earl Hollenbeck, Mr. and Mrs. Frank Holmes, Mrs. Elsie Joyce, Jack Joyce, John Kobza, Fred Link, George Lowery, Ken and Ina McDowall, and W.D. and Mrs. McDowall, J. Motil, J. Oczkowski, Mike Prozak, Sicotte, Spellman Bros., Harold and Ruby Vroom, L. Warren, A. Wojtyla, Harry Zurowski. Map hand drawn by the author.*

Coalfields School, located west of Pincher Creek, was the first school that I attended. I started January 8, 1933, the day I was six years old, even though I had to ride eight miles round trip every day. This picture shows how small the school was for 40 pupils in grades one to 10.

This photo was taken in 1979. When I attended to Coalfields School, it was covered with white clapboard. Courtesy of Edith Annand Smithies, Author's collection.

However, as usual, school re-opened right after New Year's; Don was gone all day again and I was left to play alone. Winter had really settled in. "Can I go meet Don today?" I asked, after a couple of days.

"Oh, you'd better stay home, Bess; it's pretty cold today," Dad advised me. I was not happy with the situation. I could play outside with the animals, so I did not understand why it was too cold to go meet Don. Moreover, it was near my birthday, so I did not whine.

I was confident that I would be able to go to school very soon, anyway. I knew I would be six years old on my birthday, and that my dad had promised me that I could go to school when I was six. So, obviously, there was nothing to be concerned about. I bided my time.

I had learned enough about numbers by then, and my birthday was so close, that I could do the countdown to zero days myself. Now I did not have to keep repeating, "How many more days until my birthday, Daddy?"

Dad was relieved. He thought for sure that I had accepted that I could not go to school until I was six. He was right, and he was wrong.

I was taking the promise of "You can go to school when you are six years old," to mean exactly what it said. To me that answer meant that I would start school on the day that I was six years old, not the next September, by which time I would be six and one-half years old.

Starting School - A Successful Venture

Consequently, on the morning of my sixth birthday in January 1933, I was up bright and early. I had planned my day carefully. I expected my first day of school to be successful.

Cheerfully, I went to the barn to help Don feed hay and some oats to the school horses. I ate my bowl of oatmeal porridge without a whimper even though I disliked porridge so much that I could hardly swallow it sometimes. When Don got dressed in his heavy winter clothing to go to school I got dressed in my warm clothing, too.

"Where are you going, Bess?" Dad asked.

"To school," I answered happily.

Dad squatted down and took me on his knee, and spoke softly to me. "Bess, you can't go to school yet," he said gently.

I jumped off his knee, wailing, "But you promised I could go to school when I was six years old, and I am six years old, so why can't I go to school?"

Dad was trapped. He remembered that away back in September he had promised me I could start school when I was six years old and he could not go back on his word. So Dad resignedly packed another lunch and let me go. He still figured that the novelty of going to school would wear off.

Mom never got up when Dad and we kids got up. Her arthritis was so painful that she stayed in bed until the house got heated up some, usually coming downstairs around 11:00 a.m. to start lunch. The house seemed ominously quiet that morning. "Where's Bess?" she asked Dad as soon as he came in from the barn.

"Oh," Dad replied nonchalantly, "she went to school with Don this morning. I promised her she could go when she was six, you know." Mom agreed that promises had to be kept; thus it was that I started school "when I was six." I hardly missed a day the rest of the year; if Don could go, I could go.

Because I had Don to broaden my view of the world I learned very quickly. I already knew my colours, and learned to read faster than some of the other grade one children, if for no other reason than that English was their second language.

In June, I passed into grade two, along with Don. Thus it was that we were always in the same grade throughout our school years, even graduating from high school together. It was a lot of fun!

Hazards of Riding Horseback to School During Winter

My parents were rightly concerned about heading us children off to school. Riding on horseback was our only choice. Coalfields School, our first school, was about four miles away from our home.

In this 1935 picture we are ready to go riding on a wintry day. Bill, 3½ years old, is on "Rex," (just a colt). Dad is on "Scout", Don is on "Babe," and I am riding "Ribbons." Author's collection.

Spring was a very treacherous time for riding to school, especially when we were going to Coalfields School. Beavers had dammed up Beaver Mines Creek in several places causing the creek to flood over much of the flatland on either side of it. Late winter and early spring were bad times for icy roads because a Chinook[4] could blow in anytime.

A Chinook would cause the snow to melt on these already saturated flatlands. Then a freeze would come along during the night causing parts of our short-cut road to be covered with glare ice for nearly one-half mile. That ice was very dangerous for our saddle horses.

When our horses were walking over these stretches of ice they would slip and slide, and sometimes fall down. If the horses did fall, there was a great danger of them or us being injured. So at such times we had to be very skilful riders - to steady the horses' heads and help them maintain their balance, and to be very careful to avoid a broken leg or being dragged in the stirrup if one of our horses did fall. Sometimes we got off and led our saddle horses over the icy stretches, but that was very slow going.

To avoid a broken leg if your horse slips or trips and falls down, you must pull your foot quickly out of the stirrup and step onto the ground as the horse lands on its side. If you are unable to pull your foot out in time, your best plan is to relax and go down with your horse.

If your horse does fall with you, firmly pull the horse's head around as you go down. Continue to hold the horse down on its side until you are sure your foot is out of the stirrup on the underside of the horse. Next, slowly let the horse scramble to its feet on the slippery surface. You must be sure to get out of its way as it scrambles up. You also have to be sure to hold onto the bridle reins or the horse may take off on you as soon it stands up again, leaving you on foot.

Most riders, me included, would risk almost anything to prevent having their horse fall on them. The further from home we were, the more careful we were, too, though it was very embarrassing to make an obvious mistake in horsemanship in front of Dad.

We kids -,my brothers, Don and Bill, and my sister, Marion, and I - must have learned our riding lessons well. A horse never dragged any of us, even though we all rode some pretty raunchy horses in some very ticklish situations, time and time again.

However, Marion, through not fault of her own, had one very painful accident. She had the misfortune of being kicked in the face by a horse when she was nearly eight years old. That incident happened after the family returned to our ranch at Beaver Mines after being off it during World War II. Marion's nose was never quite the same afterwards.

I had my saddle horse fall on me only a couple of times in all the years, and for all the miles, that I rode on horseback. One of those times was on the hot tarmac of the highway just outside Waterton Lakes National Park. Fortunately, only my pride was injured.

Dad, a Blacksmith

Getting to school safely and on time was always important, so Dad put shoes on our horses when their hooves started to get tender. Dad's was a skilled "farrier," or a blacksmith, and could shoe his own horses. Thus, he did not have to make time-consuming, costly trips to town to the blacksmith to have our horses shod, as did most farmers and ranchers. Dad's uncle, Claude Vroom, and his dad, Oscar, had been blacksmiths, too. Dad inherited their aptitude and their blacksmith outfit. Dad also made some cash shoeing horses for other people.

Dad shod any and all horses that were brought to him. To protect his overalls he wore a leather blacksmith's apron. Sometimes Dad was injured doing such a strenuous, dangerous job.

The forge[5] was the dominant piece of equipment in my dad's blacksmith shop. Dad's forge was in one corner of the blacksmith shop.

Being a blacksmith is a hard, hot job; Dad stripped to the waist for the task. We kids liked to watch him as he laboured, perspiring and sometimes cussing, becoming covered with soot and blackened by the smoke of the forge, as he hammered the red hot metal to the desired shape.

Before Dad could shoe our horses he had to make the shoes fit the horses' feet. For that task he had to have his forge going full blast. We watched enthralled as Dad pounded the white hot metal with a heavy mallet to make the shoes the size and shape of each hoof of each horse individually. On such occasions we gladly turned the wheel that operated the bellows to blow air into the forge to fan the fire to produce greater heat.

We were intensely interested when Dad was shoeing our saddle horses. We knew that once they had the specially fitted metal plates on their hooves that we would be much safer on our daily ride to school. We could also travel a little bit faster because we did not have to worry about the horses slipping on the ice or wincing when they stepped on a stone.

Preparing horses' hooves for shoeing also requires special skill and care. Even at the present time, horses have to be shod by hand by people skilled in the trade. As in Dad's time, there are few people who possess this valuable skill. Shoeing a horse that is quiet and well trained is a demanding task. But shoeing one that is at all wild, as in the case of the bronc that broke Don's leg, is extremely difficult.

When shoeing a horse, Dad first used hoof cutters to trim off the broken edges of the hoof that had grown out during the past several months. Then he rasped the hoof until it was smooth and even, taking care to rasp just the right amount so as not to cut into the "quick," or soft part underneath the hard shell of the hoof. The cutting and rasping done, Dad selected a set of near-fitting horseshoes and put them on the horse's hoof.

"Horseshoes" are flat pieces of metal shaped like a horse's hoof. Dad had dozens of sets of horseshoes of various sizes hanging on a rail along the wall. After Dad found the correct size he began the fine fitting and shoeing of each hoof individually.

Dad heated the selected shoe in the forge, removing the shoe when it was white-hot. Then he pounded each horseshoe on the anvil with his heavy hammer until the metal was too cool to mould. Next he fitted the shoe on the horse's hoof, setting it up against the hoof he was shoeing at the time and making a mental note of where the shoe had to be flattened or widened.

Then, Dad grasped the shoe with his blacksmith tongs and buried the blue-gray iron in the fire again. He turned the wheel that worked the bellows to fan the flames to get the horseshoe white-hot. Then he removed the white-hot horseshoe with his tongs, and pounded it some more.

This heating, pounding, fitting routine was repeated until Dad had the best fit possible on the horse's hoof. When he was satisfied with the fit Dad enlarged the horseshoe nail holes with a small metal punch, then plunged the hot metal shoe into a bucketful of cold water to "temper," or harden, the metal. As he did so the water sizzled and spattered and clouds of smoky steam billowed toward the rafters of the blacksmith shop.

The final step in the horse shoeing process is nailing the shoe onto the horse's hoof with a hammer made specifically for that purpose. Dad took great care not to bend the malleable horseshoe nails and also not to let a misguided nail touch the quick, which would cause the horse to go lame.

Depending on the horse and its use, Dad either put shoes on all four hooves, or just on its front hooves. Generally, workhorses were shod all around because their hind legs were used for pulling their load. Saddle horses, on the other hand, were often shod only on the front feet, especially in the spring and summertime.

During the icy, spring thaw time, Dad often shod all four of our saddle horses' feet. In addition, for travel over the treacherous ice of spring-thaw time, Dad put corked shoes on all four hooves of our school horses. If the horses were shod only on their front hooves they could stand on their front legs without sliding, but their hind legs slipped out from under them.

Making corked horseshoes for riding on icy roads was much more difficult than making flat, uncorked horseshoes for summer wear. Corked shoes had to be shaped and fitted in the same way as plain shoes. In addition to the shaping and fitting of the horseshoes, Dad had to shape small pieces of metal and use a metal punch to make eight holes in each horseshoe — two near the toe and two at the heel on each side.

This 1920s picture shows Beaver Mines Creek in flood near the home of my Uncle Harold and Aunt Ruby Vroom. If a late winter freeze came while the creek was flooding, this area would be glare ice, similar to what we rode over on the way to Coalfields School. Courtesy Ruby Peters Jaggernath, Author's collection.

Then he got the corks and the horseshoe white hot at the same time and carefully placed each cork in its hole and welded it in, as a potter does with a piece of clay, or as a child does when making Plasticine models. The main difference was that Dad was working with hot metal that would sear flesh upon contact, and which required great strength and endurance to manipulate. Shoeing a couple of school horses on all four feet was a full weekend's job; we kids watched with great anticipation and helped however we could.

Even with corked shoes on our horses, during a winter freeze-up after a Chinook, for example, we had to ride slowly and carefully over the nearly one-half mile of glare ice. This added at least 15 to 20 minutes to the total of one hour, which it regularly took us to ride the four and one-half miles.

Later in the year, during spring flooding, water some two to three feet deep covered about one mile of a short cut past the Zurowski place. This shortcut took about one-half mile off the total distance to school.

Spring run-off was, in some ways, worse than icy-roads time. During spring run-off, Beaver Mines Creek, already overflowing its banks in low lying areas because of the beaver dams, was spread out even further over the valley floor. It flooded over a mile of our short-cut road.

During spring run-off, a stretch of road that was dust dry in late summer might be covered with over three feet of water. Then walking was very difficult for the saddle horses, firstly because they could not see what was underfoot, and secondly, because their footing was extremely slippery on the muddy bottom.

At such times we really had no alternative but to take the long road around. At least by then the days were warmer and the extra 20 or so minutes would not mean further risk of frozen toes and hands.

"Silver," A New Saddle Horse

After I started school, I could not go riding and horse hunting with my dad very often. I loved going to school, but really missed the long, exciting rides with my dad.

One day, in the spring of 1933, to my surprise and delight Dad brought home a new saddle horse for me to ride to Coalfields School. "Silver" was a palomino, a gold-coloured horse, as gentle as a lamb. James Riviere, a friend of our family, lent Silver to Dad for me to ride. James had done me a big favour, albeit unknowingly - he had taught Silver to lie down.

Silver was trained to lie down at a certain signal. I didn't know this until one day I was practising leading him around in a small circle. All of a sudden Silver lay down on the grass. At first I was really puzzled by his behaviour. I thought there must be something wrong. So I made Silver stand up again and led him around in a circle once more. Sure enough, he lay down on the grass. After that, all I had to do was lead Silver around in a little circle and say, "Come on, boy, lie down," and Silver would lie down any time or place.

I was quite small, and only six years old, and Silver was a regular-sized horse. Previous to that I had developed a method of getting on a tall horse bareback. I would wait until the horse put its head down to eat grass, then I would swing one leg over its ears and get on its neck, facing backwards. Startled, the horse would lift its head and I would slide down onto its back. Then all I had to do was right myself and I was on my way. Other times I would lead a tall horse up beside a fence or a step by the barn or my mother's mounting platform, anything to give me a few more inches in height, and climb on from there.

After I discovered that Silver would lie down for me, I had him lie down while I put my saddle on his back. Then, I would have him get up carefully and stand still while I did up the cinch.

When I was ready to leave for school, or the post office, or wherever I wanted, I would get Silver to lie down again. Next, I settled myself firmly in the saddle and grabbed hold of the saddle horn. Then I nudged Silver in the ribs, saying encouragingly, "Come on, Silver! Get up, boy!" I hung on tight as Silver scrambled to his feet. Then I sat up straight and, well balanced on Silver's back, I nudged him in the ribs and went on my way.

Some of the big boys at Coalfields School would tease me, as I was getting ready to ride home. They might, for instance, deliberately make my horse move so that I had even more difficulty getting on. After I discovered that Silver would lie down for me, I made him lie down when I wanted to come home from school. Then I got on his back, had him stand up, and started for home.

That gave me another problem with the big boys for a while. They were pretty impressed with how my horse would lie down for me, and wanted to have him lie down for them. At first I refused to let the boys touch Silver, but they persisted so eventually I reluctantly handed the reins to one of them. To my great satisfaction, they had no success.

Whenever the boys tried to make Silver lie down, he just acted as if he did not know that trick. "Lie down, Silver, lie down," they would command, shaking the bridle reins as they did so, but to no avail; Silver would not lie down. They had not caught on to leading Silver in a circle, and I said nothing about it.

This July 1933 picture shows me as a confident rider at 6½ years of age. I am sitting atop "Silver," as he gets up from a lying down position.

"Silver" was trained to lie down. When I wanted to get on Silver, I would have him lie, get myself into the saddle, and then have him stand up.

One day when I was at Mrs. Bruce's I was telling her how Silver was trained to lie down. "Let me see you make him lie down," Mrs. Bruce suggested. I made Silver lie down.

"Now let's see him get up," Mrs. Bruce said. Just as Silver was "sitting up," she snapped this picture. Mrs. Mabel (Edward) Bruce photo, Author's collection.

"You do it, Bessie," they told me.

As soon as I took the reins and led Silver around in even a partial circle, saying, "Come on, Silver, lie down," he lay down.

"How do you make your horse do that, Bessie?" they demanded, but I would not tell them my secret. The boys had me get Silver to do his lying down trick over and over, but they never did catch on to how to make Silver lie down.

Finally, pretty impressed with my horse handling ability, they admitted defeat. After that the big boys did not bother me. They left my horse alone, too.

"Dickie," My Own Shetland Pony

The Pete LaGrandeur children, who were attending Coalfields School when Don and I went to school there, rode Shetland ponies. Shetland ponies are small-sized ponies that are just the right size for small children to ride.

"Daddy," I would say wistfully whenever the moment seemed right, and especially when I had done my chores very willingly, "I wish I had a little horse to ride to school. Then I could get on him really easily and it would be more fun."

"Well, we'll see, Bess," my dad answered cheerfully.

Then, at the beginning of July, when I was six and one-half years old, and had successfully completed grade one and passed into grade two, I got my wish - sort of. Just as I was wondering what to do for the summer holidays, Dad came home one evening leading the smallest horse I had ever seen. He had kept his promise. Here was a Shetland pony for me to ride.

"Here's a pony for you, Bess," Dad said cheerily. He pointed proudly at the small horse he was leading. "He's a little stallion owned by Dick Smith in Pincher Creek. He has leant him to us for awhile. I've named him Dickie. I've got a little saddle for you to use on him, too."

I thought Dickie was a great idea, since I was so small that getting on a regular-size horse was a real struggle for me. The idea of having a pony "just my size" seemed like Heaven to me. Dickie looked small enough that I could mount him in the regular fashion of horseback riders - standing on by the left side of the horse with the right foot on the ground and reaching up to the stirrup with the left foot. I could hardly wait to ride him.

"Can I ride him right now?" I asked eagerly.

To my disappointment Dad replied, "You'll have to wait a day or so, Bess, until I can fix this saddle. I'll have to clean it and oil it up and put a new handhold on it."

The saddle actually had been a saddle used by a jockey on a racehorse, but had fallen into disrepair. There was not a regular pommel on the front of the saddle. Instead, there was a curved handhold made of bone, it looked like to me. "I'll have to take your saddle into the blacksmith shop and make a new handhold on the front of it for you," Dad continued. I wriggled with impatience, but there was nothing to do but wait.

The next time Dad started the forge he heated an iron rod to white hot. Then he cut a piece off and hammered it into the correct shape. Finally, Dad tempered the new handhold. When the handhold had cooled, he fastened it firmly to my little saddle making it ready for use.

Our re-training of Dickie was Dad's payment to the owner for the use of him to breed our mares. Our part-Morgan mares then had half-Shetland foals, which were lovely to ride when they were three or four years old.

However, there was another "fly in the ointment," so to speak. It was an unexpected problem that had to be solved before I could really enjoy riding Dickie. Dad did not mention this to me before I got on Dickie to ride him to Beaver Mines, but some town kids had spoiled Dickie.

We called children who lived in Pincher Creek, the town nearest our ranch, "town kids." It was only 17 miles in distance, but was nearly five hours away by team and wagon, so we did not see these children very often.

With regard to Dickie: first and worst of all, according to Dad's teaching of us, the town kids did not know how to look after their pony. He was just a toy to them. All of our horses were working animals, either for riding or for hauling heavy farm loads. Secondly, and just as bad, if not worse, the town kids had teased Dickie until he was very ornery.

This is a picture of the "little saddle" that dad bought for me when we first got "Dickie," a Shetland pony stallion. A few years later, Bill used this saddle for several more years while riding on our half-Shetland ponies, which were sired by Dickie. Dad always kept our tack in good shape. By the time Bill grew out of the saddle, Dad had mended the stirrup leathers and the tapederos, the leather coverings over the front of the stirrups.

The stirrup leathers are stamped "Great West Saddlery Co. Ltd., Horse Sage Brand, Trademark No. 380."

Dad kept the saddle well oiled, so the leather has stayed in fairly good shape. I still have this saddle. Photo by Edith Annand Smithies, Author's collection.

I had never ridden a horse that was truly ornery because most of our saddle horses were part Morgan, which is a breed of horses characterized as willing workers. Shetland ponies are less even-tempered than Morgan horses, so it was not long before Dickie got to be quite mean, and justly so. He would kick and bite and throw the town kids off, even quite big boys whose legs nearly touched the ground, when they sat on poor Dickie.

Sizing up the situation, Dad offered to "re-break" Dickie, that is, get him over his bad habits, if we could use him as a stallion for a few years. And so, months later, I discovered that the real reason for having Dickie on loan at our ranch, was so that Dad could start a new line of horses. He wanted to raise half-Shetland ponies that would be about the size of Mom's mare, Babe.

However, as I was the only one who was small enough to ride Dickie, the job of re-training Dickie fell to me. The first day I rode Dickie was a Saturday, ostensibly, to get the mail, but secretly, to show off MY Shetland pony.

The family of Pete LaGrandeur, who was with Dad and me in later years on a grizzly bear adventure, had ridden Shetland ponies for several years. Now I had my own Shetland pony; I couldn't wait to show him off. I was not aware of Dickie's history, hence was not prepared for the ordeal of my first ride on him.

As soon as the chores were done on Saturday morning I saddled Dickie and mounted up. The first problem was that he would not leave the barn doorstep. I tried every way I knew to make Dickie move. By then I was six or seven years old and was quite a good rider. But Dickie would not budge.

Dad came to my rescue. "Here, Bess, I'll just give him a flick with the bullwhip," Dad offered, trying to encourage to me.

Our bullwhip[6] was a long quirt that had a short braided leather handle, about six inches long. This sturdy handle enabled the wielder to get a good handhold. The bullwhip had a lash about eight feet long, tipped with separate thongs of leather. Originally it had been used to prod ox trains to a faster speed.

Dad stood back and flicked the lashes around Dickie's hind legs. Dickie kicked up his heels again. Surprised, I was flung forward, and was just able to save myself by wrapping my arms around Dickie's neck.

"Sit up, Bess!" Dad commanded. I sat up. About the time I got myself "squared away" again, that is, had got hold of both bridle lines and was seated firmly and upright in the saddle, Dad flicked Dickie with the whip again. Dickie kicked out, and I lurched forward around his neck. When I had righted myself, Dad flicked Dickie again. Dickie kicked out; I lurched forward and clung to his neck. When I had righted myself, Dad flicked Dickie again. This process was repeated all the way to the water trough at the spring near Gus Gamache's gate, about one-quarter mile from the barnyard.

Finally, Dickie lit out on the dead run. By then, I was so shook up and so humiliated by this spoiled pony's bad behaviour that I made Dickie run faster and faster.

I kicked Dickie repeatedly in the ribs; one nudge would make our usual saddle horses jump to a start. When Dickie tried to slow down, I "whipped him on both sides," that is, swung the ends of my bridle lines from side to side so that the tips of the reins would flick Dickie under the belly.

I made Dickie run, probably another one-half or three-quarters of a mile, until he was sweating and panting and could run no more. I then let Dickie proceed, very docilely, at a walk for another half mile or so until he was cooled down. Then I touched Dickie with my heels and he broke into a slow trot; I touched Dickie again and he willingly went faster; I touched his ribs a little harder, and urged, "Come on, Dickie." He broke into a gallop. Ever after that, he was a perfectly behaved pony.

I was the only person who ever rode Dickie while he was at our ranch, and for as long as we had him he never misbehaved again. He had learned his lesson well. Even though he was smaller than Don's saddle horse, Dickie would keep up as we rode to school. He even learned to love to race with the horses of the other kids that we joined up with along the way to and from school.

Miss Ida Genovese and "The Sleeping Beauty"

When school started in September, I rode Dickie to Coalfields School, which led to a near mishap at Christmas concert practicing time. I was anxious to get to school the first day because I expected to see my beloved Miss Clements, but I was disappointed. We had a new teacher, Miss Ida Genovese, for the 1933-34 school year. Again the class size was about 45 pupils, some of whom were more than 16 years of age.

But Miss Genovese jumped right in with both feet, as the saying goes. In those days, the mounting an elaborate Christmas concert often ensured a teacher's ranking as a "good" teacher.

In this late spring 1934 picture, I am wearing my Coalfields School Christmas concert fairy costume and holding Dickie by the bridle reins. My hair was in long ringlets, which Mom curled by wrapping my hair around long strips of white rags. This was done when my hair was freshly washed and left to dry overnight.

This picture was taken in the field across the road from our ranch house at Beaver Mines. In the background is part of the road to Beaver Mines, a corner of the oat field, the lane (with a wire fence on each side), the "big garden," part of the "little pasture," and the "big hill."

Shortly after taking this photo, Mom went down East for a month. Author's collection.

In that department, Miss Genovese got full marks. She put on the most elaborate Christmas concerts of any teacher I ever had. Miss Genovese's production of the operetta *The Sleeping Beauty* was the concert that I remember most vividly. I was in grade two at the time. My part in the operetta was that of one of the six fairies who danced around the sleeping beauty, protecting her as she slept.

My white crepe paper costume had gauze wings with gold stars on them and a very short, frilly skirt. With my long blond hair in shining ringlets, I thought I looked like a fairy. The skirt was so short that when my mother saw me on stage she was worried lest I had forgotten to put on my special costume panties. The costume panties were made out of a bleached 100-pound flour sack and were shorter than I usually wore. But Mom need not have worried; the panties were safely in place.

We did a quite a bit practising at school. However, as Christmas concert day drew near, we trekked over to the W. D. McDowall home a few times to practice our singing accompanied by Mrs. McDowall at the piano. There was no piano at the schoolhouse; Mrs. McDowall's piano was one of the very few in the district, so we went there to practice singing. Mrs. McDowall lived about one and one-half miles from the schoolhouse in the opposite direction from where Don and I, and many of the other children, lived. But no matter what, the Christmas concert songs had to be practised.

Some of the children walked to school, so they walked over to McDowall's. However, I was one of the lucky few who had a horse to ride. At that time, it was Dickie.

One mid-December day, as we trudged along towards Mrs. McDowall's, I got bored with our slow progress. So I decided to ride Dickie over a small bare-of-snow hill that was beside the road, instead of following along at a snail's pace with the children who were walking. A west wind was blowing quite steadily. As luck would have it, just as I topped the little hill a strong gust of wind caught hold of Dickie and blew the both of us right down the other side of the hill into a snow bank. Don and some of the bigger boys came back to rescue me.

For the dress rehearsal and for concert night, Mrs. McDowall, who had raised eight children of her own, went to the Beaver Mines Women's Institute Hall to play the piano. It went off without a hitch.

The next summer Mom wanted to take a picture of me in my fairy costume, but I insisted on having Dickie in the picture. Mom framed the picture, taken as I stood in the sunny hay meadow west of the house, so that some small trees, the lane and the big hill show. Dickie stood quietly beside me as I carefully held his bridle reins so he wouldn't move. By then, I truly loved Dickie and thought we made a splendid pair.

Photo OVERLEAF (page 44) - The opening of the Mountain Mill Church in 1906 was a momentous occasion for families in the Beaver Mines district. My dad, Ralph Vroom, along with his parents, Oscar and Alena, his brothers, Harold and Alfred, and his sister, Marion (Cyr), were among those attending the first church service.

Although the custom in the 1930s was to baptize children as babies, for one reason or another I was not baptized until 1934, when I was seven years old. Mr. and Mrs. Frank & Louise (Riley) Holmes were my godparents. The Louise Bridge, which crosses the Bow River in downtown Calgary, is named for Louise Riley.

My baptismal ceremony was held on a bright sunshiny day in late spring or early summer. We travelled the eight miles to Mountain Mill Church by team and wagon. Our whole family went to the service.

Getting ready to go and getting to the church on time was a big procedure. All the regular chores had to be done. Then we had to change into our "good" clothes and travel for nearly two hours, which seemed like a long way to me. I generally rode horse back where ever I wanted to go, so travelling by team and wagon was almost unbearably slow. The round trip, including the church service and visiting, would take nearly seven hours.

This 1922 photo shows the west end of Mountain Mill church, located about 6 miles east of Beaver Mines. The small child in a white dress at the church door with her back to the camera is Alma "Jo" Ballantyne (Johnson). The girl on the right in the white dress is Grace Currie - she's running to get her horse.

By the time I was baptized my younger brother, Bill, born September 16, 1931, was nearly three years old. Mom took advantage of the situation and had Bill baptized at the same time.

My sister Marion, born October 3, 1938, also was not baptized when she was a tiny baby. By the end of October the roads were bad and getting to church was very difficult. When winter set in, the roads were impassable.

To add to my mother's travails, the following February-March 1939 our whole family, except Don and Dad, had scarlet fever. Then, about the end of March when she was barely six months old, Marion contracted pneumonia. The roads were so bad - snowdrifts left over from winter and axle-deep mud in places - that the doctor could not get out to our ranch, and we could not get to town. As there were no antibiotics, pneumonia was a very grave illness. Many families lost at least one child to the dread disease.

Marion became so ill that my mother feared she would die. Mom had been raised in the Anglican Church in Ambleside, England. She knew that, in the case of imminent death, an emergency baptism could be performed by a lay person, using spittle - if no water is available -and making the sign of the cross on the person's forehead and saying, "I baptize thee in the name of the Father, the Son and the Holy Ghost. Amen."[7] The baptism is then reported to Parish authorities when the emergency has passed. So Mom, unwilling to risk my sister's dying without her being baptized, baptized Marion herself.

My older brother, Don, was baptized in about 1926 at the Mountain Mill Church after Mom and Dad returned to the ranch after living at a logging camp near Rossland, BC, for a few years.

Ralph and Mollie attended the 50th anniversary service of the Mountain Mill Church on June 1, 1956. My children and I are looking forward to attending the 100th anniversary service in June 2006. Courtesy Alma "Jo" Ballantyne Johnson, Author's collection.

Charlie Mitchell, husband of "Sis" Mitchell, holding his niece, Mae "Sissie" Vroom on her 1ˢᵗ birthday in August 1917. The family has a number of other pictures of Sissie that day. Several were sent to Sissie's father, Harold Vroom, who along with his younger brother, Alfred, was fighting in the trenches in France during WWI.

The buildings in the background include a small sloped-roof structure which may have been Archie Vroom's original homesteader shack. The log barn with high hay loft was built by Charlie after he bought the place from Archie Vroom, and before the ranch was owned by Ralph Vroom. Visible above the barn roof are the big fir trees which were at the top of our big garden when I was a child.

Harold was the first of Oscar and Alena Vroom's sons to enlist in the Canadian Expeditionary Force (CEF) in WWI. On March 1, 1916, he rode his saddle horse into Pincher Creek and joined the CEF, 192ⁿᵈ Battalion. Ruby was left to run the ranch by herself. Their son, Oscar, was only 5 years old and Ruby was pregnant with their daughter Sissie.

In October 1915, barely four months after his marriage to Margaret Coulter of Hillcrest, AB, Alfred Vroom followed his older brother into the CEF. Men who enlisted in the CEF had to provide their own saddle horses. The Vroom brothers were paid $2.00 per day for their horses and 10 cents a day for themselves.

Margaret and Ruby did not know their husbands, Alfred and Harold, had gone overseas until Margaret received a post card from Alfred in November 1916. His postcard, mailed from Moose Jaw, SK, as the troop train passed through, said he and Harold were being shipped overseas. Margaret was only 16 years old.

Harold and Alfred arrived in England together on the Empress of Britain. Both of them were sent on to France with the 192ⁿᵈ Battalion. They served in France during some of the bloodiest battles of WWI.

In the meantime, in 1915 their brother, Ralph, joined the CEF 82ⁿᵈ Battalion, and went to Sarcee Camp near Calgary for training. His knowledge of and skill in handling rough broncs earned Ralph the job of breaking horses for the army. However, when a bronc he was riding "accidentally" flattened a row of army tents, including the officers', he aggravated an old knee injury. Ralph was given an Honourable discharge.

Disappointed by the turn of events, Ralph spent the rest of the War years helping his aging parents, who lived on a place at Mountain Mill, later owned by Fred Link. Ralph also worked for various other ranchers in the district, many of whose sons had gone overseas with the CEF. However, Ralph got his turn in WWII when he served Overseas with the Royal Canadian Artillery for nearly four years.

Ruby Mitchell Vroom was left to run the ranch by herself. In this photo, it is likely that Charlie and Sis were looking after baby Sissie, enabling Ruby to do her ranch work. Spring was crop-planting time; summer was haying time; in the fall, vegetables from the garden and crops in the fields had to be garnered for winter storage; in the winter, ice for cooling food in the summer had to be cut from the frozen creek and hauled home and stored. These were back-breaking jobs that required long hours outside. It was a blessing for Ruby that her family was able to help out. Courtesy Ruby Peters Jaggernath, Author's collection.

This photo, circa 1930, is the beaver dam that was about 100 yards below the Beaver Mines Creek bridge. Behind the dam, stretching back among the trees, is the deep pool where I swam "Two Step".

On hot summer days, on our way home from Beaver Mines, we would unsaddle our horses, get on them bareback and ride into the creek. I remember swimming Two Step, a 17-hand tall horse, in this deep hole when I was about 8 years old. I was alone at the time, and knew that I was living dangerously.

As Two-Step swam along I looked down through the still, slightly murky water. I could see snarled willows lying on the bottom and two-foot high stumps of cottonwood trees the beavers had chewed off to make their dam.

After going about 50 yards downstream I decided I had better turn around before I got into trouble. I carefully reined Two Step in a wide circle to ensure he would not flip over and throw me into the deep water. The creek banks were covered with a deep muck of slimy mud. For me and Two Step to get out of the creek would have been very chancy. I made it safely back to the bridge, saddled up and headed for home. Once that far down the creek was enough for me. I never did it again. Courtesy Katherine Bruce, Author's collection.

---

[1] On ranches when I was a child, the biggest meal of the day was the noon meal, which was called "dinner." The evening meal, which we called "supper," also had to be a hearty meal to satisfy the appetites of hard working ranchers and ranch hands.

[2] On modern maps the pass through the Rocky Mountains west of Lethbridge, AB, is called "Crowsnest Pass." I am using the original spelling, "Crows Nest Pass," which referred to the area where a tribe of First Nations people, the Crows, camped for periods of time in the late 1800s and early 1900s.

[3] Farmland is fertile soil on which crops can be grown. Many immigrants had worked as farmhands in their homelands, and laboured hard to own their own farms.

[4] A Chinook is a flow of warm air from the Pacific Ocean. This warm air spills over the Rocky Mountains in southern Alberta and spreads out to cover an area as far north as about Calgary and east to the Saskatchewan boundary. A strong wind often accompanies a Chinook. Chinook is also the name of a tribe of First Nations people.

[5] A forge is a specially built fire in which metal can be heated to white hot so it can be placed on an anvil and pounded into another shape.

[6] Bullwhips were not usual equipment for horse breeders. Bullwhips were used by ox train drivers to prod their slow-moving oxen along the hot, dusty wagon trail, as they hauled freight from Fort Benton, Montana, on the Missouri River, to Fort Macleod, NWT, in the late 1800s. When Dad roamed the countryside as a young man, he got the bullwhip in a trade.

[7] From *Common Prayer--Church Hymns*, pre-1891, page 190. This small book was presented to my maternal grandfather, George W. Tyson, on Christmas Day, 1891.

DAILY DANGERS OF RANCH LIFE

My Childhood Constraints

As a child on an isolated ranch in the Alberta foothills, I had an amazing amount of freedom, with few constraints. This was made more remarkable by the fact that I was a girl. What constraints I did have were natural and logical. This applied to Don, too. The first and most important rule was to look after our saddle horses well. The next rule seemed to follow naturally from the first - we were to keep ourselves safe.

My successful, satisfying experiences as a young child enabled me to develop a positive attitude that has stood me in good stead all of my life. Even my attitude towards raising my own family was shaped to a degree by my childhood experiences. I really did not know, until I was in my forties, that in many parts of the world, and even in Canada, girls and women do not have equal rights, nor equal opportunities, with boys and men.

Since my first awakening to the plight of many women, I have been an ardent supporter of women's rights - to be free to participate fully in all aspects of society, and to receive equal pay for work of equal value. The older I become, the more determinedly I support those principles.

Along with rights, of course, go responsibilities, whether one is a boy or a girl, a man or a woman. Women have proved themselves to be strong, loyal, and ardent workers. Life for the whole world can only get better as the talents and energies of women are more fully realized and utilized.

My dad did not make a bunch of rules, but those he did make were necessary and practical. If we got ourselves into some kind of a "jackpot," as Dad called an undesirable predicament, it was generally because we had carelessly, or sometimes deliberately, neglected to follow one or another of these rules. In other words, we had not "used our heads," and considered what the consequences of any given action might be.

We children had what I would call natural, or situational, constraints. We always suffered one way or another for not obeying any given rule. We learned when young to use our own judgement with regard to our behaviour in various situations. We were encouraged to use imagination, and sometimes to rely on intuition, in solving our problems. Even today I try to approach problem solving in this manner.

In most families, the parents teach the children, and the children learn from each other - with the older children generally teaching, or trying to teach, younger siblings "what they should know," that is, essential knowledge, in the opinion of the older siblings.

My brother Don and I were taught by my father and mother by direction, and by example. If we blatantly disobeyed, we were punished in what my parents considered an appropriate manner. Don, who is very much like my mother, but also has many traits of my father, taught me by example. I can never remember Don being mean or unkind to me. I considered Don as an equal, and I think he thought the same of me. We needed each other to carry out many of our schemes.

Because Don was older, he understood a lot of things before I did, so most of our schemes were probably his ideas. I figured out some of the details and helped carry our plans to fruition by giving Don unquestioning support. One such time was when we built a two-wheeled cart, and I trained a couple of our saddle ponies to be a team so that they could pull our cart.

Don and I made a good pair and respected each other. Mom and Dad felt that between the two of us we could look after ourselves fairly well in most circumstances.

Long after we were grown up Don paid me what I considered the supreme compliment. ".... In those days," Don assured his enthralled audience during one of his story-telling times with family and friends, "I'd rather chase horses with Bess than any man in the country."

I have often quoted Don when I want to impress upon someone, who looks a little skeptical, what a really expert horseback rider I was in my heyday on our ranch!

Eye to Eye with a Bronc

There were always a variety of animals around our ranch. From an early age, I learned to respect animals, but not to be afraid of them.

Often I would run after the "kids." But other times, I would sit on the ground contentedly holding a kid on my lap, and be amused for some time. When I first learned to walk, I steadied myself by holding onto our collie dog. I also loved to play with the cats, and would hold them by the hour.

As used by us on our ranch, and even by me to this day, a "close call" means a time when a person or animal is in danger of serious injury, yet escapes being injured. They may escape injury through good luck, by making a wise last-minute decision, by being quick-witted and well prepared for any eventuality, or simply by the grace of God.

In spite of my parents' watchfulness, and careful teaching, I was, from time to time, in a very precarious situation. I have had many "close calls."

The first close call that I had while working or playing with the horses occurred when I was about one and one-half years old.

The grass in the house yard grew faster than one horse could eat it down, so Dad decided that two horses could graze in the house yard. He got in the habit of keeping a second horse in the house yard, one was a tame horse for Mom to ride. The second horse was often a "bronc," or a "bronco," a wild or partly tamed horse, that Dad was currently breaking. That habit was nearly my undoing at a tender age.

This 1928 picture shows our patient collie dog letting me hold onto him to steady myself while I was learning to walk.

However, living on our ranch, with its many animals, was fraught with danger. The horses, mostly because of their size, were especially dangerous.

Adding to the danger was the fact that Dad had so many of them. He kept between sixty and seventy-five head most of the time when I was a young child. In addition, not all of these horses were your tame, plough horse type.

Most of our horses were quite spirited, to say the least. Some of them were practically outlaws. Others were outright ornery and untrustworthy.

At this age, I was closely supervised by my mother, and kept from most dangers. But she could not protect me from everything - a host of angels has served me well. Author's collection.

The cats liked to have me play with them, as in this picture taken in the spring of 1928. I had the cats trained so that they would lie placidly while I played with them by the hour.

Our cats lived in the barn; to play with them I would bring them into the house. In the early spring, when there was still snow on the ground, I would run out to the barn wearing only my nightgown and mittens - no coat or shoes - to get the cats I wanted to play with that day.

We children always knew when there was a new litter of kittens. We liked to find them before their eyes were open even a crack. However, the mother cat did not like us to play with her brand new kittens. Whenever we found them, she would pick up the kittens by the scruff of the neck, one at a time, and move them to a new hiding place. Author's collection.

By late spring of the year I turned one year old I was quite mobile. Whenever I got the chance I followed Don outdoors into the house yard. I could walk unsteadily over the rough ground of the house yard, but I liked to "run on all fours," that is, I sort of ran along the ground on my hands and feet, not on my hands and knees. When I got a few years older I could imitate all the gaits of a horse.

In this 1929 picture of me at 2 ½ years old, I am holding a "kid." In the background are the goat house, barn, and the small corral behind the barn.

The big garden site was just north of the two corrals near the barn; these were the little corral and the small corral. And it was to the northeast of the big corral. The big corral did not have a pole fence until 1935. Author's collection. (See Map 1 House Yard, Barnyard, and Corrals, 1936.)

I could walk like a horse, and trot, gallop, and "single-foot," that is, imitate a horse's gait where the horse moves its front and hind leg on the same side at the same time, giving the rider a sensation of rocking back and forth sideways. Single-footing is sometimes referred to as pacing, especially when the speed is increased.

I had been used to having the goats, and other animals, around the house yard from the time I was about six months old, so was not afraid of animals. When I spied Dad's bronc grazing just outside the back door of our house, I headed straight for it. I was very fond of horses and always regarded them as my friends. So, quite unafraid, I toddled unsteadily up to the bronc and stood with my feet apart peering up at him. The bronc was far more curious than I was. In fact he was downright terrified, as my dad described the scene at a later date.

Dad, who was coming in from the barn, stopped in his tracks at the house yard gate. There, to his horror, was I practically in between the bronc's front legs. "There was Bess," Dad related, "looking up into that bronc's eyes. He just stood with his front legs splayed apart, and his head down - nostrils flaring, not daring to move lest he step on Bess."

Dad was transfixed; he could not risk moving lest he startle the bronc causing it to inadvertently jump on me.

About that moment Mom made a periodic check out the kitchen door. Taking in the scene with one quick scan, she made a fast decision that probably saved my life. Mom knew how I loved raisins, so she called out, "Come and get some raisins, Bess!"

Hearing my mother's voice I promptly dropped to my running-on-all-fours position and turned around and scooted back to the verandah, not even aware of the drama I had caused.

A Broken Leg

My brother Don had his share of close calls and outright accidents, too. Don was born two and one-half years before me, but we were always in the same grade throughout our school years.

The situation came about as the result of a seemingly "freak accident," that is, a type of accident that is extremely unlikely to occur, plus a series of other unexpected events. These resulted in my starting school just a few months after Don started.

On looking back, that freak accident, like so many other inexplicable happenings and turns in my life's course, may have been part of Someone's grand scheme for me. My life certainly took a path that no one could ever have predicted for a little girl, born in mid-winter to a mother, whose body would soon be wracked with painful rheumatoid arthritis, and living on an isolated ranch in southwestern Alberta.

Don and I both loved to watch Dad while he worked, especially with the animals. With great patience he let us follow him around. Mom always warned us, "Be very careful and stay out of the way." We did our best to comply, and mostly succeeded. However, when Don was only four years old, he had his left leg broken just below the hip in a horse-related accident.

That fateful day, however, Dad was shoeing a very ornery horse near the front door of the barn. He had the horse "snubbed," that is, securely tied up with a short piece of rope, to a sturdy post at the corner of the box stall.[1]

On that day, Don was sitting on the shovel end of a scoop shovel and watching Dad shoe the ornery horse. The shovel was lying on the floor of the barn in a stall right beside the six- to eight- feet wide alley which ran along the middle of the barn, with stalls on either side. The oat box was kept there; the saddles were also stored on racks in that area.

"Stay back, Donnie," Dad warned several times. Don would move back, but eventually he crept up closer again until he was sitting directly behind the horse Dad was shoeing. Don's short legs dangled over the end of a scoop shovel.

Suddenly, in a burst of fear, anger, and orneriness, the horse reared back on its haunches. The strain on the halter shank, which had held the animal's head firm, was too much and it broke in two, leaving the horse with no support.

The horse tried to catch itself, but its hind foot caught on the edge of the stall floor, which was made of four-inch-in-diameter logs, making a four-inch drop-off to the alley floor. The horse literally sat down on Don's lap as he sat on the shovel in the opposite stall with his legs hanging unsupported. Don's left thighbone snapped in two.

Dad and Mom got Don over to the house. Then Dad rode to Beaver Mines to phone the doctor in Pincher Creek, some 17 miles away. Dr. Walkey came out by car and set Don's leg on the couch in the dining room.

Don's leg was in a cast for about six weeks, but he was not bedridden. Don was soon able to crawl around on all fours. I brought him things he could not reach himself, learning early from my parents to be helpful and generous to others.

Because of his broken leg, Don's rate of physical growth was slowed down somewhat. Moreover, Mom and Dad didn't want six-year-old Don to ride on horseback alone for the four and one-half miles to Coalfields School. So, Don's starting to school was delayed by two years and he did not start school until he was eight years old.

Getting Bucked Off

Other than Don's broken leg, I cannot remember us children having any serious injuries involving the horses. That was true even though we were bucked off our ponies every now and again, especially in the early summer when the ponies were fresh off the range.

To some extent, our lack of injuries reflected Dad and Mom's careful tutoring of us with regard to being careful around the horses. But we did take many calculated risks. Thus, I am sure, there was a certain amount of luck involved in our having few injuries.

It just may have been coincidence, but I seemed more likely to get bucked off my horse when I was showing off a bit, or really not treating my horse quite right, according to my dad's instructions. My dad's rules were pretty simple: You don't race your school ponies; you don't gallop your horse downhill; you always treat your horse gently.

I loved to race my pony. I got a real thrill out of riding down a steep trail on the run when chasing a herd of horses. Running my horse downhill was allowed, and indeed necessary, when we were chasing horses. However, running my horse downhill just because I was in a hurry was not all right.

Ribbons, one of my horses that had a bit of a rebellious streak in her, would buck at the slightest provocation. She was a very smart horse, and had to be watched constantly. Whenever Ribbons sensed that I was sitting relaxed in the saddle and not paying strict attention to her, she would pile me then and there.

One such day I was coming home from Beaver Mines. The mail and a loaf of baker's bread, which Mom did not often buy, were tied onto the back of my saddle with the saddle strings. We had company at home and I was anxious to get back as soon as I could. I thought it would be all right to push Ribbons into a gallop when I was almost at the bottom of Prozak's Hill.

Unknown to me, one end of the sack with the bread in it had come untied. As soon as she started to gallop, Ribbons caught sight of the bouncing bread out of the corner of one eye. Right on the spot she just ducked her head and started to buck, sort of bouncing on straight legs and kicking her hind end up in the air - "crow-hopping" my dad would have called it.

Since I was going downhill, and was already slightly off balance, Ribbons piled me on the second jump. I landed unhurt in the soft dust. Ribbons took off down the road, the bread still flapping up and down. After a few hundred yards the bread fell off. A short distance further on Ribbons stopped to graze on the green grass by the roadside.

Feeling embarrassed because my horse had caught me off guard, but relieved that no person was around to see me, I got up and dusted myself off. Then I walked as quietly as I could along the far side of the road allowance to try to get past Ribbons so that I would be between her and home, and thus more likely to be able to catch her. After a few minutes of gentle talk, and by making a cautious approach, I got hold of the bridle lines and mounted Ribbons again. I rode home carefully, expecting a second bucking off, but Ribbons did not try it again that day.

In this 1937 picture I am riding "Ribbons." The picture was taken in the house yard, looking eastward. Our root house with its new gambrel roof is in the background. Author's collection.

Another time, Don and Bill and I were heading up the road towards Gladstone Valley School. We had made Bill start off first because he always rode more slowly than we did and, we felt, held us up. I was riding a three-year-old called Ginger. I had trained Ginger the spring before, when he was a two-year-old, and was very proud of the fact that, up to that time, nobody but I had ridden Ginger.

Usually, Dad did not "break our horses," that is, train the horses to ride, until they were three years old. However, because I was small and light, he let me break Ginger when he two years old.

I was really happy that mid-June morning because I had a new horse to ride to school. We had been coaxing Dad for weeks to let us ride some of the horses that had been out on the range all winter instead of our usual ponies which we had been riding to school for several months.

Finally, Dad had let us run in the bunch of horses that included Ginger. I worked with Ginger all weekend and thought I had him under control. However, by Monday morning Ginger was still pretty snorty.

Ginger, like Ribbons, was just watching for his chance to buck me off, and he got it. As we started off up the road, Don's horse got just a neck's length in front of me. I felt that I had to be at least even with Don, so I gave Ginger a sudden dig in the ribs with my heels. Like Ribbons, he ducked his head and started bucking. I stayed on for a few jumps, with Dad calling from the barnyard, "Stay with him, Bess!"

After the first few jumps Ginger headed into the ditch and I went off head first, sliding right down a little sapling and landing in the thick grass. Ginger turned and raced back toward the barnyard, the stirrups flapping up and down and further frightening him. He ran right past the barnyard, not stopping until he got to the water rough, about one-quarter mile further on. Don wheeled his saddle horse around and took after Ginger to try to catch him. When Ginger finally stopped, Don caught hold of the bridle lines and led Ginger back up the road.

We children rode four miles to Gladstone Valley School (eight miles round trip). Mom snapped this 1938 picture of Bill and me, just as we were ready to leave for school. I am riding "Rex," and Bill is on "Pickles." This was Bill's second year of school. Author's collection.

In the meantime, I had picked myself up and was limping and crying back toward the barnyard, with Dad standing watching me. That was very embarrassing. Not only had my horse caught me off guard, but Dad had also seen the whole event.

Another of Dad's cardinal rules about riding horseback was that if your horse bucked you off, you had to get back on it right away just to show the horse who was in charge. "If you don't get back on your horse right away," Dad assured us many times, "You will never be able to ride that horse. It will buck you off every time."

When I got back to the barnyard and Dad was sure I was all right, he told me that again.

"I don't want to ride Ginger now," I whimpered.

"You've got to, Bess," Dad urged me. "You're already late for school, and you don't have another horse to ride. You don't want to spoil him."[2]

So, like it or lump it, I had to get back on Ginger. We made it to school without further objections from Ginger. However, whenever I wanted him to go faster, I moved very cautiously.

Dad was right. Ginger never again bucked with me when we were starting out for school, but I had to watch him continually for the next few weeks. He would jump a little when I was getting on, or he might wait until I was on and then give a few hops, but he never bucked me off.

Another day, when I was on the way home from school and had stopped to talk with Mrs. Stillman, our neighbour one-half mile to the south, one of their animals suddenly came on the scene. Ginger pretended to be startled, and used that for an excuse to duck his head and start bucking. I was taken somewhat by surprise because I thought Ginger was over that bucking silliness, but I managed to pull my bridle reins up short and make Ginger lift up his head.

A horse cannot buck very well with its head up, so Ginger soon settled down. I talked softly to him, patted his neck, and repeated over and over, "That's okay, boy, just settle down now, settle down. You're a good, good horse. Easy, boy, easy." Ginger eventually became one of my best horse-chasing mounts.

A New School and New Hazards

A big part of the danger of living on our ranch was that we had to go so far to get to school. And just when we got established in one school - Coalfields School - we had to transfer to another school - Gladstone Valley.

When Don and I started school at Coalfields School there were no large school divisions. Each school was a separate district with its own school board. Which school each child attended depended upon the location of the quarter section on which the family's home was located. Large school divisions, along with their consolidated schools, did not come into being in Alberta, or Saskatchewan, until the 1940s.

My parents owned two quarter sections, the west quarter and the east quarter, which were located one on opposite sides of the road. The west quarter was located across the road from our house and was in the Coalfields School District. The east quarter, where our house was situated, was in the Gladstone Valley School District. The taxes from the land where a family's home was located went to that school district, so school boards paid close attention to which school each child was attending.

The Gladstone Valley, known locally as "the Valley," is a wide, bowl-shaped area southwest of Pincher Creek that was formed by glaciers during the last Ice Age. Ridges of hills form natural boundaries on the north, west, and east sides, while the main range of the Canadian Rocky Mountains forms the southern boundary. Over the eons, Gladstone Creek, a relatively small, but swift-flowing, stream cut its way to the bottom of the valley.

Gladstone Creek rises, about ten miles east of the Alberta-British Columbia border, on the eastern watershed of the Rocky Mountains in a valley between Table Mountain and Mount Gladstone. The creek flows through a cut toward the north end of Gladstone Valley, where it joins Mill Creek.

It tumbles over rocks and waterfalls as it rushes toward the Castle River. Eventually, these waters flow into historic Hudson Bay by way of the Oldman River, the South Saskatchewan River, and the storied, mighty Saskatchewan River. Crossing Gladstone Creek on horseback was always exciting. Our small horses could hardly stand against the current when the creek was full in the spring.

Don and I attended Coalfields School for grades one and two. However, when I was in grade three, the school boards decided Don and I should be attending Gladstone Valley School.

Though both schools were about four miles from our home, the Gladstone Valley School route presented a different set of hazards.

In the wintertime, none of the farming area roads were snowplowed. The snowdrifts along the Coalfields School road were not that deep. But in the Gladstone Valley, which was deeper into the foothills, the drifts were very deep. Often, for weeks on end, our road to school was covered for a distance of about three-quarters of a mile with hard-packed snowdrifts up to three feet in depth.

At such times Don and I would ride the tallest horses that Dad owned. Dad had a couple of gallant saddle horses - "Red Cloud," a bright sorrel, and "Two-Step," a well-broken, brown sway-backed gelding. Both of them stood over 17 hands[3] tall.

Until we got Dickie, and Dad brought me home a small, child-sized saddle, I had always ridden an adult's saddle with the stirrup leathers shortened to fit me. On a horse as tall as Red Cloud or Two-Step, the stirrup was a long way up! To mount such a tall horse at home I would lead it up beside the mounting platform which Dad had built for Mom, and clamber on from there.

Away from home, I had to climb up a wire fence, a very dangerous exercise, to get on a tall horse. When I was at the Beaver Mines Store and Post Office, I led my horse up beside the platform, which was along the front of the store, and mounted from there. Sometimes, my horse would step away from my mounting perch and my legs would be stretched widespread, with one foot in the stirrup, and the other on my perch. It's a wonder I wasn't killed!

Double-Decking "Two-Step to School

Though we sometimes got very cold riding to and from Coalfields School, we never got as cold as on the ride to Gladstone Valley School. This was mainly because the Coalfields School road was quite sheltered by large areas of trees and bush for most of the way.

We also had two places where we could stop in Beaver Mines. We always passed the home of Mr. and Mrs. Frank Holmes - good friends of my parents - where we could warm up. Kindly Mrs. Holmes often gave us a cup of hot chocolate, too. Then on mail days, we would stop in at the Beaver Mines Store and Post Office to pick up the day's mail. We often bought some small grocery items to save Mom or Dad an extra trip to the store. Both these havens were about half way home from school. (See Map 2.)

There were no such warm-up places on the Gladstone Valley School route. We had to ride all the way home without getting warmed up, so it was quite a bit more rigorous.

One winter, when Don and I were about ten and eight years old, we double-decked Two-Step to Gladstone Valley School. Mounting Two-Step was sometimes a challenge. We loaded ourselves at our convenient home mounting platform each morning, so that was easy.

Getting on at school to come home, though, was much more difficult, as we did not have the convenience of the platform. Don would help me scramble up Two-Step's front leg to grab hold of the saddle horn and pull myself up behind the saddle. Then I would grab Don's hand and he would scramble up into the saddle in front of me.

We did not look very dignified doing this, but the only alternatives were to ask the teacher to help or to walk home, neither of which we wanted to do.

We often played with toy trains at home, so when we rode double-deck on our horse we extended our play. Don was the "engineer", sitting in front in the saddle and controlling the horse with the bridle reins. I was the "fireman", sitting behind the saddle and nudging Two-Step with my heels to make him go faster. Sometimes we got in a race with the Sicotte boys, who rode on horseback in the same general direction as we did. Dad forbade us to race our horses, but we did it every once in a while, knowingly risking Dad's displeasure. He did not always find out about our racing.

Occasionally, we would get going too fast for the trail conditions. Sometimes when we came to the turn-off into the Stillman shortcut trail, which ran through a hilly area sheltered by thick stands of trees, we were going too fast, and Don could not make the powerful horse slow down for the turn. At such times, Don would pull as hard as he could on one bridle rein and steer Two-Step into a deep snow bank.

Don and I usually had our signals straight, but once I was kicking Two-Step with my heels to make him go faster, while Don was pulling up on the reins trying to make him slow down. That day, Don had headed Two-Step into a three-foot-deep snow bank. Two-Step did not slow down very much, but he did not slip and fall down with us, either. We were very good riders!

The other children, some of whom did not even have saddle horses, used to tease Don and me, and our horses.

"Daddy," we whined one day when the situation seemed intolerable, "the kids at school are teasing us. They tease our horses, too."

"You guys are big enough to look after yourselves," Dad answered, not wishing to get involved in our scraps with the neighbours' children, "but don't let anyone touch your horses." We understood what he meant.

The final straw came in mid-June when a couple of the boys strung a rope across the path from the schoolyard gate to the barn and pretended to be going to trip our horses. Don, who was then about ten years old, going on eleven, was filled with indignation over the continuing harassment by the other children. In a flash he jumped off his horse and tore into our tormentors with his fists.

Later that same week I had a fist fight with one of the boys; he was threatening to drop a piece of old desk iron on my horse as I led it out of the barn. With our dad's warning ringing in our ears, we were absolute tigers when it came to defending our horses. From that time on we got considerable respect from all the other children; none of them bothered our horses anymore, either.

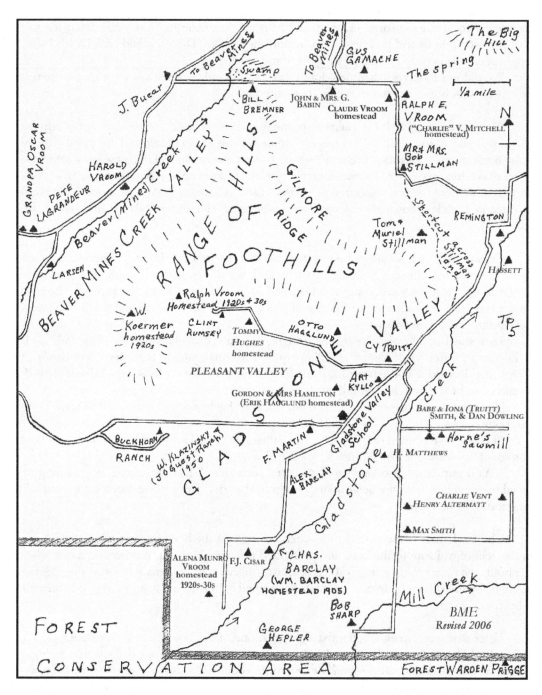

MAP 3 GLADSTONE VALLEY AND BEAVER MINES CREEK VALLEY, 1930s

MAP 3 *The map "Gladstone Valley and Beaver Mines Creek Valley, 1930s" shows the location of the homes of various people who lived up Gladstone Valley, and in Beaver Mines Creek Valley, when I was a young child. Beaver Mines Creek Valley was separated from Gladstone Valley by a range of foothills. Pleasant Valley enters Gladstone Valley from the west.*

Names of neighbours shown on the map include Henry Altermatt, John and Mrs. G. Babin, Alex and Margaret (Martin) Barclay, Charlie and Sonia (Chiesa) Barclay, C. J. Barclay, Bill Bremner, W. and Mrs. Cisar, Dan Dowling, Gus Gamache, Erik and Mrs. Olga Hagglund, Otto and Mrs. Anna Hagglund, Gordon Hamilton and his mother, Mrs. Hamilton, George and Mrs. Hepler, P. and E. Klazinsky, Art and Christie Kyllo, Floyd and Mrs. Martin, Henry and Mrs. Matthews, Forest Ranger and Mrs. Prigge, Glen's Grandfather Remington, Clint and Mrs. Rumsey, Bob Sharp, Babe & Iona (Truitt) Smith, Max and Mrs. Smith, Bob and Agnes Stillman, Tom and Muriel Stillman, Cy and Phyllis Truitt, John and Melcina Truitt, and Charlie Vent.

Homesteads and other ranches shown are Ralph Vroom's 1920s homestead (SW¼-28-5-2-W5), Alena Munro Vroom's 1920s homestead (NW¼-29-5-2-W5), Claude Vroom homestead (NE¼ -34-5-2-W5), Charlie V. Mitchell homestead (NW¼ -35-5-2-W5) and Tommy Hughes.

This map also shows the location of some Beaver Mines Creek Valley homes such as John and Mrs. Bucar, Wm. Koermer, Pete and Edith LaGrandeur, Louie and Mrs. Larsen, Harold and Ruby Vroom and my Grandpa Oscar Vroom.

Also shown: the Buckhorn Ranch and the JO Guest Ranch (1950), which are located between the two valleys.

Harry and Bessie Truitt's home and Elk Lodge were in Beaver Mines Creek Valley, a couple of miles past my Grandpa Vroom's place, further west into the foothills. Map by the author.

This picture shows all of the Gladstone Valley School pupils in 1936-37, the year I was in grade five. Back row, L to R: Don Vroom and Frank Cisar. Middle row, L to R: Gordie Kyllo, Hughie Fenton, Howard Martin, Bessie Vroom, and Roy Kyllo.

Front row, kneeling, L to R: Mary Martin and Josephine Hepler.

In grades 5 & 6, my teacher was Miss Elva Ballantyne. She boarded with Mrs. Hamilton and her son, Gordon, who lived very near the school, on what had been the homestead of Eric and Olga Hagglund. Elva married Sam McClelland, and lived at Beaver Mines.

My teacher in grades 3 & 4 had been Mrs. Jessie (Rev. Gavin) Hamilton. Author's collection.

Jackie, a Runaway Dartmoor

My dad was very concerned about what horse I should ride to plough through the deep snowdrifts en route to Gladstone Valley School. Dickie was not quite big enough to face the hard four-mile ride to school every winter day. Dad thought that I really should have a bigger horse for my daily ride to school. Riding in the good weather of spring and fall was no problem, but he was worried about the winter riding. Rainbow and Ribbons' colts were not old enough to ride yet.

This September 1935 picture shows me riding Jackie, using an adult-sized saddle with the stirrup leathers shortened to fit me. I am wearing the red tam that my Great-aunt Bessie Vroom of Nova Scotia knitted for me, when she was visiting Aunt Marion Cyr in 1935. I loved that little tam, and wore it constantly until it was in shreds. Authors's collection.

So, the summer I was seven years old, Dad brought home a sturdy, Dartmoor pony, about eleven hands tall that I named "Jackie". Jackie was a handsome dark bay with a wavy black mane and tail. He carried his neck in a proud bow when he walked. The saddle I was using at the time was a full-sized saddle. Dad had shortened the stirrup leathers for me.

Jackie had one very bad habit - he loved to run and when he got started running he "would run away with his rider," that is, he was out of my control and I could not stop him no matter where he was heading. His rider just had to sit tight and hope he did not put his foot in a hole and fall.

Jackie never fell with me, but he did fall with one on the older boys, Glen Remington, and broke Glen's arm. That accident happened when Glen boldly declared, "I bet I can stop that horse of yours, Bessie." So I let him try. As soon as we started running our ponies on a flat stretch of road, Jackie took off like the wind. The rest of us did not want to travel at that fast of a pace, so we trailed along at our usual speed. About a mile further along the road we came across Glen lying stretched out across the road, cradling a broken arm.

Glen had yanked and yanked on the bridle reins, but to no avail. Jackie had the bit clamped between his teeth and he ran full speed until he did stick his foot in a hole in that country road. Glen was quite a big boy and had pulled Jackie's head to the side so that when Jackie tripped he could not stay upright. When Jackie fell he pitched Glen over his head and onto the hard road, breaking Glen's arm. Jackie scrambled to his feet and ran the rest of the way home without a rider.

When the rest of us found Glen, we got him up on one of our horses and double-decked him back to his grandfather's home where he was living. Glen's Grandfather Remington then had to take Glen by about fifteen miles to a doctor to get the broken bone set.

After that, when Jackie ran away with me I let him have his head and did not try to stop him right away. I did my best to help him avoid falling, and he never fell again; I loved to ride Jackie.

Sadly, however, within a couple of years Jackie got "hoof rot" in his right hind foot. In hoof rot, a horse's hoof shrivels up; then the horny covering loosens and falls off. Jackie had to be destroyed. But I do have this picture of me sitting on Jackie, his neck in a proud bow, wearing a red tam hat knitted for me by my Great-aunt Bessie Vroom.

A Vicious Ram

To keep myself entertained on weekends, I played with the goats. We had a herd of about 30 goats of various sizes and colours. They were wonderful playmates. There was only one cloud on my playing-with-the-goats horizon and that was a vicious black-faced "ram," a male sheep used for breeding purposes. Dad had got the ram from Uncle Dominic Cyr.

Unbeknown to Don and me, our cousin Eugene had taught the ram to "bunt." The ram would run into a person from the side or from behind with enough force to knock them down.

Dad knew about the ram's meanness, but the ram was well bred. Our ranching operation needed a new ram, and the price was right, so Dad brought the ram home. Dad trusted us children to take care of ourselves if need be. His faith in us was rewarded. We were quite ingenious at solving various problems. Dealing with the ram was no exception, though it took us awhile to figure out the best way to handle the situation.

But my younger brother Bill was not so lucky. When he was about three and one-half years old he was old, he wanted to be with the "big kids," out playing with Don and me.

Sometimes he would wander out of the house yard and up onto the side hill before Mom noticed he was gone. Generally, though, Mom or Dad, or Don or I would see him in time and nothing untoward happened to him. Then, he started following me when I went to chase the goats. Of course, he was not old enough to know about the bad habits of that black-faced ram. Eventually, however, the inevitable happened - the ram caught Bill in the open.

On that unfortunate day in about mid-June, Dad was working round the barn when he heard my Bill yelling at the top of his lungs, "Waah-aah-aah!" Dad, judging the sound to be coming from up on the side hill northeast of the barn, looked out the back door of the barn. Sure enough there was the little fellow standing unsteadily on the side hill above the corrals.

Dad looked out just in time to see the black-faced ram square off and charge at Bill, knocking him flying "…about thirty feet down the hill," Dad said. The little fellow scrambled up determinedly. Bill had just got his balance back when the ram charged again. That time he just lay there yelling until Dad ran up and rescued him.

The ram stared belligerently at Bill's rescuer. As Dad carried the small child back to the house yard he warned, "Son, you have to stay in the house yard; that ram will get you every time you come out by yourself."

Bill heeded Dad's the warning for a few days, but soon he wanted to be with us big kids again.

"Take Bill along, you fellows," Dad said with a no-nonsense tone in his voice. And that was the beginning of Bill's "tagging along" with Don and me on our various adventures. We had to take Bill with us even when we did not really want him to come.

Fortunately, Bill was not with me another time, when I was out working with Dad, and the vicious ram caught me unawares. Dad and I had just returned from the stack yards. The "stack yards" was a fenced-in area south of the house where several haystacks were located.

Haystacks were made during haying season in the summer time. The "haystacks were piles of loose hay which were waterproof when built in an orderly manner and "topped off," that is, finished off in a special way. "Loose hay" is hay that is not baled.

The animals were fed outdoors at the stack yards during the winter. The stack yard fences kept the animals from eating a whole haystack at once.

One fateful winter day, our team of heavy workhorses, Mike and Pearl, were hitched to the hayrack and standing in the big corral near the goat house. I was supposed to be holding onto the lines. For some reason, I decided that I had to run over to the house for something or other, so I tied the harness lines[4] loosely to the front of the hayrack.

Without thinking about the ram, I headed off across the big corral towards the house.

Out of nowhere, unseen by me, the ram suddenly appeared. I turned to try to run the few steps back to the hayrack, but the ram lost no time in doing his dirty work. He knocked me down right beside the team. The ram would not let me get up and kept bunting me along the snow-covered ground until I was right under the front sleigh runner of the empty hayrack.

I lay as still as I could, hoping against hope that nothing would startle the team, or that they would not become restless move forward. If the team had stepped just another foot forward, the heavy sleigh would have been on top of me and I would have been seriously injured.

For what seemed like an eternity, but which must have been only a few minutes, I lay there hardly daring to breathe. The ram stood guard, hoping to get another whack at me. Luckily, the ram eventually tired of keeping what must have seemed like a fruitless vigil and wandered off to find something else of interest.

I waited another few minutes, until I was sure the ram was far enough away, then I started talking quietly to the team. To make sure that my movement did not startle the horses, I eased myself out from under the sleigh runner.

So as not to attract the ram's attention again, I slowly got to my feet, and quickly scrambled back onto the hayrack. I stayed there, breathing sighs of relief, until Dad returned from his other tasks and we took the team back to the barn. Then I quickly went out the front door of the barn and scooted back over to the safety of the house. I had enough outdoor adventure for one day!

But the lure of playing with the goats outweighed our fear of the ram. In the wintertime the goats liked to stay around the buildings, so were always available to play with. However, before we could play with the goats, we had to make sure that mean ram was nowhere around. Even though Don and I watched out for the ram, he caught us unawares a few times and knocked one or the other of us spinning. But one of us would always have time to escape! Then, the escapee would distract the ram with a pan of oats, and the other one of us would get away. The ram never did knock both of us down at the same time.

Eventually, however, Don and I got tired of never knowing when the ram would appear to bunt us down or into some imminent danger. So we developed a strategy to deal with the ram.

We would bait the ram by enticing him over to the pole fence between the barn and the blacksmith shop. In the short stretch between the gate and the barn there was a place in the fence where the poles were a little further apart than usual and where we children crawled through instead of opening the gate each time.

Don would climb up the pole fence carrying Dad's lariat. A "lariat" is a rope about 15 to 20 feet long. Dad used a lariat for roping horses in the corral or for tethering his saddle horse over night if he were "out on the trail," riding in an unsettled area where there was no barn or corral.

Don would then lean over the top rail of the fence and make a huge loop, or "noose," in the lariat so that it hung down in front of the hole in the fence.

In the meantime, I would get a pan of oats and shake it in front of the hole in the fence. Of course, all the sheep, including the ram, would come on the run trying to get a treat. Don would wait patiently, and I would try not to give away too many oats, until finally the ram was eating oats alone and only his head was through the noose.

We would wait until the ram was completely absorbed in eating oats. Then ever so slowly and carefully, Don would begin to tighten the noose around the ram's neck.

After we had done this a few times, the ram became very wary of our friendly, oat feeding overtures, so we had to become very crafty in carrying out the procedure. If the ram backed out of the noose, other sheep would crowd in to get at the oats, and we would have to start over again.

Sometimes, to get the ram's attention and lure him over to the fence, I would go into the big corral where the sheep were and get the ram to chase me. I would run full speed over to the fence, nimbly scramble through the hole, grab the pan of oats and keep the ram preoccupied while Don tightened the noose again.

Once we had the noose tight around the ram's neck, we wrapped the rest of the lariat around the corral poles to make good and sure that he did not get loose. Then we would go and play happily with the goats without fear of being attacked by the renegade ram.

When we finished playing, we would unwind the lariat from the fence rails and turn the ram loose. He would glare at us for a few seconds, and then walk defiantly back to the herd.

We never did tame that ram; he was always a mean animal. The ram even caught Dad unawares one day and knocked him down, so Dad understood Don's and my frustration with the ram.

I do not know if Dad knew how Don and I solved the problem of the vicious ram. But even if Dad did know, he would never have objected, as long as we did not injure the ram. As it was, our "solution" just hurt the ram's pride a little!

This is the original location of Gladstone Valley School, on the southwest corner of Harry and Bessie Mitchell Truitt's homestead quarter SE¼-22-5-2-W5. The school yard looks exactly as it did when I attended for grades two through seven in the 1930s.

Mrs. Jessie Wilger (Rev. Gavin) Hamilton taught me in 1934-35 and 1935-36, the years I was in grade 3 and grade 4. This photo is taken looking south, from the house rented by Mrs. Hamilton and her son, Gordon. The house had been Eric and Olga Hagglund's original homestead house (this quarter is now owned by George and Kay Kettles Hagglund). During the years when Mrs. Olga Hagglund lived there, the teacher boarded with her.

In the medium near foreground is a barbed wire fence that runs straight north and south along the quarter-section line immediately west of the school.

When I attended the Gladstone Valley School, a barbed wire fence also enclosed the school yard. During the day, in spring and early fall, this yard was large enough to pasture several school ponies. In the winter, they had a barn for protection against the cold westerly winds. The barn is the building furthest to the right in this photo.

During the winter, the ponies had to stand all day in the unheated barn, with no feed. This was one reason why Dad forbade us to race our ponies on the way home from school, even though we were sorely tempted. If we ever broke that rule, Dad would invariably find us out, and we were in trouble.

The ride to Gladstone Valley School was much colder than the ride to Coalfields School, which was probably why Mom and Dad started us off at Coalfields School. On the road to Gladstone Valley School, there were much longer stretches of open road. Along these stretches, a howling winter wind from the west, which we faced into nearly every day, would sweep down on us from the main range of the Rocky Mountains. (See Map 3.)

Often we arrived at school with frozen hands and feet. On those days, before we could do any writing, we would spend nearly an hour warming up around the big wood heater, which was located in one corner of the schoolroom.

The school yard had room for a softball diamond. We played "Two Batters Up," which meant that the first two children to put a foot on home plate before school, or at noon or recess, were the first two to get to be up to bat. *Touching the base first was important for we younger children - if a strong batter, generally an older child, got up to bat first, the rest of the children might not get up to bat at all that day.*

Since Don and I rode four miles to school, we were never first to school in the morning, except for one morning in mid-June. Mom and Dad were away overnight and Charlie Riviere was staying at our place. Don and I told Charlie we get up really early the next morning. Charlie could not understand why we wanted to get to school that early, but we were insistent - we **had to** *leave home by about 7:00 a.m., meaning that we wanted to be at school by 8:00 a.m., so we could be the first and second batters that day.*

Charlie obligingly fed our ponies, then fed us breakfast and sent us up the road. As we rode along the short-cut trail winding through the tall timber across Stillman's place, it was so early I could see the stars shining. It seemed like a long time before any other children showed up at school to play ball with us.

The school yard was also big enough that we could pack patterns in the snow and play "Fox and Geese", and other games, as long as the snow lasted in the winter. When the snow melted, we would scratch the outlines of the trails into the bare ground, so that we could keep on playing our favourite game, but that didn't work very well.

The fence around the school yard encompassed a grove of scraggly poplar trees on a little hill behind the school. We played a game called "Run, Sheep, Run" on that hill. Just beyond the little hill, on the outside of the fence, was a small stream or a spring, where we kids used to go for a cool drink in late spring. By the time we returned to school in the fall the creek may have dried up.

A shed, shown in this photo at the left end of the school, was used to store wood and coal for the big wood heater that stood in one corner of the classroom, providing the only heat. Frank Cisar and his sisters were the school janitors in the 1930s. The school toilet - with a boys' and a girls' side - was located near the school yard fence and shows in the above photo between the school and the barn.

Mill Creek valley is on the extreme right of the photo. Then, between Mill Creek on the right and Whitney Creek on the left, is the nearest mountain in this photo, known as "Round Mountain". Round Mountain was aptly named by Bob Sharp for its shape. Bob was the son of an early settler in Gladstone Valley. Gladstone Creek runs right to left, just behind the school. A bit northeast of the school, Whitney Creek joins Gladstone Creek to form Mill Creek.

Victoria Peak is in the centre of the picture. The long ridge sloping off to the left runs out to Corner Mountain. (Although the name "Corner Mountian" was used by us, and is still used by some locals, the mountain appears as "Prairie Bluff" on modern topographic maps.)

Tom and Alice Dalager and their children, Tilman, Clara, Neil, Marian, Eileen, and Yvonne from Eastend, SK, Art and Christie Kyllo, and many other families, lived on the Harry Truitt place for varying lengths of time in the 1930s and later. However, the buildings on the Harry Truitt place are located to the left of the photo and cannot be seen from the angle at which this picture is taken. The nearer buildings, in the hollow on the left of the photo across Gladstone Creek on its south side, are the Matthews homestead place. Mr. and Mrs. Charlie Matthews and one of their sons, Wesley, lived here for several years in the 1930s.

Henry Altermatt's buildings are located above the Matthews place, beside the grade which runs upward from left to right along the low hill in the middle left of the picture. The road continues on to Charlie Vent's place. Charlie Vent, a bachelor, was found dead one spring when neighbours went to look for him. A tree fell on Mr.

Vent sometime during the winter and pinned him to the ground. The bears found his body and ate it.

In 1934, Dad and I rode along that road for a ways to get to the trail that took us along the east edge of the mountains to Alice and Alphie Primeau's ranch. This was the summer I went to stay with the Primeau's when Mom was down East, at Dr. Locke's clinic, for treatment for her rheumatism. I subsequently went to stay with Mrs. Nellie Gladstone (Henri "Frenchy") Riviere at the George Gladstone place on Drywood Creek.

I thought it was wonderful to be with the Rivieres'. Living there when I stayed with them were Nellie, her son George and his wife, Margaret Clark ("Maggie"), and their two children, Nellie and Henry. As well, there were Nellie's son James, and daughters, Inez (Rae) and Frances (McWhirter).

"Nichemoos , widow of Kootenai Brown, was living in her little cabin near Nellie's house. Frenchy was up at his cabin at their Victoria Peak ranch, near the headwaters of Pincher Creek. Frenchy visited a couple of times while I was at the Riviere's. I stayed with Nellie for a while and then went back to Primeaus'. They took me to Pincher Creek. There I stayed with my Aunt Marion and Uncle Dominic. I attended St. Michael's Catholic School, taking grade 3 until the end of September, when I returned to our ranch at Beaver Mines.

This photo was likely taken by Mrs. Mabel (Edward) Bruce, who was a good friend of Mrs. Hamilton. While riding from Beaver Mines to Gladstone Valley to visit Mrs. Hamilton, Mrs. Bruce would stop at our ranch to visit with Mom.

The features in this photo were first identified by John Russell, who, with his dad, Andy, rode this area on many occasions over the years. John's identification was subsequently confirmed and expanded by George Hagglund, a long-time Gladstone Valley resident, and by my brother Donald, who has an infallible sense of direction. To all of them, I am indebted for their assistance. Courtesy Katherine Bruce, Author's collection.

---

[1] The box stall was a closed in area of our barn used to confine animals without tying them up with a halter shank.

Sometimes, a very wild, easily spooked horse was kept in the box stall. At other times, Dad put a calf in there when he wanted to keep it away from its mother for some reason. Occasionally a goat, or a sheep, might be in the box stall for various reasons.

[2] To spoil a horse is to let it get away with disobedient or bad mannered behaviour. Horses learn very quickly when they have their rider buffaloed, or intimidated.

[3] A hand is a measurement of about four inches. A 17-hand tall horse would stand nearly six feet tall at the withers (the highest part of the back, at the base of the neck).

[4] Harness lines are long leather straps that are attached to the bridle bit. A harness is an arrangement of leather straps and metal buckles, rings, and snaps, which is put on an animal so it can be hitched to a vehicle to pull a load. A bridle bit is a metal bar that is put in a horse's mouth and used to start, steer, and stop the horse.

MY FOUR-LEGGED PLAYMATES,
THE SHEEP AND GOATS

Young Teachers

For most of the time Don and I lived on the ranch, Bill was too young to take much of a part in Don's and my playing. Often, too, Don was busy helping Mom, and I had free time on my own. I must have had a strong urge to teach something or somebody even at an early age. This was borne out late in my life. By the end of my paid working career I had nearly thirty years of service as a classroom teacher.

I started out my practice teaching, as it were, by teaching the animals on our ranch what I thought they should know. When I was about three years old I taught all the cats to lie on their backs. As I got older I played with the goats and horses that my dad raised on our ranch.

I especially liked teaching the goats, which were just my size. When I was six or seven, I trained some of the goats to do various tasks. From about eight years old up through my teens I worked with, and helped to train, some of our horses.

In the task of teaching the goats, I had the help of an excellent dog that we called Tippy. He was a sort of slate blue and white pinto dog, and was probably part Border collie.

It got so that all I had to do was yell, "Here, Tippy! Here, Tippy! Tippy!" and the goats would come running up to me to be caught. They stood quietly while I put a rope around their necks and were docile while I played with them.

But the goats, as I said, were smart. It did not take them long to figure out that Tippy was not always there. Then they would not come when I yelled, "Here, Tippy! Here, Tippy!"

When this happened I would wait until some afternoon when Tippy was around. Then I would have him catch all of the goats that I liked to play with several times that afternoon. After that, for quite awhile, the goats would come running up to me when I called, "Here, Tippy! Here, Tippy!"

They would look expectantly up at me as if to say, "Take me! Take me! Don't let the dog get me." When they stopped running up to me, I would teach the same lesson over again. Eventually, however, I grew tired of that game, too. I was getting older.

Basically, I could play with the horses for only a short period of time in the summer. To fill my playtime the rest of the year required considerable ingenuity. I had very few store-bought toys. Those that I did have interested me for only brief periods of time, maybe on a very cold, blustery day in winter, or on soggy, wet days in the spring and summer. I liked to be around the animals, even if that meant working really hard. Many times, however, the work seemed like play, or could be used as an opportunity for playing.

In this 1937 picture, Don and Bill are standing beside "Tippy," my goat-catching dog. Tippy was a blue and white Border collie. Herding animals was in his blood. He just loved an opportunity to show off his expertise.

We always had a dog on our ranch but none of the others matched Tippy for chasing goats. Tippy was so smart that I quite easily trained him to catch whichever goat I wanted and hold it by the hind leg until I came up with a rope for its neck. Often I would play with several goats in an afternoon to give Tippy practice and to keep the goats in form. Author's collection.

There always seemed to be an opportunity for playing while I was "helping Dad," even if all I had to do was hold the lines of the team's harnesses. The team was trained to stand without having their lines held, but I felt like I was helping. Indeed, I was helping Mom by being somewhere safe with Dad!

One daily wintertime task was feeding the animals over at the stack yards. Every day about dusk the cattle, sheep and goats gathered expectantly beside a haystack in one of the stack yards waiting for Dad to throw out some hay for them.

It was while Dad was throwing out the hay in the evening that I took very fast rides. These "fast rides" were a kind of game that Don and I played, where we hung onto the hair at the top of the sheep's or goat's hips then ran fast along behind the animal as it tried to get rid of us.

Generally speaking, I did not think the sheep were much fun to play with; to me they were too wild and/or stupid. Perhaps I felt that way because I never could tame and train the sheep like I trained the goats. Besides, sheep were smelly and oily. Nevertheless, sometimes when I felt like having some excitement, I would get a handhold on a sheep just above its hips.

When I gave the wool a yank the sheep would run as fast as it could, generally into the midst of the feeding herd. Then I would let go of the first sheep and grab hold of a second one.

Then the second startled animal would bolt off with me hanging on behind. Gradually I would work up to a fast, wild sheep, and would go flying across the stack yards until I was flung off into the snow.

Playing with the Goats

There were no restrictions to playing with the goats, so for a few years that was one of my favourite activities - spring, summer, fall or winter. I had a lot of fun playing with the goats. They were small enough that I could handle them by myself when I was quite young and small.

This 1934 picture shows me riding "Smokey," one of my favourite goats. I am using the little saddle that Dad got for me to use to ride Dickie. Dad made the bridle that I am using on Smokey especially for my goats. Courtesy Don Vroom, Author's collection.

I really did enjoy playing with the goats. I could play undisturbed by anyone and in a setting that was generally safe enough that my mother did not have to keep too close an eye on me.

I could hold onto the hair on the top of the goats' hips and run behind them, pulled along at what seemed like break-neck speed. I could chase them on foot, lead them around, or harness them to a little sleigh in winter or a little wagon in summer.

Actually, I rode the goats very little, much preferring to ride a horse. The goats were not strong enough to carry or pull much weight, but they were fun to play with, and gave me many hours of pleasure and some very good exercise.

Another advantage of playing with the goats was that they were more available than the horses, especially in the wintertime. That's when Dad took most of the horses to pasture out at the Peigan Indian Reservation near Brocket.

The only horses that were kept at our ranch in the winter were a team of workhorses[1], a couple of saddle horses, and our school ponies. They were not for playing with.
Chasing in the goats was a hard task, but one that I enjoyed almost as much as chasing horses. Getting them down to the corrals required a lot of energy and tenacity. Moreover, in the summer time, it was a necessary task if I wanted to play with the goats.

The main difference between chasing in the goats and chasing in the horses was that I had to chase the goats in on foot for the most part. The goats ranged on much steeper hillsides and much rougher terrain than the horses. In the spring they had to be brought in so that they could be milked, and thus provide much-needed nourishment for the family before the cows came fresh.[2]

Chasing in the goats was always fun. The task became increasingly challenging as summer progressed and the goats ranged further and further away from the home corrals.

Here is a 1979 view of a steep, rocky hillside in the little pasture of our home ranch, down which I chased goats and horses. I chased the goats on crutches one summer.

Stories about my adventures near or on these mountains are told in this book. Several landmarks, which figured prominently in these childhood experiences, show in the background. The main range of the Rocky Mountains forms a magnificent backdrop; left to right are Victoria Peak, Round Mountain, Windsor Peak (formerly Castle Mountain) right of centre, and a small piece of the ridge that runs southwest to northeast along the top of Table Mountain. The Castle River flows through a wide valley behind these mountains.

My son, Dave Annand, is seen here with the family dog, "Charlie". Courtesy Edith Annand Smithies.

Even so, I continued to bring in the goats so that the coyotes would not sneak up on the sleeping herd and kill one or two of them during the night. An added motivation was that once the goats were in the barnyard I could play with my favourite goats, and continue to train the rest of the goats as needed.

Because I liked playing with the goats, and they liked me, bringing in the goats became my regular task. When I was a little older, I applied the same ardour and determination to chasing in the horses. A couple of goat-chasing episodes demonstrated how much determination I needed in dealing with the goats.

One such example was when I still had to use crutches to get around after having had my right leg tendons badly torn in a skiing accident. "That Bess sure has a lot of grit," my dad would say. That made me work still harder at what I was trying to do.

Even though my leg hurt, I wanted to play with the goats. But, before I could play with them, I had to chase the herd in off the side hill above our home corrals. Dad made me a pair of little crutches that were just the right size for me.

Getting up the hill using my crutches was a real struggle. At first I had to take the long way round to get to the top of the side hill. I went about one-quarter mile up the little creek, struggling slowly along the trail at the bottom of the side hill.

Then I took another trail, making a big switchback that brought me out at the top of the side hill. I would come out of the trees above where the goats were grazing at the top of the side hill or sleeping in the shade of the "big fir trees," a group of large fir trees that grew just east of the top of the lane.

Once above the goats, I would yell "Whoo-oo-p! Whoo-oo-p," in my loudest, most commanding manner. The startled animals would leap to their feet and instantly start running toward the goat pen in the barnyard. To try to keep up with them I would hold my crutches securely under both arms. Then I would kick with my weak leg, fly through the air, and land ten to twelve feet further down the hill on my strong left leg.

I used my crutches for balance when I landed. After awhile I could go almost as fast as I would normally run. Miraculously, by the end of summer my injured right leg was as strong as the other one. For a few years, if I were really tired, my right leg would develop a dull ache. As I got older and continued an active lifestyle my leg became stronger and stronger and does not trouble me at all any more. If I had not been such an active child, however, I could have ended up being lame all of my life. What a shame that would have been!

Bill Learns to Survive

One beautiful, sunny spring Saturday, when I started out to run in my goats, Mom said quietly, "You'd better take Bill along today, Bess."

My parents taught us children to look out for each other. Whether we were a boy or a girl, older or younger, we were to look out for and help each other. This was not easy because we, as children, did not understand the developmental differences between us. I was two and one-half years younger than Don, but Bill, my younger brother, was four and one-half years younger than I was. This spread in ages is not much difference in adults, but in children, it is a big difference.

71

It seemed to me I had always been able to keep up with Don, though he may have made some allowance for me that I was unaware of! "Look after each other, you two," Mom always said. So when we were children and Bill was old enough to trail along with me on my exploits, I felt it was my duty to teach him endurance, fortitude, and tenacity.

Bill was four and one-half years old the spring that Mom insisted I take him along with me on my private adventure. I was just past eight, but quickly thought of our age difference for an excuse not to take Bill along on one of my goat-chasing exploits.

"He's too little," I protested.

"He's not too little, Bess," Mom said firmly. "Take him with you, please." I argued back and forth a little, until Mom asked in an exasperated tone of voice, "Bess, do you want me to call your dad over here?"

I knew that if Mom had to call Dad to get me to obey her I would get some kind of punishment, though I didn't know exactly what. My punishments varied according to the seriousness of my misdemeanor.

"Oh, all right," I said half-heartedly. Then on second thought I added, "What if he gets hungry?"

"He won't get hungry. He ate a good breakfast," Mom answered. [3]

"But what if he does?" I said defensively.

"Bess, do you want me to call your father?"

I knew I had no leg to stand on. Dejectedly, I headed toward the little pasture to get the goats in so we could play with them. Bill couldn't run as fast as I could, but came along without complaining. After awhile I found out he was pretty good company and could help some, too.

I thought things were going quite well, but suddenly Bill started getting hungry. "We're just about to where the goats are," I said cheerfully, hoping to divert his attention away from his hunger.

"I don't care," wailed Bill, "I'm hungry."

"There's nothing to eat," I said flatly. And there was nothing in sight to eat; the berries were not ripe yet and we did not have sandwiches.

"But I'm hungry," insisted Bill, starting to cry.

"Don't be a cry baby," I said, thinking he might learn to be tough.

"I'm not a cry baby; I'm hungry," cried Bill, wiping his tears and his runny nose on his shirtsleeve.

Suddenly I thought about goat's milk. The nannies had come fresh a couple of months earlier and were still giving lots of milk.

Mom didn't know it, but when I got hungry when I was out playing with the goats I would catch one of the nannies, squirt the milk into my mouth and have a little lunch.

Map 4 *The hand-drawn map, "Trails in the little pasture and over the big hill, 1936" shows the main trails on our ranch that the horses and goats followed when we were chasing them in from the little pasture or from "over the big hill."*

It also shows the lane, the big garden, the side hill, the location of our home corrals, and the spring that was the source of the "little creek." Map hand drawn by the author.

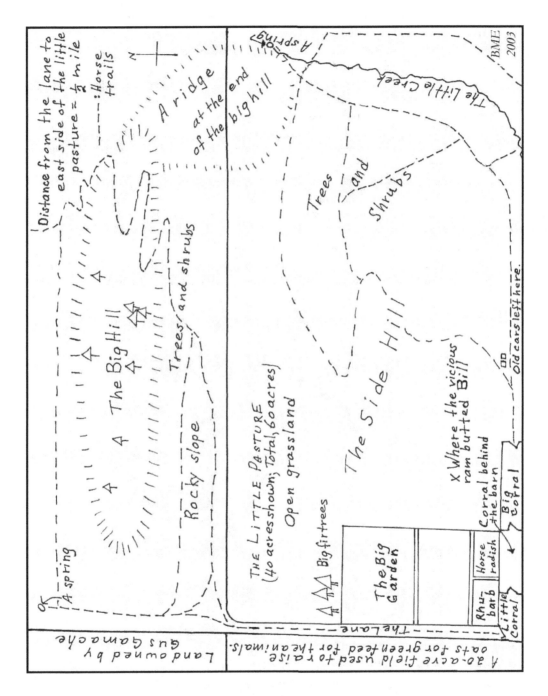

MAP 4 TRAILS IN THE LITTLE PASTURE AND OVER THE BIG HILL, 1936

Once when I had my cousin Rita Cyr along, I showed her how to have lunch "on the trail" — away from the house, too.

"How would you like some milk, Bill?" I asked lightheartedly.

"There's no cow," bellowed Bill.

"I could catch a goat, and you could have goat's milk," I said optimistically.

"No, you can't; they're too wild," protested Bill.

"You just watch," I answered in a chipper tone of voice.

We walked quietly along for awhile. When we came to where the goats were lying in the shade. I did not want to startle them.

"You stay here," I said to Bill in a low voice. "I'll catch one."

And off I went before Bill could object again. I caught one of "the nanny goats," a female, without any trouble, put a short rope around her neck and led her back to where Bill sat waiting.

"I have no cup," Bill blurted out, tears welling up in his eyes again.

"That's all right," I said in a matter-of-fact tone of voice. "I'll squirt it into your mouth. Just bend down here and open your mouth; I'll show you how it's done," I continued confidently.

Dad was Overseas with the Canadian Army from March 1941 to January 1945. This Christmas card, "The Goatherd," post marked Nov 17, 1941, must have reminded him of home.

Upon the advice of our family doctor, Dr. Brayton of Pincher Creek, Dad was brought home from Overseas on compassionate leave before the end of WWII because my mother was so ill. Author's collection.

The goat stood quietly while I squirted the milk in short squirts into Bill's mouth until he said he was full, and would drink no more.

I didn't know if I'd done the right thing, so I didn't say anything to Mom when we got home. Bill taking his cue from me, didn't say anything either. He did not, however, seem to have as good an appetite as usual come mealtime. I really did not like goat's milk and did not drink much of it, so I was as hungry as a bear and ate my usual amount.

This went of for several weeks. Bill would eat a hearty breakfast and dinner; the two of us would go off playing in the afternoon, and Bill would not eat his supper. But he stayed healthy and was getting fat and chubby.

Mom and Dad tried everything they could think of to get Bill to eat, but still he refused. Mom, especially, got more and more worried. "I wonder what's wrong with Bill," Mom mused one day. "Maybe we should call the doctor." Neither Bill nor I said a word.

Mom rode to Beaver Mines and phoned our family physician, Dr. Walkey of Pincher Creek. After Mom had explained Bill's symptoms, the doctor said, "I'm going out to Gladstone Valley in a couple of days. I'll call in and have a look at Bill."

"He looks fine to me," Dr. Walkey pronounced after he had examined Bill a couple of days later. "He's sure a healthy-looking little fellow. Just keep and eye on him."

My secret was discovered and the mystery solved when Bill eventually got tired of drinking goat's milk. When that stage came I had to develop a new strategy. I would catch Bill, then catch a goat and throw Bill onto the ground under the goat and hold him there, while I squirted milk into his mouth. If Bill would not open his mouth, I splattered milk in his face. When he opened his mouth to yell I squirted milk in it, causing him to let out a sort of muffled holler.

One day Dad, again working around the barn, heard a ruckus out behind the goat house. I was always careful to feed Bill at a spot where Mom could not see the procedure if she looked out the kitchen door. Dad went to investigate. Peering around the back corner of the sheep shed, which was attached to the barn, Dad got the surprise of his life.

There, behind the goat house and out of sight of the house, was Bill, a nanny goat, and I going through our snack time procedure. Dad stood for a couple of minutes chuckling at how cleverly I had figured out how to keep Bill from getting hungry "on the trail." Then, remembering how worried Mom was, he took action.

"What are you doing, Bess?" he called out.

Guiltily, I jumped to my feet. There was no use denying what I was up to.

Dad took appropriate action, and that was the end of my feeding Bill goat's milk. Bill's appetite returned to normal and we went on with our summer adventures. By then the saskatoon berries were ripe and we ate berries for little snacks, always being careful not to eat too many and spoil our appetites for supper.

Smokey and Baby Darling

I had all the goats named. Their names generally reflected their colour or their disposition. Smokey and Baby Darling were two of the bigger goats in the herd and were my two all-time favourites.

Smokey was named for his colour. His shaggy coat was smoky buckskin, a duller colour than a palomino horse, but of roughly the same shade and with a tinge of greyish-blue to his hair. Smokey had a white blaze, or stripe, down his face. He was the first goat I taught to drive and to pull a little sleigh or wagon.

Baby Darling was named for his disposition. When he was a kid, Baby Darling was a really sweet animal. He loved to be petted and brushed, and was soft and cuddly.

Baby Darling grew to be a tall, light brown goat and, like Smokey, had white stripes on his face. As Baby Darling grew older he was easily trained to pull a sleigh or wagon and became a willing worker. When Baby Darling was two years old, he was tall and strong. I decided it was time he was taught to do "something useful," so I put him to work.

Smokey was also a tall, strong goat, but was inclined to be what I called "lazy." Smokey did not work energetically, but he was a very even-tempered, steady worker. I did not notice that Smokey was lazy until Baby Darling came on the scene.

Smokey was a few years older than Baby Darling and was the first goat I trained as a riding goat, and then as a driving goat. Dad made a "little harness," an arrangement of leather straps and metal buckles, rings, and snaps that just fit Smokey and with which I fastened him to my sleigh or wagon.

Bill practiced his riding skills by riding around the house yard on a goat. Here is Bill in 1935 on Smokey, the goat I trained to pull my sled and wagon. Author's collection.

Dad also made a "little singletree," a wooden bar onto which to hitch the traces, out of a piece of kindling wood. [4] It was about 12 inches long with a loop of baling wire at each end to hook the goat harness traces onto. [5]

I was quite small at the time, probably six or seven, and spent many happy hours driving Smokey around in the barnyard. I even used him to haul wood from the big woodpile by the shack to the woodpile on the back porch, a distance of about thirty feet!

As a child, I would do "play work," playing with toy articles or small animals pretending to do grown-up tasks, for hours upon hours. I gradually learned many skills, some of which I have used throughout my life when doing "real work," that is, work for which one is responsible, and which enables a family or a community to function smoothly and live together peacefully.

Every day I still use some of the skills that I learned as a child. My optimistic attitude, which has stayed with me throughout my life, has made my life pleasant and rewarding.

When Baby Darling was about three years old, and tall and strong, Dad asked one day, "How would you like to have a team, Bess?"

"Okay!" I answered cheerily. So dad made a second little leather harness that just fit Baby Darling, and whittled another small singletree.

"I think you should drive your goats in tandem, Bess," Dad advised, when the second harness was made.

"What's that?" I asked, my curiosity piqued.

"That's when you drive your team one behind the other, instead of side by side," Dad explained.

I was really curious about that, as I had never seen any kind of a team except where horses were driven side by side. I could hardly wait to get started. So Dad put a ring on either side of the wide band of Baby Darling's harness that fitted around his body just behind his front legs. Smokey's tugs were then hooked onto Baby Darling's harness.

Smokey was an older goat by then and not so able to pull a load, so Dad thought Baby Darling should be the wheeler. Being the "wheeler" meant Baby Darling was hitched closest to my sleigh or wagon, and thus did most of the actual pulling. He was easier to train because he was closer to me, and had to work harder than Smokey did.

Since he was used to being steered, Smokey was a good choice for my "lead," or front, goat, in my tandem team. Smokey had a little halter, a head harness with a band around his nose, which Dad had made especially for him, and which had long reins attached to each side of the halter. I held these reins and pulled one or the other to make my goat team go where I wanted them to go.

I drove my team around the barnyard and over to the stack yards practicing with them every day. And that was how I taught high-spirited, willing Baby Darling to be a play-work goat.

By then I was about eight years old, and was too heavy to ride the goats. However, now that I had a team, I felt I could go further afield, and so began memorable adventures with my beloved goat team.

One fairly mild winter day, I started out to drive the two and one-half miles to Beaver Mines. The snow was not very deep and I was following along in the tracks made by sleighs pulled by teams of horses driven by people who lived up the Gladstone Valley. People like the Truitts and Barclays, who lived south of Dad's place, over a small ridge in the Gladstone Creek Valley, passed by our place periodically en route to the Beaver Mines Store and Post Office.

Travelling by goat team was slow, there was no doubt about that. I also had to walk quite a bit of the way because the goats were not strong enough to pull the sleigh with me on it for more than a few hundred yards at a time. So I walked behind the sleigh, scrambling over ridges of hard-packed, drifted snow.

Eventually, we passed "John Babin's corner," the point where Dad's west quarter met John Babin's home quarter, about one-half mile from my home. After facing a brisk west wind all the way, I was tired. After some thought, I decided I probably could not make it to Beaver Mines with my goat team that day.

We had reached a sheltered stretch of road, so I turned my goat team around and stopped to have a good rest. I rather carelessly laid the reins on the ground beside me. I was just getting my wind back, and was thinking of moving on, when I noticed my goats had started going without me. All of a sudden, they were full of energy, trotting along the snowy road about twenty-five feet away from me. I scrambled to my feet and started to run after them, not able to move very quickly in my heavy winter clothing

This is a panoramic view of our ranch, looking northeast, from atop Gilmore Ridge, about two miles to the west. The ranch buildings, in the east quarter, are visible in the upper centre of the photo. The "big hill," where the goats ranged in the summer, is in the far distance. Author's collection.

"Whoa, Smokey! Whoa, Baby Darling! Whoa!" I called out, but my goat team did not stop. Within about fifty yards, however, I had almost caught up to my sleigh. As I ran doggedly onward, I thought despairingly, "I am going to fall down from tiredness. I will never catch up. But I don't want my goats to get home without me."

Just before the goats turned the corner to head up the final half-mile to our ranch yard, I gave one final burst of speed and lunged forward. I just managed to flop onto the sleigh, where I lay panting to regain my breath. As soon as I got onto the sleigh, Smokey and Baby Darling wanted to stop. After giving them a little rest, we carried on.

I was so tired that I rode the sleigh most of the way home. Even though I was exhausted, I had to look after my goats before I went into the house for my own food. I took the harnesses off of Smokey and Baby Darling, and let them out in the big corral where they could get feed and water near the goat house.

Although Smokey was a very good lead goat, and would go wherever I steered him, he seemed to get lazier and lazier. He just would not keep his traces tight, with the result that Baby Darling had to do most of the pulling. I did not think that was fair to Baby Darling, so one day about mid-June I decided to try an experiment. I switched my goats' order in the tandem set-up, putting Baby Darling as the lead goat and Smokey as the wheeler.

The dog in this March 1929 photo is hitched to a homemade sled with an apple box fixed on top. The Bruce family used it to haul small packages from Ballantyne's Store and Post Office to their home. This picture is taken looking eastward from a short distance north of the Bruces' home at Beaver Mines. Behind the car is part of the large slag heap that was on their land. The slag was from what once was one of the main coal mines at Beaver Mines but which had been closed for many years when I was a child.

The hill in the background is the north slope of the "big hill" where I chased herds of horses when I was child. The "big hill" was north of my father's ranch, so the ranch is south of this hill. Number One coal mine, which was still operating when I was a child, is on the west side, facing the camera, but does not show in this photo.

I hitched Smokey and Baby Darling to a small sled, in an arrangement similar to this, with a nose band and harness. I usually drove my goats close to home, but on at least one occasion, when I was about seven years old, I started out to drive them to Beaver Mines, a distance of two and one-half miles each way.

By the time we'd travelled only a little more than one-half mile, however, I was tired and the goats seemed to be tired. So, I turned them around, and headed for home. Suddenly, the goats had a burst of energy that had me running to keep up with them! Michael Bruce photo, courtesy of Katherine Bruce, Author's collection.

What a schmozzle! All of a sudden Smokey was really energetic. Used to being the lead goat, Smokey tried to get in front of Baby Darling. Baby Darling, on the other hand, used to being the wheeler, tried to get behind Smokey. Round and round my goats turned, still hitched to the wagon and to each other, until they were completely entangled and nearly choking.

When they finally settled down, unable to move, I tried to untangle them. Whenever I got them partly undone, they went in their circle again. Finally, I decided to unharness them. They were so ensnarled that I could barely undo the buckles, and even had to cut one or two straps.

By the time the whole operation was done I was completely frustrated. To make matters worse Dad, who came out of the barn to see what the commotion was about, did not help me out of my predicament. He even may have shown some amusement at the scene.

My struggling with Smokey and Baby Darling probably was a very funny sight, but I was not amused. I let the two goats run back into the big corral, and hung up my tangled harnesses.

I do not think I ever again harnessed up my goats. The magic was gone. I guess I had outgrown them. After that the goats were for meat and milk only. Smokey and Baby Darling both eventually died of old age.

Bunny

When the kids were younger than three months old, they were left at the home corrals with a nanny goat. In the springtime the nanny goats took turns acting as a "baby sitter." Each day, one nanny goat, a different one from the day before, did not go out to pasture, but stayed in the big barnyard with all the kids, while the rest of the herd went up on the high hill to graze. The kids would sleep in sun all day. One of their favourite spots was on the tiers of a pile of lumber that was stacked beside the goat house. I would play with them after school and on weekends and begin the taming down process.

Of course, the kids had had nothing to eat all day, so were ravenously hungry by evening. When the main herd of goats returned about sunset, the kids would run bleating half-way up the side hill, find their mothers, and begin suckling right on the spot.

Generally, one or two kids or lambs were born to a nanny goat or ewe, but sometimes triplets were born. In such a case, one of the three was always very frail. If on his morning rounds Dad found triplets, he would always bring the weakest one, whether it was a kid or a lamb, into the house. Mom would make a bed for the tiny creature in a box behind the kitchen range, and feed it by hand.

I have seen my mother revive lambs and kids that were so weak they could not even open their mouths. Mom would hold the shivering little animal on her lap, gently open its mouth and feed it some water-weakened ewe's or nanny's milk, sometimes with a drop or two of brandy, kept especially for that purpose.

Gradually, the frail young ones gained strength, and would be fed by bottle until they were big enough to eat grass. Sometimes, one of a set of twins would die and the smallest of a set of triplets could be "put on" that ewe or nanny, that is, the mother animal could be persuaded to adopt a young one that was not her own. Similarly, a ewe or nanny with only one offspring might be persuaded to adopt one of the triplets, feeding it as if it were her own.

Even though she had no formal training, my mother was a very good practical nurse, both for humans and animals. Most of the smallest kids or lambs from the sets of triplet were saved by Mom's persistent, instinctive care.

Early one March morning Dad came in to the house gently cradling a limp newborn kid that he had wrapped in an old blanket. "Here's a little fellow that's really bad off, Mommy," Dad said with grave concern in his voice. "The other two kids from that nanny look okay. But this little guy doesn't look to me like he's got a very good chance. He's got a 'double-jointed hind leg'[6] and a 'bunny foot.'"[7]

These two abnormalities were the main reasons why the little black and white kid had not been able to get to his feet.

"Let me see him," directed Mom in a professional tone of voice.

"I'll put him on the table here," Dad said, gently setting the helpless animal down. The kid was so feeble it could not lift its head from the blanket.

Normally, newborn kids are able to stand up within an hour of their birth. This little fellow just lay there, not moving a muscle, his eyes closed.

My mother looked compassionately at the pitiful little creature. The kid just lay there shivering. Don and I crowded close on either side, excited as always by the arrival of a new offspring.

"Keep back, you guys. Let Mommy look at him," Dad directed. "Put some more wood on the fire, Don," he ordered. I drew back for a couple of minutes, but soon I was crowding close beside Mom again.

"Let me pet him," I pleaded.

"Just let him be," Mom answered, wiping the little kid dry with an old towel. "He needs to sleep. And bring in some more firewood, please. We need to keep him warm."

I stood and looked at the little goat. He was a brown and white pinto with white stripes on his face. Even in his near-dead state he looked sweet and playful. "He would be a wonderful pet," I said longingly. "I hope he lives. He would be so much fun to play with."

Slowly I reached out my hand and began to stroke the little goat. "You'll be all right, little goat," I murmured softly. "You'll be all right."

The helpless little goat just lay there without moving, his eyes closed, breathing in short and shallow breaths; as if even just breathing took all the strength he could muster.

The soft touch of a small child's hand seemed to relax the little fellow. He seemed to sense that love and hope were surrounding him. The weak little kid relaxed even more under my soft petting, and just lay there, his life totally dependent upon the humans that stood beside him.

My mother examined the weak little kid carefully, gently lifting the little animal's legs one at a time to test them for strength. When Mom came to the kid's right rear leg, she paused and examined it more carefully.

"This leg is double-jointed all right," she said softly, her voice full of concern. "See how weak it is. It just flops back and forth when I lift it. The tendons and muscles are underdeveloped. But I think we can fix it. And look at this little foot," mused my mother. "It has no hoof."

"What do you mean?" I asked, peering closer.

81

"Well, just look at it," Mom said. Then I, too, examined the little goat's hind leg looking at the spot where a solid hoof should have been. Sure enough, there was no hoof on the right hind leg. The leg ended at the ankle with hair growing on the end of it.

Our animals were often given a certain name because of some identifying physical characteristic. My dad named this little kid "Bunny" because it had "bunny foot."

Mom knew instinctively what to do for the helpless little creature. In spite of how sore her hands were with arthritis in the joints, she put a figure-eight bandage on the double-jointed leg to hold it at about a ninety-degree angle. The joint healed in that position. Bunny never could straighten that leg nor bend the joint any further shut, but he could walk on it.

Nothing could be done about the little animal's bunny foot, however. Thus, in combination with his stiff leg, Bunny always moved, whether walking or running, with a limp.

One day Bunny had a close call. I was not watching him closely enough, and was not prepared for what happened to him.

Bunny had become my special pet and followed me everywhere, even to the "outhouse"; that is, an outdoor toilet, separate from, but near, the house. An outhouse usually has one hole over a deep pit. Our ranch house, however, had once been used as a schoolhouse, so the outhouse had a boys' and a girls' side.

I generally used the girls' side. The outhouse had been built to meet the needs of boys and girls of different sizes, so each side had three holes ranging from small to large. I, being small at that time, maybe eight years old, would use the smallest hole.

Goats are very curious, active animals. Suddenly one day, Bunny, by this time bigger and stronger, hopped up onto the outhouse seat. He circled around and around the biggest hole, peering curiously into the depths below. "Be careful, Bunny," I warned, "You'll fall in." But my warning came too late. Just at that moment Bunny, forgetting in the excitement of the moment about his missing hoof, lost his footing and fell through the hole. He desperately tried to save himself from falling, catching hold of the edge of the seat and hanging on with his front legs.

I jumped off the toilet seat and ran over to try to get hold of Bunny, but I was too late. By then the weight of Bunny's body, swinging below, had pulled him off from his leg hold and he had fallen into the pit below.

Peering down into the half darkness below, my voice filled with exasperation, I moaned, "Now look what you've gone and done, Bunny! How will I ever get you out?"

Bunny was not hurt by his fall. He looked up pleadingly at me. "Don't worry, Bunny," I reassured him, not knowing quite what I would do. "I'll get you out," I promised, "you just stand still."

Deciding that I needed some advice in the situation, I ran into the house, calling out, "Mom! Mom!" I cried. "Bunny fell down the toilet hole."

"What did you say, Bess?" my mother asked, not quite believing her ears.

"Bunny fell down the toilet hole," I repeated, with a tone of apology in my voice. "I'm sorry, he just did it."

"Well, we'll have to get him out," my mother replied calmly, not wasting time inquiring about the details.

Setting down whatever work she was doing Mom followed me up the trail to the outhouse.

"I was just sitting there, and he jumped up on the seat and fell down the hole," I explained anxiously as we neared the outhouse.

"It's okay, Bess," Mom said reassuringly. "Let's see what we can do for him. Maybe we could use a rope."

"I know where Dad's rope is," I volunteered hastily. "I'll go get it. Then maybe we can put a loop around Bunny's neck and haul him out that way." Mom looked a little doubtful, but, before she could voice her protests, I ran out the outhouse door and over to the barn as fast as I could. I did not like the thought of Bunny staying down the toilet hole for very long.

Once over at the barn I reached up and took down Dad's lariat. Back I raced to the outhouse. I made a medium-sized loop in the lariat and lowered it down through the hole through which Bunny had fallen. After several tries I finally got the loop round Bunny's neck and carefully pulled it tight.

With much effort I hauled the struggling, choking Bunny up out of the toilet hole. He was covered with muck. "Look at him!" I cried, my voice filled with consternation, "He's all dirty! How can I clean him?"

"He needs washing," my mother answered calmly. "Take him down to the pump and try washing him there," she suggested helpfully.

This is 4½-year-old Bill Vroom in the spring of 1936 on "Pickles" with "Bunny," a bunny-footed kid, by Pickles' front legs. Bunny, a goat born with a double-jointed hind leg was around the house yard all summer while his leg strengthened. Just before Mom snapped this photo, Bunny limped over to Bill and stood by Pickles' front legs. Author's collection.

Bunny struggled nearly making me lose my grip on him, whenever I poured the cold water that I pumped from the well over him. "Stand still, Bunny," I urged as no matter how hard I tried I could not hold Bunny and pour clean water over him at the same time.

After several minutes of struggling I got a brain wave that helped me to solve my problem. "I know what I'll do with you, Bunny," I said to him confidently, "I'll wash you in the dam."

So saying I took Bunny to the nearby house yard dam, which we kids generally referred to it as "the little dam".

As I tried to wash him off, Bunny struggled some more. This time he slipped out of my grasp and slid down the steep bank and into the water. Goats are not natural swimmers. Poor Bunny nearly drowned, but I got him out in time.

Bunny was saved! But, after that, I closed and locked the door to keep Bunny out whenever I was using the outhouse.

I spent many happy hours with Bunny. In the late spring when the dam was full of water from spring run-off, we children got the idea of using Mom's wash tub as a boat to sail around in the little dam. The water was still too cold for comfortable swimming, but we were fine in the tub.

By mid-summer the dam water was warm, but it was really too low for us children to swim in. So we rode our ponies down to Beaver Mines Creek to swim and to play in the shallow creek above the deep hole. But I found a way that I could still play in the dam.

I taught Bunny to "sail in the wash tub." He would stand still with his legs braced and ride around the dam in the wash tub as I had done in the springtime. I walked around in the water pushing the tub and talking lovingly to Bunny.

This is late spring, 1936, and the house yard dam is full to the brim. Bill and Don are standing beside the big cottonwood trees on what we kids called "the island" in the little dam. They are reflected in the still water. Author's collection.

84

Bunny, thus comforted, would sail around in the tub by the hour. Sometimes, on a really warm day, he would stand in the tub with his eyes closed, almost asleep.

That pastime ended, however, when I thought it would be fairer, more equal, for other goats, if I gave them a turn, too. I intended to give all the other kids a turn, one at a time, regardless of how big or wild they were. So one day I caught a "neophyte kid," one that had no experience at sailing in the washtub. I put it in the tub with Bunny. That was not a very good idea. Bunny did not like the company.

The neophyte kid, probably quite frightened at the time, did not like being in a washtub either, and tried to jump out. The washtub tipped and both non-swimming kids ended up in the water. I had to jump in and rescue them. I did not pull that stunt, as my dad would say, again. But I did do some other unusual things which had unexpected outcomes. I was ever the experimenter.

Henry Hits the Stew Pot

When we wanted to play in the goat house we first tied up the ram. Once the ram was disposed of, we chased the goats into the goat house for one of our favourite wintertime activities, a kind of tag game which we called "Riding the Goats." We could not sit on the goats' backs as we were too heavy. And, besides, that was too slow. So, we made up an exciting alternative.

"Riding the goats," meant running behind the easiest-to-catch goat, and grabbing on to the hair on its rump at the top of its hips. I would give the hair a little jerk to make the goat start running. As the goat charged into the middle of the herd of about twenty to twenty-five goats, I would let go and grab hold of another startled goat. Then I'd give its hair a jerk and go flying around the pen again.

The rest of herd milled around trying to get out of my way as I came running along behind my goat. They crowded into one corner or the other of the small building, which was about twelve feet square. I would start with an easy-to-catch goat. I knew which goats were faster than the one I was holding onto. I would manoevre skillfully to get the excited goat that I was holding onto up beside the one I wanted to transfer to. Then I would let go of the first goat's rump hairs and grab a second goat, getting a faster goat each time.

"Come on! Get him!" I shouted as I urged each goat in turn to go faster and faster. Once I had some momentum going, I sometimes would grab a faster goat "on the fly." I wouldn't wait for the goats to bunch up in a corner, but would make the transfer on the run. The goats, milling around in the small pen, stirred up the dry manure dust until the air was so thick with dust that I could hardly breathe, but I would keep on. Gradually, I worked up until I caught our very fastest goat, a male goat named "Henry."

Terrified, but unable to escape, Henry would go careening around the goat house at breakneck speed. By the time I got going fast enough to get hold of Henry's hip hairs it would be suppertime.

I generally played alone with the goats when they were outdoors, but often Don joined me in my goat house playing. That added to the noise and shrieks and created even more dust in the small building. Every once in awhile Mom would look out the kitchen door to see where we were.

As long as she heard lots of yells and thumping and bumping in the goat house, Mom knew that we were okay.

When Mom had supper ready she would go to the kitchen door and call, "Yoo-oo-hoo-oo!" That was a very welcome sound, even though we were reluctant to leave the goats. For all our work, we had probably been playing with them for less than an hour by the time we got the ram tied up and the goats chased into the goat house!

Even if Mom had not heard us shrieking and shouting, she would have known from the smell of us where we had been when we went into the house, reeking of goat scent. Mom never complained, however, thankful once again that her children were safe at the end of another day.

Henry was a goat so wild that I considered him to be "thorn in my side," that is, a nuisance. Henry was a stranger, a new goat, amongst my herd of goats. Unlike my other goats, he had not been played with and loved ever since he was a tiny kid.

Henry was a brown, horned goat, which Dad had got from one of our neighbours, Henry Altermatt, who lived "up the (Gladstone) Valley." Henry Altermatt lived about six miles closer to the Rocky Mountains than we did, in the general area through which Gladstone Creek ran. Although Henry was a challenge when I was playing "Riding the Goats" in the goat house, he was not really dangerous like the vicious black-faced ram. But he was a nuisance, nevertheless.

As a child, I loved to go up in the pasture above our ranch and pick bouquets of spring flowers for my mother. My favourite wild flower was, and still is, the fuchsia-coloured shooting star.

Here I am, in May 1935, on a hill near our ranch looking for shooting stars. When I picked flowers in our pastures, most shooting stars had only one or two flowers to a stem. A four-headed shooting star was a rarity.

I was delighted a few years ago to discover a patch of shooting stars in Beacon Hill Park, a beautiful park close to my home in Victoria, BC. My delight grew as I found more and more multi-flowered shooting stars. A 12-flowered specimen was the most splendid I found.

Since my discovery, each Spring I return to the same spot in Beacon Hill Park to make sure "my" shooting stars are still there. As I gaze at them, I am transported back to the spring days of my childhood when I roamed the hills with gay abandon. Michael Bruce photo, courtesy Katherine Bruce, Author's collection.

I could hardly believe that one of my goats would not learn to co-operate with me. One winter day Dad was talking seriously with my mother about how we needed fresh meat. When I heard the word goats, my ears perked up. "I guess I'll have to butcher Smokey or Baby Darling," Dad remarked with a worried tone in his voice. "I don't think we have any other big wethers."[8]

At the words "butcher Smokey or Baby Darling" I was really alarmed.

As Dad continued talking, I thought of Henry. "It would be better to have Henry gone than to lose Smokey or," I reasoned to myself. Out loud I said cheerily, "There's Henry!"

"Who's 'Henry'?" Dad queried, since he did not know the names of all my goats.

"He's that wild goat you got from Henry Altermatt a while ago," I explained, feeling proud of my knowledge about the goats in our herd.

"Oh, yes," Dad mused.

So Henry hit the stew pot. I think Dad knew all along that Henry was a young wether, and just wanted to see what I would say to the idea of losing Smokey or Baby Darling, and what I would do to defend them.

However, without Henry in the goat house, my riding-the-goats game definitely was not so exciting anymore. This was a sign, I guess, that I was outgrowing the goats. I was getting too old to play with them - something like the child in the song about the magic dragon!

This herd of Ralph Vroom horses is ranging on the Gilmore place, which my dad leased for summer pasture during the 1930s. It was only about a mile west of our home place. This photo, taken looking northeast, shows the west side of the range of hills which we viewed looking west from our ranch.

The great hazard to we kids was that, to get to this pasture, we had to ride cross Beaver Mines Creek. The entire length of the creek was a tangle of beaver dams, which made it very swampy and dangerous.

The last time I rode by way of the short-cut west from Babin's corner, my horse was knee-deep in slimy muck and had to struggle to maintain his footing. I was very frightened. After that, I decided discretion was the better part of valour, and took the long way round - going by road via Beaver Mines before turning and heading south up the other side of Beaver Mines Creek Valley. Although this added an hour to the ride, my horse and I were safe. Author's collection.

One day when Don and I were riding to Beaver Mines we came upon an amazing sight - hundreds of giant puffballs strewn across a small, open flat beside the "little" creek a few hundred yards past Babin's corner.

There before us were hundreds of these roundish, mushroom-like fungi. The whole area was covered with the soft gleaming-white growths, ranging in size from a few inches to nearly a foot in height. This August 1927 photo is like these puffballs. Michael Bruce, the photographer, set the stick upright beside the puffball, showing it was about a foot high.

Maida Durham Bird of Victoria, whose grandfather, Arthur Durham, homesteaded at Arrow Lakes, Manitoba, remembers, "South of Winnipeg there was this big farm where hundreds of mushrooms grew. We picked them up and took them home, then skinned and sliced them in thick slices and fried them in butter. Were they ever yummy!" "Sometimes," Maida continued, "when we were playing golf in the field we hit a piece of a broken up puffball, and it went, 'Squish!' Michael Bruce photo, courtesy Katherine Bruce, Author's collection.

---

[1] The horses we called workhorses were big, heavy horses, such as Percherons. They were used for pulling various loads in a sleigh or wagon.

[2] The cows came fresh means our milk cows had calves and began producing milk again. Dry means they were producing no milk.

[3] A good breakfast was usually a bowl of home cooked cereal and milk. Sometimes we had toast, which was toasted on the hot lids of our wood-burning cook stove.

[4] The little singletree could be attached to the front of our little sleigh in winter and the toy wagon in summer.

[5] Traces are the heavier straps of the harness used to attach the work animal to the vehicle being hauled.

[6] A double-jointed leg is a limb having a joint that bends backwards as well as forwards.

[7] A bunny foot is a leg with its hoof missing; the leg ends at the ankle joint and has hair growing over the end of it.

[8] Wethers are castrated male goats that have had their testicles removed so that they cannot breed the nanny goats and thus cause inbreeding in the herd. Inbreeding occurs when animals that are closely related to each other breed with each other. Smaller and sometimes deformed animals can result from inbreeding.

ADVENTURES WITH THE HORSES

We used three types of horses on our ranch - working horses, saddle horses and ponies. The horses that we used to do certain tasks every day were considered to be "working horses." We could not play with them just for the sake of playing - we had to be doing some useful task when we used them.

Our big workhorses were used for pulling heavy loads and various kinds of equipment on our ranch. We did not ride them. As soon as I was able, I loved to drive the work team to help Dad do whatever task was at hand.

In this book I use the words "saddle horses" and "ponies" almost interchangeably. Saddle horses and ponies are used mainly for riding. Until I was about eight years old, most of our saddle horses stood about fourteen or fifteen hands tall, although some were as tall as seventeen hands. Then Dad started breeding ponies.

"Saddle horses" were horses used for riding purposes, generally only one person on their back at a time. They were lighter and more slimly built, than workhorses, and were used for general ranch work. Dad always rode a saddle horse, sturdy animals that were able to stand a full day's ride doing regular ranch work in hilly terrain.

Dad used the saddle horses to bring horses home from pastures that were further away, and to do other ranch work, such as branding colts and calves.

We children used the saddle horses more than we used workhorses. As we grew older, we rode saddle horses to school.

Caring for Our School Mounts

On the weekends we also rode our saddle horses down to Beaver Mines to get the mail and, occasionally, a few groceries. Mom bought much of our food in bulk, so large quantities of food were hauled home by team and wagon, or by sleigh.

We children also used saddle horses to chase in horses from up on the big hill. I often used a saddle horse to get the cows at milking time, though sometimes I had to walk to bring in the cows. I did not like walking for the cows.

Our school mounts worked very hard. They were considered to be "working horses" because we rode them four miles to school and back every day, rain or shine, and often under harsh conditions.

The trail to school was uphill and downhill. Sometimes the road was muddy; sometimes it was icy; sometimes our mounts had to plow through three feet of snow. Sometimes the temperature plunged to forty-below zero Fahrenheit, and we arrived at school half-frozen. It took until morning recess for our hands to get warm enough to hold a pencil, even though our desks were crowded around the one-room school's heater.

We rode the same horses to school everyday from about the end of October to the end of May. So our playing on the weekends was mostly done on foot.

Here I am in 1939, driving Mike and Pearl, a team of our heavy workhorses. I am standing on a load of wood that I hauled from the stack yards. Bill is kneeling in the middle of the load.

After Mom took the picture Bill and I unloaded the blocks of wood onto the woodpile. Every day Dad chopped and split some of the blocks for firewood and kindling. I was driving this team when the "vicious ram" knocked me down and butted me under the sleigh runners. Author's collection.

Our "school ponies" were smaller-sized saddle horses. Looking after our school mounts, and keeping them healthy, was of utmost importance. After a day at school we had to take care of our ponies and see that they were comfortable for the night before we could eat our own supper. At six years of age, I was expected to look after my own horse.

Upon arriving home each day, we first fed and watered our ponies. Then we made sure that our tack was properly stored. We hung our bridles on a peg on the wall and carefully set our saddles on saddle stands made with a horizontal two-by-four. When our riding equipment was neatly stored we ran over to the house where Mom was always waiting for us with a snack to hold us until our supper was ready.

In the spring, summer and early fall our ponies had the run of the school yard, so could get a little bit of grass to eat during the day. We kept them in the barn on weeknights, but on weekends they were kept in a small pasture near our ranch buildings.

However, in the wintertime, our school ponies had to stand all day in the cold school barn without any feed or water, so, by the time we got home at night, they were both tired and hungry.

Overnight and on weekends in the wintertime we kept our school ponies in the barn at home for warmth. We fed those oats and hay, which had been garnered and stored during the summer and fall.

I am standing in the shallow water of Beaver Mines Creek holding up a log in this 1932 photo.

Sometimes we stopped and played in Beaver Mines Creek. Early in the summer, the water was deep enough just below the bridge that we could swim on logs. We would each get a 10-foot long pole and lie along the top of it. We paddled with our hands to move ourselves along.

Sometimes we swam our saddle horses in the deep water a little further down the creek, where beaver dams had made the water ten to twelve feet deep. Mrs. Mabel (Edward) Bruce, Author's collection.

Although we tried to let our ponies rest on the weekends, going for the mail on weekends was considered work for our school ponies, too. Sometimes, in the spring and early fall, we also used them to hunt for and chase in other horses to ride to school. This gave us a change of mounts and gave our usual ponies a rest.

By the time I was six years old, I often rode alone to Beaver Mines on my pony. Sometimes, when Don was with me, we worked in a little playing at the home of some of the neighbour children on the way to or from Beaver Mines. However, Mom and Dad knew how long it should take us to get to the store and back, so we did not linger along the way very often.

One day, later in the summer when the water was low, Mrs. Bruce came along on her saddle horse while we were playing in the creek. As she often did, Mrs. Bruce took these two charming snapshots, on this page and the next, of us at our play.

If we stopped to play for awhile, we would make our ponies trot a little so that we would get home at the right time. As long as our ponies were not sweating when we got home, we were okay. But racing our ponies on the way home was definitely forbidden. We were very proud of how fast our ponies could run, and sometimes, we did race with other children who also rode on horseback to school.

However, I finally "learned the hard way," to obey the no-racing rule

That happened the time when we raced our ponies coming home from Gladstone Valley School, and Dad happened to come along a couple of hours later. He could tell by the horses' tracks that we had been galloping them.

When Dad asked me if I had been running my pony, I innocently said, "No." Right away I knew I had been caught in a lie, but it was too late.

In this 1932 picture, I am holding Mrs. Bruce's big straw hat, while Don, who is being extremely careful not to get the hat too wet, pours water into it. Mrs. Mabel (Edward) Bruce photo, Author's collection.

But Dad always had a way of meting our appropriate punishment. He knew that I disliked walking anywhere more than anything else. So to punish me he said, "Well, Bess, you'll have to walk to school for a week."

I took my punishment stoically; I knew I had disobeyed my parents. I did not whine and beg, but every morning I cheerfully asked, "Is it a week yet?"

"No, Bess," Dad would say. Then I would trudge along road the four miles to school. After a few days, Mom persuaded Dad to relent, and I was able to ride again, but I always remembered that lesson.

Some of our horses had such quiet, gentle natures that they could be trusted year in and year out, early spring, or late fall. Don's black, half-Shetland mare, Babe, for instance, and all her colts and their colts, had that same gentle nature. Babe, in fact, was my mother's favourite mount.

Horses like Babe never had to be "topped off." The ones that did were ridden very warily for a few days each spring when they were first brought in off the winter range, until they remembered what being a saddle horse meant and were gentled down again. After a few springs, even these horses eventually settled down and became excellent mounts. Such a horse was

"Ginger," a sorrel, part thoroughbred, gelding that I broke all by myself when I was about ten years old.

Many of Dad's horses were of the so-called "range-horse breed." Range horses are beautiful animals, both physically and by nature. These horses are, generally speaking, very gentle and trustworthy once they have been trained as saddle horses, yet they never become lazy or sluggish. They have tender mouths, and need to be ridden with a "light hand," that is, with a light, gentle hold on the bridle reins.

In addition, range horses have great stamina and agility. They can run for miles, when need be, as in horse chasing, and can leap over unexpected obstacles. If, while you are riding a range horse in headlong pursuit of a herd of horses, there is suddenly a deadfall[1] or a windfall across the trail, a range horse will leap over it, hardly breaking its stride.

Of course, you as a rider must be prepared for any obstacle, or you will be piled in the bush, and have to walk home. Your horse would keep going on the chase. Most riders try to avoid that circumstance. Walking anywhere always made me feel quite vulnerable and powerless. When I was on horseback, however, it was a different story. No one could catch me. Fortunately, I was never forced to walk home from a horse-chasing expedition.

So intelligent are these range horses that, when well-trained, they scarcely need to be reined at all; a gentle pull on the reins is all that is needed to stop them. A light pressure on either side of their neck will turn them in whatever direction the rider wants to go. This is called "neck reining." A "well-reined horse" responds quickly to gentle neck reining. Many saddle horses of the range-horse breed are strong and agile, and can "turn on a dime," as the cowboys say, meaning that they can whirl 180 degrees standing almost on one spot.

Jerking our ponies' mouths was absolutely forbidden. "Don't you ever let me catch you jerking those ponies," Dad warned us. One telling was all we got.

These beautiful, intelligent horses can also be trained to "knee rein." The rider can guide them simply by leaning slightly to the side in the direction of the turn and exerting pressure with the opposite knee.

Having a horse that knee reins well is a great advantage in many working ranch situations, as when a person wants to "cut out," or separate, a certain animal from a herd. The animal naturally does not want to leave the herd and keeps dodging back and forth. A knee-reined horse can dodge back and forth just as fast, and the desired animal is successfully cut from the herd in short order.

Range horses are also the breed often used by rodeo riders in calf roping, wild cow milking, and steer decorating events in rodeos. Pick-up men at the rodeo generally ride range horses to do their tasks. "Pick-up men at the rodeo" are cowboys who firmly lift cowboys off a bucking bronco after they have completed their 10-second ride in the saddle bronc-riding event in a rodeo. The horses enjoy the challenge and the excitement as much as the riders do. A well-trained rodeo horse is a valuable mount in any event, with a good roping horse probably the most highly valued.

Although we spent a lot of time playing with and riding the horses, we children had remarkably few injuries. This was due in part, no doubt, to the gentle nature of many of Dad's horses, and to the fact that Dad's horses were all very well trained. The really mean, untrustworthy horses were of a cross breeding that resulted in their developing into surly, mean tempered creatures. Dad got most such horses as a "to boot" in a trade or sale, that is, as a little something extra over the price the person was willing or able to pay.

This general lack of serious injuries - hurt feelings did not count - was due, too, to Dad and Mom's careful tutoring of us children. We learned how to mount and dismount our horses safely, how to calm a frightened mount, and how to manage a startled one. We had to trust our mounts and we had to get them to trust us. This they willingly did, as long as we behaved in a kind, consistent, and firm, manner.

We kids were allowed a great deal of freedom around the horses. That we were expected to be careful went without saying. Being careful was critical to our good fun, and even to our survival; we were often several miles from home in hilly, tree-covered country. Finding us if we had an accident would have been like looking for a needle in the proverbial haystack.

Building Up Our Own Herd of Horses

My dad earned most of our family's cash income by breeding and selling saddle horses. He used his wide knowledge of caring for horses to keep our horses healthy. His skill at handling horses enabled him to train any horse to be a quiet, reliable saddle horse.

Riding to school on freshly trained horses or on horses in training[2] was an excellent way to get horses tame enough to sell as gentle saddle horses. Don and I, and later Bill and Marion, had no shortage of fresh horses. Some of our fresh horses were pretty "rough." They were barely halter-broken, let alone used to having a saddle or rider on them, when we first rode them. I was piled more than once.

To encourage us children to take more of an interest in the raising of horses, and to reward us for our contributions to our ranch economy, my dad and mother decided to let Don and me start our own herd.

So early one summer morning, when I was about six years old, Dad said to Don and me, "I'll give each of you fellows your own brood mare.[3] The colts of these mares and their colts will belong to you, too. You can break the colts yourselves, and you will have some gentle horses to ride. You can pick out which mare you want."

Don and I were overjoyed and spent many happy hours planning what we would do when we had a big herd of horses. Don and I already knew which mare we wanted, and these mares were "in foal."

I wanted "Rainbow," and Don wanted "Leaf." They were pregnant by the stallion Dad was using at that time — a brown part thoroughbred that had belonged to man called "Kokie" Bosley. The "Kokie Bosley stallion" sired some very fine saddle horses while Dad owned him.

Many of Dad's horses at that time were part Morgan. A "Morgan" horse, according to *Webster's New World Dictionary*, 1970, is "any of a breed of strong, light harness or saddle horses" named after Justin Morgan, the New England breeder who developed the breed in the eighteenth century. Most of Dad's horses stood 14 or 15 hands tall and some as tall as 17 hands, depending on the cross.

Although they were sturdy mountain horses, on the whole our horses were not very fast. We loved to race them anyway, and they loved to race. We practiced our fastest saddle horses for the children's saddle pony race at the Castle River Stampede each summer. My first brood mare was typical of Dad's herd. She was a bay and white pinto mare and was part Morgan. I called my chosen mare "Rainbow" because she had different colours! Rainbow was not too tall, about 14 hands maybe; she had slender, clean-cut legs, and a beautiful, quiet disposition.

Rainbow had only two colts after Dad gave her to me. I called Rainbow's first colt "Ribbons." "Ribbons," sired by the Kokie Bosley stallion, was a brown "filly," a young female horse.

Rainbow's second colt was a clear bay, male horse with a white star in his forehead and a white blaze down his nose. I called him "Rex" because I thought he looked like a king. Rex was sired by Dickie and, hence, was a half-Shetland.

I always wanted my horses to look cheerful. In this 1935 picture, taken in the house yard, I am leaning forward on Rex, trying to make him smile.

Rex became one of my favourite ponies. He was only about 12 hands tall and was slimly built, showing more Morgan horse traits than Shetland pony traits. He could run very fast. I won the 13-hands-and-under race at the Castle River Stampede a couple of summers in a row with him. Author's collection.

Unfortunately, Rainbow contracted "sleeping sickness," a disease fatal to horses in those days, and died. I wanted to be with Rainbow to comfort her as she lay suffering and dying on the barn floor.

I crouched beside Rainbow with my arms around her neck, crying as if my heart would break. "Yoo-oo-oo hoo-oo-oo, Bess," my mother called when I did not come into the house at lunchtime. I paid her no heed.

Soon my mother was at the barn door.

"You'll have to go back to the house, Bess," Mom said firmly. "We don't want you catching sleeping sickness from Rainbow."

With great sadness, I kissed Rainbow "Good-bye" and reluctantly left her in God's hands. I was sure that my animals, namely the horses and goats, went to heaven when they died.

When Ribbons turned four years old, she became my second brood mare. Ribbons' only colt while we were on our ranch in the 1930s was a clear bay, half-Shetland male colt sired by Dickie. The colt had a white spot on each flank, so we named him "Two Spot." Getting two male colts in succession resulted in my herd growing very slowly.

When Two Spot turned three years old, I trained him for riding all by myself. Under my dad's careful tutelage, I had "handled" Two Spot since he was a colt. First, I petted and brushed him, then led him around the corral. I rubbed him all over with a blanket, and, eventually, set my saddle on his back. When I finally mounted Two Spot, and nudged him with my heels, he moved off gingerly, but did not buck. After that I finished him off, by teaching him to neck rein and to perform the usual tasks that horses were expected to do.

Don chose "Babe", the smaller-sized black mare with a white blaze in her face that my mother liked to ride at that time, as his first brood mare.

Babe's first foal, sired by the Kokie' Bosley stallion, was a brown male colt that we named "Nickle." Nickle was just the right size for Bill, who was about three years old by then. Bill called the colt "Pickles" because he could not pronounce an 'n'. So Nickle became known as "Pickles" to all of us.

Babe must have had some pinto breeding in her, because when bred to Dickie, a plain brown stallion, she had pinto colts. Don's second brood mare, "Leaf," was a beautiful bright bay horse with a wavy mane and tail. Leaf was livelier than Rainbow and a little "closer coupled," that is, shorter in the back. Leaf's first foal, that I remember, was a bright bay half-Shetland pony, sired by "Dickie." Don named him "Laddie."

The fact that Dickie was used to breed mares much taller than he was led to a temporary setback in my dad's half-Shetland breeding program. At first Dad used the culvert over the creek between the house and the barn as a platform for Dickie to stand on. Dad would have us back the mare that was to be bred up to the culvert in the house yard creek. Then Dad would get Dickie standing on the culvert and the operation proceeded.

That idea worked fine until one summer day when my mare Rainbow moved a step during the breeding process. In his excitement, Dickie forgot that he was on a precarious perch and took a step forward. His hoof missed the edge of the culvert and Dickie fell upside down in the creek - a very undignified position for a stallion. Dad got Dickie up, and re-positioned him on the end of the culvert. However, Dickie refused to perform.

Dad took Dickie back in the barn for a while so he would calm down, and then brought him out again. Dickie still would have nothing to do with breeding Rainbow.

Then Dad thought of a novel use for Mom's mounting platform "I know what we'll do," he exclaimed. "We'll have Dickie stand on the mounting platform to do his duty." So for the rest of the breeding season that was the routine that was followed.

We would position a mare firmly beside the platform. Then Dad would lead Dickie carefully up the steps to the top of the platform and the procedure went smoothly thereafter. I do not know why Don was given two brood mares while I had only one. It was probably because he was older, but I did not understand that at the time, and the question kept bothering me.

"It's not fair!" I said to myself. "If Don has two horses, I should have two." However, there was nothing I could do about it right then. I just had to accept my situation.

Since a mare has to be four years old before having a colt, and a "good brood mare" has only one colt per year, it was going to take quite awhile for me to build up much of a herd starting with one mare. This was especially true since my brood mare, Rainbow, died, and I had to wait for her colt, Ribbons, to be old enough to have colts.

On the other, hand Don's brood mares bore mostly male colts, so his herd also grew slowly. Nevertheless, we kept our hopes up, and were finally rewarded. Babe lived on to produce several more foals. Ribbons, Rainbow's colt, had one foal while we were still on our ranch in the 1930s.

Here is 5 ½-year-old Bill is on "Pickles" in 1937. By then Bill was riding the little saddle that Dad had fixed up for me to ride Dickie. Pickles had a wavy mane; his coat was at its summer best and was bright and shiny.

Visible in the background are the tops of the "big fir trees," the barn with its gambrel roof, the blacksmith with its new gambrel roof, and the carpenter shop with a shed roof. Author's collection.

After Pickles and Ribbons were born, Dad bought, or traded for, a bright bay Morgan stallion owned by Joe Kovatch. Dad named the new stallion "Dandy." Renowned to be the best Morgan stallion west of Winnipeg, Dandy had one obvious fault. He had a crooked front leg, which made him unsuitable for riding. However, Dandy sired a number colts of various colours, all of which turned out to be very amiable, intelligent, hard-working saddle horses after they were trained.

The Castle River Stampede

We always attended the local stampede, the "Castle River Stampede," which was an annual sports day consisting mostly of horseback riding events. The stampede grounds were in a flat, open area, half encircled by a big bend of the Castle River. The stampede was held at a location about eight miles south of Burmis, Alberta, and eight miles northwest of our ranch.

The grassy hillside, where stampede spectators sat, was once a riverbank. This low hillside to the east of the arena formed a natural amphitheatre, created over thousands of years as the riverbed gradually shifted westward.

The day's events featured various contests, such as wild steer riding, calf roping, wild cow milking, saddle bronc riding, bareback bronc riding, thoroughbred horse races, and saddle horse races for boys and girls about fourteen years old and younger.

The Castle River Stampede was timed to take place just before or after haying time. The competitors were mostly local cowboys who owned ranches, or worked as cowhands on ranches, within about an eight-mile radius of the stampede grounds. However, it did not matter if haying was completed or not, attending the Castle River Stampede - often called simply "the stampede"- was a MUST for our family.

Getting ready for the stampede was the most exciting time of the summer for Don and me. We always had our favourite horses polished to a glistening sheen for the event. We energetically cleaned and smoothed their shining coats with a currycomb and horse brush - two pieces of equipment for grooming horses.

To add to the excitement, one couple, the Ekelunds, friends of ours living west of Twin Butte, always rode by our place a couple of days before the stampede. They would be leading a packhorse, prepared to camp near the stampede grounds.

"There go the Ekelunds!" was a cry that sent us flying into the barnyard to wave to them as they went by. We knew for sure then that the stampede was near at hand.

One reason for my excitement about the Castle River Stampede was that I could race my fastest pony in it. For that one occasion, Dad made an exception to the no-racing-our-ponies rule. We still could not race our horses or our ponies on the way home from school, but we could race them on weekends to practice for the Castle River stampede.

Once I learned the difference I had no problems. However, the ponies that we chose to race generally were not the ponies that we rode to school anyway. Our school ponies had to be very strong and sturdy, even though they were also fairly fast.

But, our racing ponies were the fastest ones in Dad's herd. A big part of the reason for chasing in herds of horses on the weekends was so that we could determine which pony was the fastest and thus which one we would ride that year to the Castle River Stampede.

About the middle of June, after the range horses had had time to get used to eating green grass and were fattened up again after a long, hard winter, Dad would finally say, "Well, I guess you fellows had better start practicing." We knew what he meant! We could start practicing for the races for boys' and girls' ponies held at the stampede. What joyous news!

On the very next Saturday morning we were up bright and early. There were no complaints about feeding and watering our ponies that day; we were going to be doing our favourite activity - running in a bunch of horses. I still remember the thrill of those wonderful chases. I really think the horses, both our saddle horses and the herds we chased, enjoyed it as much as we did. It was a battle of wits and wills.

We pretty well knew ahead of time which ones of our ponies were the fastest, so on Sunday mornings we saddled them up. Dad would stand beside the road at the barnyard and get Don and me all lined up. Then he would command, "Go!" and we were off like a shot, racing along the dirt road to the bottom of the hill by the big potato patch.

The "big potato patch" was the largest of our three potato patches. It was located in the west quarter about one-quarter mile south of our house beside the road leading past one of our neighbours, the Stillmans, and into Gladstone Valley.

We would race our ponies a few times each weekend, then we turned the herd lose in the pasture that ran up and over the big hill. Next weekend we ran in another herd and tried out a few more racing horses. We did that until we were sure we knew which ones were the fastest, and therefore which we would each ride to the stampede.

One of my biggest childhood disappointments happened the summer I was 11. Search as I would, I could not find the herd of horses that had my chosen mount for that year's races in it. When the big day of the stampede finally arrived, I still had not found those horses. So I had to take second best.

I felt pretty discouraged, but Dad and Mom re-assured me. "You will do okay, Bess," they said kindly. And I guess I did.

In this photo, taken about 1930, the chuckwagon drivers are driving their teams up to the starting line. At the Castle River Stampede only two outfits could race at once because the track was relatively narrow. If more than two outfits were entered, they had to race in heats, two at a time. The winners then raced each other.

Watching the race was very suspenseful. There was always a chance that a piece of equipment, like a camp stove, would fall off the rear end of a wagon, creating a hazard for oncoming drivers. Fortunately, there was never a serious chuckwagon accident at the Castle River Stampede. Courtesy of Katherine Bruce, Author's collection.

BRAND CERTIFICATE of Ralph Vroom's horse brand.
This brand — XV bar (XV) on the right thigh — was on all of our horses at Beaver Mines. I have maintained the registration of this brand since the late 1950s. In 1997, I took advantage of an opportunity to purchase the brand for a lifetime. It is a treasured memento of a happy, adventurous childhood. Author's collection.

I did not get downhearted about it for very long, but set about practicing the best horse that I had available. At that time our family consisted of my mother and dad, my older brother, Don, my younger brother, Bill, and me. My sister, Marion, was not born yet. No doubt the hustle and bustle of getting all of us ready helped to take my mind off my disappointment. We had to get our horses saddled and a team "harnessed" and hitched to our buggy for the eight-mile trek to the stampede grounds. We made quite a cavalcade!

The next weekend when I rode up into the pasture, I found my preferred racing horse grazing large as life on an open hillside. I was not impressed!

Mom took this photo of us just as we were ready to leave for the 1937 Castle River Stampede. Dad is riding "Fly" and leading "Moonshine," an outlaw and Dad's fanciest saddle horse. (Only Dad could ride "Old Moon," as he called him.)

To Dad's left is "Blondie," our packhorse for the day. I am on "Rex", Bill is on "Pickles," and Don is on "Leaf." The horses are alert and anxious to be on their way.

Dad is wearing a beaded vest and beaded buckskin chaps, which were handmade by a Stoney Indian woman. We children are dressed in our "Sunday best" clothes. We're wearing our new caps - red and white triangles with a green celluloid visor.

Visible in the background are part of the "little corral," the road to Beaver Mines, and the hills northwest of our ranch and south of Beaver Mines. Author's collection.

On the morning of the stampede we hurried up with the chores and got dressed in our best stampede clothes. We generally had new slacks for the occasion, though not always the colour we wanted. Frequently, Simpson's or Eaton's mail order house was sold out by the time Mom's order went in, and a different colour was substituted. One year we had red, white and green baseball caps with green see-through visors.

Dad always rode his fanciest horse, a buckskin outlaw called "Moonshine", on the day of the Castle River Stampede. Before we headed off from our ranch, Mom lined up Dad, Don, Bill and me in the barnyard for picture taking.

My mother took some precious pictures of us children when we were "all dressed up," wearing our newest and best clothing, and on our ponies ready to go some place special, like the Castle River Stampede. Before we rode off, Mom always came out to the barnyard and took our pictures. To do so, she disregarded the pain she endured at every step. My mother knew what was important in life.

After the picture taking, Mom mounted her horse, and off we went for a long day at the stampede. At that time Mom was able to ride on horseback, in spite of her arthritis. In fact, horseback riding was more comfortable for her than walking because her feet were so sore.

To add to the merriment of the day, Dad dressed Bill as a prospector for the 1936 Castle River Stampede parade. Bill's "whiskers" were a piece of sheepskin with the wool on it.

Dad put a small pack on Baby Darling and tied it with a real "diamond hitch." Bill rode Smokey, and led Baby Darling. Author's collection.

My dad was a great person for trying to add a little fun or merriment to almost any situation. One summer he dressed Bill up as a prospector to enter in the Castle River Stampede parade. Dad made a beard for Bill by cutting a piece out of the pelt of a sheep that still had the wool on it. He tied the makeshift beard onto Bill's face with a piece of binder twine knotted at the back.

To make Bill's outfit even more authentic, Dad had Bill ride astride Smokey and lead Baby Darling, two goats that I had trained to ride a few years before. Baby Darling was a light brown goat with white stripes in his face. By then he was as tall as Smokey was.

Dad had also loaded Baby Darling with a small pack bundle, complete with a diamond hitch, a special knot used to keep a load securely fastened atop a pack animal.

Before going to the Calgary Stampede when I was about fifteen years old, my only experience with midway rides was at the Castle River Stampede. For the first few years of the Castle River Stampede's existence there were no midway rides. The stampede was strictly for horse-related events - cowboys riding bucking broncos, young people riding racehorses, and the kids' saddle-pony race, in which I always took part.

After a few years, one of the organizing committee had a new suggestion. "We should have a merry-go-round to give the children something to do," W. D. McDowall asserted. So a small merry-go-round was set up beside the racetrack. The trouble was that, in the mid-Thirties, very few children could afford the five cents required for one ride.

I was fascinated by the brightly-coloured merry-go-round horses, and by the lively music box tunes. But I rode the merry-go-round only once, just to see what it was like. I was disappointed, because I had lots of real horses to ride all the time.

In this 1935 picture, "Judging the parade at the Castle River Stampede," you can see six numbered chutes for the bucking horses. As each cowboy rode a mount, another bucking horse was moved into the chute. A wide gate on the chute allowed the horse to buck out sideways.

In the background are the banks of the Castle River as it made a bend to half-encircle the flat area used for the stampede grounds. The day Bill rode "Smokey" in the parade, the goat got away and ran to the top of these cliffs. Getting him down was quite a job. Courtesy of Ruby Peters Jaggernath, Author's collection.

So after that, if I had five cents to spend, I bought an ice cream cone. Ice cream in those days was made with thick cream from a nearby rancher's dairy cows. We never had an ice-cream mixer, so the process was mysterious to me as a child.

To make ice cream, the rich cream was mixed with eggs, sugar and vanilla. Then the sweet mixture was put in a bucket with a lid and a handle on the top, and placed into a tub of chipped ice, which had come from a nearby rancher's icehouse. People took turns turning the handle around and around until the ice cream was thick. The finished product was delicious! I can taste it until this day.

One year, coming home from the stampede late in the evening, a friend offered to buy me some candy at the Beaver Mines Store and Post Office.

"We've had so many customers today that we're out of candy," said the storekeeper.

"I want a can of lye then," I said resolutely.

"A can of lye, Bessie? What for?" asked the storekeeper incredulously.

"I just want it," I replied.

"Okay, then," said the storekeeper and handed over the can of lye for the few cents I had been given for candy. I picked up the small brown bag and continued on my way home.

"Here's the lye," I said proudly to Mom when I got home.

"What lye?" Mom asked, mystified.

"Remember the time I bought candy when the store was out of lye?" I asked, prompting Mom's memory.

"Yes," said Mom, "but why are you bringing lye now?"

"Well, tonight when I went to buy some candy on the way home from the stampede they were out of candy, so I bought lye instead." My mother accepted the lye graciously, probably wondering at the way my mind worked, even when I was only nine or ten years old.

Castle River Stampede Day did not always end happily for our family. I can recall two very serious accidents in which our family was directly involved. One accident, resulting in a colt being killed, happened when I was a young child. The other accident, in which my dad was nearly killed, occurred after I was grown up.

"Watch out!" my mother called out urgently. "You'll hit that colt." Unheeding, the driver of a late-model car kept on going down the road. He struck the colt of the mare that Mom was riding as the colt was walking, blinded by the headlights of the oncoming car, up the middle of the narrow dirt road. Mom was riding along on a trail beside the car tracks. The colt had strayed, unnoticed by Dad or Mom, onto the road.

"He just knocked the colt down and drove over it," Mom recalled somewhat bitterly later. "You could see the car bounce as the wheels rolled over the colt's legs. The driver didn't even stop."

The colt was badly injured, but was not killed outright. Dad had no choice but to hit the colt on the head and put it out of its misery. That was an expensive stampede outing, as the sale of horses was our main source of cash.

A second accident, one that nearly killed Dad, occurred after World War II. Mom, Dad, Bill and Marion had moved back out to our ranch after having been away for several years during the War. During that time Dad had served Overseas for four years with the artillery branch of the Canadian Army.

In July 1947, Dad, who was by then 56 years old, had his leg broken while riding a bucking horse at the Castle River Stampede. The accident was no fault of his. He had entered the contest "just to help make a show," that is, to add to the entertainment.

When a cowboy has ridden a bucking horse for ten seconds he is entitled to "dismount," or get off the bucking horse. Dad once said, "Those 10 seconds are a very long time."

To dismount safely, a pick-up man rides up alongside the bronco-rider, puts his arm around the cowboy's waist and lifts him off. This enables the cowboy to get off the bucking horse without being kicked by the flying heels of his mount. After the rider is safely off, other cowboys come out to haze the bucking horse into a holding pen. On that fateful day, Dad rode his bucking horse till the whistle blew at the end of 10 seconds. The pick-up man rode up beside Dad and leaned over to reach for him. However, the pickup man's saddle horse was not well trained for the job. Suddenly the two horses shied away from each other.

In the split second before that sudden movement, Dad "loosened up for the pickup" and relaxed his leg-muscle grip on the saddle to get ready to swing into the pickup man's arms. In a split second, Dad realized that the pick-up man did not have a good hold on him and that he was going to be dropped - a bronco rider's worst fear. He made a last-minute effort to right himself on the still-bucking horse, but it was too late.

Dad missed his grab at the saddle horn and fell to the ground with a thud. Because of the angle of his body, Dad was unable to kick both his feet out of the stirrups as he fell. His left foot got hung up in the stirrup. The bronco dragged Dad along the ground beside it. Now frightened by the object hanging from him, the bronco kicked and bucked wildly along the arena.

Pete LaGrandeur riding a bronc at the 1923 Castle River Stampede. In the background are many cowboys, mounted on their horses, watching the "show". Pete was Dad's good friend. Cowboys rode in the smaller stampedes around Southern Alberta to practice their riding and roping skills in preparation for competing at the Calgary Stampede, which is now famous throughout the world.

The son of homesteaders, Moise & Julia Livermore LaGrandeur, Pete grew up at LaGrandeur Crossing, a stage coach stop on the Oldman River just west of the Peigan Reserve (Piikani Nation) at Brocket, AB. At the 1924 Calgary Stampede, Pete was the Canadian Bucking Horse Champion and the Canadian All-Around Champion. Pete was inducted into the Canadian Rodeo Hall of Fame in 1991. Author's collection.

A hush, such that you could have heard a pin drop, fell over the crowd of spectators. Moments before, they had been cheering wildly, urging on one of their favourite cowboys. To the crowd's horror, Dad was dragged for the entire length of the arena with his left foot still in the stirrup.

Dad had held his body tense for a short distance, trying to protect his head. Then a sideways kick knocked him cold and he was dragged, hanging totally limp, until the horse reached the other end. The startled arena men caught the horse and quieted it. Another man gently took Dad's left foot out of his boot and laid his battered body out straight in the arena's dust.

When a crew arrived with a stretcher, they thought Dad was dead. Nevertheless, they loaded Dad carefully on the stretcher, put him in the back of a pickup truck and drove with haste to St. Vincent's Hospital in Pincher Creek.

Miraculously, Dad lived through this ordeal, even though he sustained a number of serious injuries. The most apparent injury was a broken thighbone in his left leg, a very serious break. He also had a concussion and many cuts and bruises.

Dad's concussion was made more serious by the fact that, several years before, he had plummeted backwards off the top of a load of hay when the trip rope on the hay fork broke as he was unloading the hay into the loft of our barn. He sustained a mild concussion that day, but was out haying the next morning.

A couple of days after Dad's stampede accident, I arrived home from my teaching job for summer holidays on our ranch. Upon arriving in Pincher Creek, I was horrified when I learned that Dad was in the hospital. Full of concern, I hurried up the hospital to see him. Mom was sitting beside him. Several of my cousins were standing in the stuffy room that hot July day giving Mom moral support.

Fortunately, a lot of the haying was done already. Dad was in the hospital about 10 days. Bill and Marion looked after the chores. I pitched in to help, and we carried on with the haying. Within a few days of his release from hospital, Dad was out helping turn over the haycocks, or small piles of raked hay, to let the hay dry after a rain. He worked with a full-length leg cast for the rest of haying season.

Ralph Vroom is the fourth rider from the right (dark shirt) in this line-up for the judging of the 1936 Castle River Stampede parade. You can see the corral where the bucking horses were held in pens, before being released to buck the length of the arena. When the cowboy had ridden 10 seconds, a pick-up man rode up alongside and lifted the rider to safety. Dad once said, "Those 10 seconds are a very long time."

On the far left, are five Indians chiefs from the Peigan Indian Reservation at Brocket and the Blood Indian Reservation at Cardston. Vehicles are parked along the left side of the corral. In the foreground is one of the refreshment stands, made of rough boards, which was set up for the day. Courtesy of Ruby Peters Jaggernath, Author's collection.

---

[1] A deadfall is a tree that has fallen over. A windfall is a tree that the wind has blown over.

[2] "Horses in training" is an expression that refers to horses that are not yet tame and reliable enough to sell or trade to novice riders.

[3] A brood mare is a mature female horse with many desirable qualities that make her suitable for breeding.

FORTY MILES ON A LOAD OF POLES, AND OTHER MEMORABLE OUTINGS

Riding to Visit Grandpa Oscar Vroom

Don was two and one-half years older than me, and was a much better help in the house. I had very little interest in housework, so Mom let me play outside with the animals and accompany Dad as he did his chores.

Mom and Dad had numerous farm animals, including horses, cattle, goats, sheep, chickens, and occasionally a pig or two. All of these animals had to be fed and watered every day. In the summer they could graze in the pasture and drink from a stream, but in the winter we had to feed them hay or other fodder, and pump water into a trough for them.

I learned to be quite a helper, doing many little jobs that did not require a lot of strength. I also became very independent and full of self-confidence. I often accompanied my dad when he went looking for horses that had strayed out of our pastures, or when he went to visit various neighbours to check on their well being.

By the time I was five and one-half years old, I knew the countryside around our ranch well enough that I could travel a few miles from home by myself and get home safely. I could ride a horse quite well, and could make Paddy go where I wanted him to go - most of the time.

Toward the end of the summer of 1932 I got the idea I should go to visit my Grandpa Oscar Vroom. Grandpa Vroom lived alone in a little cabin near Elk Lodge, the forest ranger's station at the north entrance to the Castle River Forest Reserve, south of Beaver Mines. Grandpa sometimes rode over on horseback to visit us, a distance of about seven miles.

The Castle River Forest Reserve is in the extreme southwestern corner of Alberta. It abuts British Columbia on the west and Waterton Lakes National Park on the south. In the 1930s, logging camps and fishing parties were allowed in the Reserve. However, big game hunting, or the shooting of elk, deer, bears, or other large wild animals for sport, was not allowed. We always referred to the forest reserve area as "up the Castle River."

After the episode of visiting Mrs. Bruce unbeknown to my parents, I had to get my parents' permission to ride to Grandpa Vroom's. So I concocted a plan.

Early the next morning I was out helping Dad while he fed the animals and milked the cows. Finally I asked "Daddy, can I go to visit Grandpa Vroom today?"

"I can't take you right now, Bess," Dad answered.

"That's okay," I answered cheerfully. "I can ride Paddy over to see Grandpa by myself."

"Well, I don't know, Bess," Dad answered. "It's quite a ways." I looked at him pleadingly.

"Okay, Bess," Dad said, "but you have to ask your mother."

On the left is Grandpa Oscar Vroom as a younger man. This photo was taken about 1920 on his ranch at Beaver Mines. Courtesy Adeline Cyr Robbins, Author's collection.

Above right is Grandpa Oscar Vroom on his favourite saddle horse. In 1902, when he first came West, Grandpa Vroom took up ranching on his Sunny Vale Ranche, 18 miles west of Pincher Creek. There he raised fine saddle horses. The Vroom family owned the Crown Brand horses. They had as many as 300 head of horses at one time.

Grandpa Vroom was a very good rider. In this 1929 picture, he was nearly 70 years old. Even when he was elderly, Oscar rode on horseback to get his mail, and to visit neighbours and his son Ralph and family. Oscar died in 1933 at age 74 years, after having step-danced at a party hosted by his son and daughter-in-law, Harold and Ruby Vroom. Courtesy Marion Vroom Cyr, Author's collection.

Happily, I ran across the yard to the house where Mom was just starting her morning household chores

"Mom!" I cried out, full of enthusiasm. "Can I go to visit Grandpa Vroom today?" My mother knew how fond I was of Grandpa Vroom and him of me.

"What did your dad say, Bess?" Mom asked me pointedly.

I knew I was fudging it a bit, but I answered straight out, "He said I could go if you said I could go."

"All right, then, Bess," Mom replied. "As long as your dad says it's all right, it's all right with me." That was the answer I was hoping for. Back to the barn I raced.

"Mom says I can go if you say I can go," I panted as I ran up to Dad.

"Okay, then, Bess, I guess you can go," Dad agreed.

Joyously, I got Paddy ready to go. I teetered on the manger to put his bridle on, then led him outside the barn door and stood him parallel to the barn door step. I threw the saddle blanket over Paddy's back and hoisted my saddle on top of it. Then I mounted from the barn door step and was on my way.

"Good-bye, Daddy," I called as I rode happily out of the barnyard.

"Good-bye, Bess," he answered.

Table Mountain, which is about seven miles southwest of Beaver Mines, dominates the Beaver Mines Creek Valley.

Taken looking south from a hillside on the northwest side of Beaver Mines Creek Valley, this 1927 photo shows the whole of the northwest side of Table Mountain. The picture was taken after a fall snowstorm had covered the vertical snowslide paths and horizontal ledges. The top of 8068-foot Mount Gladstone, more than three miles south-southeast, shows past the 7315-foot peak on the northeast end (left end in this photo) of Table Mountain. My dad once told me that when he was young he and a friend raced their saddle horses along the top of Table Mountain.

This is the scenery which I could see as I rode south along the road on the west side of Beaver Mines Creek Valley. I think that I did not fully appreciate the grandeur of my surroundings when I was a young child. Courtesy Katherine Bruce, Author's collection.

I went along with no problems on that hot, sunny day. It seemed like a long way because I had to ride almost to Beaver Mines, and then make a ninety degree left hand turn and go up the Beaver Mines Creek Valley. This valley ran south toward the Castle River Forest Reserve.

Thus, the road to Grandpa Vroom's ran almost parallel to the road from our ranch to Beaver Mines. A few years later we would learn to take a shortcut[1] over the hills past Bill Bremner's place and across Beaver Mines Creek. Bill Bremner was a neighbour who lived about one mile west of our ranch.

Everything was going fine until I came to a badly damaged wooden culvert. Paddy would not cross over it. I could not get him to go around the culvert, either. He really had me buffaloed, that is, had the better of me.

Finally, two other horsemen came along, riding toward Beaver Mines. One of them was my dad's friend, Pete LaGrandeur.

I visited with Pete and the other rider for a few minutes, satisfying Pete that I knew where I was going. Then I tried to head on.

Grandpa Oscar Vroom's two dogs were his constant companions. He often sat here beside his cabin petting them and talking softly to them.

Grandpa was sitting in the sun on these steps the day I rode Paddy over to visit him. He watched with mild surprise when such a little tot, riding a tall horse, turned in at his gate. But, he greeted me affectionately.

"Have you had your dinner, Bessie?" Grandpa queried. When I assured him that I had not eaten, Grandpa continued. "How about if you sit here and talk with these fellows for awhile and I'll get us something to eat?" I was somewhat tired and hungry after my 1½ hour-long ride, and happily accepted Grandpa's invitation.

Photo circa 1930, courtesy Ruby Peters Jaggernath, Author's collection.

But Paddy had other ideas. He wanted to go with the other horses and decided to turn around. I could hold Paddy from not going back, but try as I would, I could not make him go on.

Pete watched me struggle for a couple of minutes, and then had compassion on me. Dismounting his horse, Pete said, "Here, Bessie, I'll fix him." So saying, Pete tore a strip off his saddle blanket and blindfolded my horse, putting a covering over Paddy's eyes.

I rode the rest of the way to Grandpa's with my horse blindfolded. It meant I had to travel more slowly, but I did not want to risk Paddy turning around again. I arrived safely at Grandpa Vroom's cabin, dismounted and tied my horse to the fence.

It was a very hot day, and Paddy was sweating, so I took the blindfold off him and loosened my saddle cinch. Grandpa was glad to see me and we had tea and something to eat. I watched with curiosity as Grandpa ate his potatoes off his knife, and "saucered his tea," that is, he poured his tea into his teacup saucer to cool the tea more quickly so that he could drink it right away.

After awhile Grandpa said, "It's nearly sunset, Bess; you had better start home."

So I tightened my cinch, ready to go. Grandpa helped me on and I was ready to set off. "You won't need this blindfold for your horse any more," Grandpa assured me, so I reluctantly left it.

I went along fine for a few miles. Then, as I was passing my Uncle Harold and Aunt Ruby Vroom's place, Paddy decided he wanted to go in there. Again I did not have enough strength to force Paddy to go on, so in we went. Uncle Harold's hired man, Jack Beattie, came out of the barn to see what he could do to help me.

"Will you put a blindfold on my horse?" I asked.

"You can't ride your horse blindfolded Bessie," Jack said.

"Yes, I can," I countered. "Pete LaGrandeur blindfolded him and I rode to Grandpa's."

Reluctantly Jack got a gunnysack and made a blindfold for my horse. After a couple of miles or so, when I knew Paddy would know he was heading home, and there were no more ranch gates to go past, I leaned forward and took the blindfond off.

"How did you make out, Bess?" Dad queried. I told Dad about my adventure. He was not pleased about my riding my horse blindfolded, but secretly admired my determination.

My New Table Manners

I could hardly wait for the next meal at home when I could practice eating like Grandpa Vroom.

At dinnertime the next day I carefully loaded my knife with potatoes like Grandpa had done and slowly raised it to my mouth, barely able to keep my food on the knife. My mother watched me intently for a few seconds, and then said quietly, as was her way, "What are you doing, Bess?"

"Eating," I replied innocently.

"I know you are eating," my mother continued patiently, "but you can't eat off your knife."

"Grandpa Vroom does," I countered.

"Well, you can't," my mother replied firmly. And that was that.

I was undaunted, however. I was determined to mimic Grandpa Vroom in some way. I loved Grandpa dearly.

The next day at dinnertime I asked politely, "May I please have some 'milk tea'?"

My mother looked at me curiously, but answered, "I guess you may, Bess. Just be sure to put lots of milk in it." So I poured myself a cup of tea, and added the milk. Then I saucered some of the tea in my saucer and began to drink it like Grandpa Vroom had done.

"Did you see Grandpa Vroom do that, too?" Mom asked.

"Yes," I replied sheepishly, knowing full well what my mother's next remark would be, and I was not disappointed.

"Well, just because Grandpa Vroom does certain things, that doesn't mean that you can. Now sit up and eat your meal properly," my mother admonished. Her voice had taken on a slightly sharper tone, and I knew she meant business, so I settled down after that and ate my meals the way my parents had taught me.

These buildings - a chicken coop and hay barn - were located on my Uncle Harold and Aunt Ruby Vroom's west quarter, across the road and west of their ranch house in the Beaver Mines Creek Valley. This 1930s picture was taken facing southwest. The road from Beaver Mines to the Castle River Forest Reserve ran north-south in front of these buildings, with Beaver Mines to the right.

From 1938 to 1942 this chicken coop was used as a school house, hence the moniker "Chicken Coop School". It was attended by children who lived in the valley, of families such as Bucar (Stanley Betty, Helen), Foster (Gladys, Robert), Henes (Edith), Hill (Gordon, Vada), Holmes (Betty), Kerr (Jimmy, Betty), LaGrandeur (Esther, Mary, Robin, Ramon, Doris May "Chick") and Swinney (Dave, Noreen).

Over the years, Uncle Harold modified the chicken coop several times. The original small chicken coop was renovated to accommodate their large White Leghorn operation. During the 1930s and 40s, they sold chickens, eggs and other produce in towns throughout the Crows Nest Pass. Some of Uncle Harold's black-faced sheep graze peacefully in front of the chicken coop - sheep often grazed on grass near ranch buildings, where they were safe from marauding coyotes. Courtesy Ruby Peters Jaggernath, Author's collection.

Grandmother Alena Munro Vroom

My Grandmother Alena Vroom died when I was a baby, so I never knew her. She and her family of four children travelled west by settler's train from Clementsport, Nova Scotia, in 1904. They joined my grandfather, Oscar, on his Sunny Vale Ranche in the Beaver (Mines) Creek valley, south of where Beaver Mines would later be established

Grandmother Vroom took to life on a ranch with enthusiasm. She bought a large herd of horses - they owned the Crown brand. Both she and my dad's sister, Marion, learned to ride sidesaddle.

By then Ralph was a young teenager and anxious to become a cowboy. My dad was always an avid horseman, learning his early horsemanship skills while looking after his mother's herd. She, in turn, encouraged my dad's passion for horses.

When he was about 14, dad went out to work for other ranchers in the Beaver Mines area. The lore of his gift for horse handling began to grow.

Dad was an engaging storyteller. He entertained us with stories of his life as a young cowboy - such as chasing wild horses in the mountainous Arrow Lakes area of BC, bronco-busting for the Prince of Wales at a rodeo on the EP Ranch southwest of Calgary, and his many daring adventures with horses.

This grand-looking lady, wearing a stylish hat, is my Grandmother Alena Munro Vroom, in Nova Scotia. The picture was taken about 1902 when Grandpa Oscar Vroom left for the West. Grandma and their four children joined Oscar on his 'Sunny Vale Ranche' southwest of Beaver Mines in 1904.

Grandma Vroom was raised in a life of privilege in Nova Scotia. Her widowed mother married a well-to-do hotel keeper, and Grandma was educated as a school teacher. Grandma's parents were dismayed when she fell in love with my handsome Grandpa, Oscar. Oscar was an adventurer and loved to roam. He first came to southwestern Alberta in 1886..

But Alena, like Oscar, fell in love with the West. Both Grandma Vroom and my aunt Marion(Cyr) learned to ride side saddle. I tell the exciting stories of the early lives of them, their friends and neighbours in my second book, "Pioneer Adventurers". Courtesy Marion Vroom Cyr, Author's collection.

Visiting the Jenkses on a Very Headstrong Horse

A horse can be very headstrong if the rider does not have firm control. Another example happened to Don and me one day when we were riding Paddy home from a neighbour's place.

Don and I had gone home with a neighbour family, the Jenkses, one warm summer day. We were going to play with their children for the afternoon and evening. We had ridden home with them in their car, a real novelty at that time. Dad was going to ride past the Jenkses that same day.

"I'll bring a saddle horse along for you fellows to ride home on," he said cheerily as he waved good-bye to us in the barnyard.

Sure enough, a couple of hours later, Dad rode by with Paddy in tow on the halter shank.[2] We ran excitedly up to Dad when we saw him riding into the yard. "Put Paddy in (the barn) where it's cool and feed him some hay," Dad advised us as he went on his way. We promptly obeyed, then went back to our playing.

One of the most exciting things about playing at the Jenkses was the fact that they lived in the old roundhouse. That roundhouse had at one time been the Beaver Mines terminus of the Kootenay and Alberta Railway, which ran out to the coalmines at Beaver Mines from the main line of the Canadian Pacific Railway (CPR). The junction with the CPR was between Pincher Station and Cowley, Alberta. The CPR passed through Pincher Station and Cowley en route to the Crows Nest Pass and the Pacific Coast.

In the roundhouse at Beaver Mines there had been a huge turntable — long since removed. It had been used to turn the locomotives around for the return trip, pulling the cars loaded with coal back to the main line of the CPR.

The young people of the Beaver Mines district had a lively social life. This picture shows the Beaver Mines Tennis Club, circa 1909. The tennis court was on the flat below the village of Beaver Mines, to the west of Beaver Mines Creek.

In the back row, from left, are Frank Holmes, Mr. Moodie, Mr. Morrison (holding racquet; student minister, Mountain Mill Church); Samuel McVicar, manager of the Beaver Mines coal mines, is second from right.

In the front row, second from left is Mrs. Frank (Louise Riley) Holmes in a white dress; next is Mrs. Moodie wearing a hat, with unknown small girl; then Elsie Belle Crosbie (Mrs. Edward Joyce) and Mrs. Morrison, each in a white dress and holding a racquet. Mrs. Malcolm "Mickey" (Edna) McDonald is fifth woman from right (hat and tennis racquet); Mrs. Gertrude McVicar is the third woman from the right (no hat); the two women on the extreme right, are my aunt, Marion Vroom (Mrs Dominic Cyr) in a white hat, and her mother, Mrs. Oscar (Alena Munro) Vroom, who is on the end of the row wearing a dark hat.

Other families who lived at Beaver Mines about that time, and might be in this photo are those of: Scobie, Coalfields School teacher Miss Cameron, Jack Eddy, Ballantyne, Biron, McLeod, Pope, McDowall, Dexter Smith, Ed Gamache, Kyllo, and Bouthier. Courtesy Adeline Cyr Robbins, Author's collection.

The coal at Beaver Mines had "gone soft," that is, it was no longer suitable for its original use, and the coalmines at Beaver Mines had been abandoned. The railway tracks had been torn up, but the old grades could still be seen in many places.

The old abutments for the huge railway trestle, which had spanned Mill Creek at Mountain Mill, Alberta, could also still be seen. At the time it was said to be the longest wooden railway trestle, for its height, in Canada. Many years earlier Dad, a true adventurer, had ridden a bronc across that railway trestle, for a distance of about one-half mile some 500 feet above the creek.

The meal finished, we went out in the yard to play some more with the younger children, while the older children helped with the dishes.

Just before sunset Mrs. Jenks called out, "Bess and Don, it's going to be dark pretty soon. You'd better start for home." Reluctantly, we stopped our playing, got Paddy out of the barn and headed for home.

We cut across a ploughed field to get to the road that made an S curve around a stand of willows and poplar trees before it crossed a small stream and joined the main road to Beaver Mines. When Don, who was sitting in front as we double-decked Paddy bareback, tried to turn Paddy onto the road which was familiar to us, Paddy refused to turn.

Unbeknown to Don and me, on the way to Jenkses Dad had led Paddy along a trail that was a shortcut through the bush; Paddy wanted to return by the same route. Since we were riding bareback, and with a halter instead of a bridle, Don did not have a lot of control over Paddy.

Don tugged as hard as he could on the halter shank while I clung to Don with my arms wrapped around his waist. After a few minutes, Paddy got tired of the tug-of-war.

Taking a sudden sharp whirl he headed straight for the shady path through the bush, and then proceeded back to my home ranch barnyard.

Don and I were not expecting Paddy to turn so quickly, and he piled us right in the middle of the ploughed field. Fortunately, only our pride was hurt. However, we still had to get home before dark.

There was no alternative but to walk, so we headed out.

After an hour or so we straggled into the house yard, tired and hungry. We had stopped for a drink of cold water at the "spring," a well fed by an underground water supply. It was located just after we passed the gate that led into a quarter section[3] of land owned by Gus Gamache. His quarter was located just across the road to the north of our west quarter. Because Gus lived a ways in from the road he did not see us going by.

By the time Don and I arrived on foot, Dad was home and had put Paddy away. "You'll have to do better than that next time, you fellows," was all he said about our mishap. I guess he figured we had learned our lesson.

Over the next ten years I did become an expert horsewoman. Don, Bill, Marion and I all learned well from our father, who was a real Canadian cowboy and a horse handler of some renown. As a tribute to him, Andy Russell recounts the story of my Dad and "The Wall-Eyed Stud", a wild stallion, in the Epilogue of his 1993 book, *The Canadian Cowboy: Stories of Cows, Cowboys, and Cayuses*.

In 1909, the Kootenay and Alberta Railway was constructed. The line ran from Beaver Mines to Pincher Station, hauling coal to markets in Canada and the world. The Mountain Mill railway trestle, stretching across Mill Creek valley, was the longest wooden bridge for its height in Canada. Unfortunately, the coal at Beaver Mines went "soft", and the mines ceased to operate at the beginning of World War I. But, the giant trestle stood until the early 1920s, when it was dismantled.

Seen to the south, through the huge wooden bents, is Mountain Mill church - fondly referred to as the "little white church in the valley". Dad, his parents, brothers and sister were at the first service in 1906. Parishoners, family & friends celebrated the 100ᵗʰ anniversary of the church on June 11, 2006.

Grant Smith & Company was the general contractor for the Kootenay & Alberta Railway. Contractor Bill Toban built the grades. To be closer to the work at hand, Toban set up camps on various ranches as the railway line proceeded west. There were camps on the Main and Hodgkins places east of Mountain Mill, and on the "Wash" Mitchell place west of Mill Creek on NW 1/4 12-6-2-5. The road in this photo was still used by my family when I was a child.

Local ranchers, along with their teams of horses, were hired to work on the railway construction crews. One of these ranchers so hired was W. J. Baker, who homesteaded in Gladstone Valley. Bill Baker had many horses working on the building of the roadbed. Several trestles over small creeks and coulees were constructed by the CPR construction crews, but their crowning achievement was the large wooden trestle across Mill Creek.

This photo was taken about 1914 by Mabel (Mrs. Major Edward "Ted") Bruce. The Bruce family lived on the Roodee ranch, on the west bank of the Castle River, a few miles north-west of Mountain Mill. Their son, Anthony Bruce, remembers, "In 1914 we saw the last engine and coal-car go up to Beaver Mines. It had only two *men on it and it stopped before it got to the bridge. One man got off and walked across the bridge. One could see the old bridge shake under the weight. When it got to the far side, the man who had walked across first got on and stopped and waited for the other man to walk across. I do not blame them for not trusting that bridge to take the weight of the engine."*

In 1911, Dad lived with his parents on their ranch in the Beaver (Mines) Creek valley, south of the village of Beaver Mines. On many occasions, he rode past the railway construction sites on his way to Pincher Creek. While the sites hummed with activity from morning till night, Dad watched with keen interest as the huge wooden trestle was built spanning Mill Creek.

My Dad was 20 years old and full of bravado. It wasn't long before one of the locals challenged him to prove his bravery, and skill as a horseman, by riding the bronc he was breaking across the Mountain Mill trestle. Finally, he couldn't stand the temptation any longer and took up the challenge.

The giant trestle was barely finished, and the railway tracks not yet laid, when on a sunny afternoon, Dad rode the bronc across that thin ribbon of wooden railway ties. Dad successfully completed the hazardous feat while friends and acquaintances, who had gathered at either end of the trestle, watched with bated breath. Some friends even went into the little church, to pray for his safe ride.

This story was told and retold over the years. As late as 1979, old timers like Glen "Rusty" Gold, still remembered Dad's ride. "My brother owned the bronc that Ralph rode across that railway bridge", said Rusty. Fortunately, Dad made it safely across. Mrs. Mabel Bruce photo, courtesy of Katherine Bruce, Author's collection.

Visiting Aunt Marion Cyr

Some of the happiest times of my young life were when I went to visit my Aunt Marion Cyr. She was my dad's younger and only sister, and I loved her dearly. Aunt Marion lived on a farm about two and one-half miles southeast of Pincher Creek. A total of nearly twenty miles separated us. Travelling that distance by saddle horse or team and buggy would take four and one-half to five hours of steady travelling.

As a family, we did not visit back and forth with the Cyrs very much. Neither of our families could get away from home for more than one day at a time. We hardly ever stayed overnight. So it was a "red-letter day," a very happy occasion for us children, whenever we did visit Aunt Marion or she came to visit us.

Like us, Aunt Marion and Uncle Dominic and their six children were very busy on their farm. They raised various crops, as well as beef cattle, hogs and sheep for meat, and ran a dairy farm for extra cash. All of Aunt Marion's children worked hard at home, as we did as we got older.

Two of my cousins, Adeline and Esther, could cook as well as their mother. Alberta, the oldest child, often helped out in the fields. Like most farm boys of that time, Eugene worked like a man from the time he was younger than twelve years old. Vera was more inclined to work outside, too. Rita, the youngest, helped mostly inside.

Except for Vera, they all walked to school, except in the coldest weather. Then they drove to school with a horse and "cutter," that is, a light sleigh. In the early spring, when the weather was still quite cold, they had a cart. The rest of the time, most of them walked to school, cutting across a neighbour's pasture and through a coulee, a distance of about one and one-half miles. Vera rode on horseback, so had to go around by the road.

Vera and Rita used to race, starting when they both left the house —Vera to saddle up her horse, and Rita walking. They arrived at St. Michael's School in Pincher Creek practically at the same time as each other every morning!

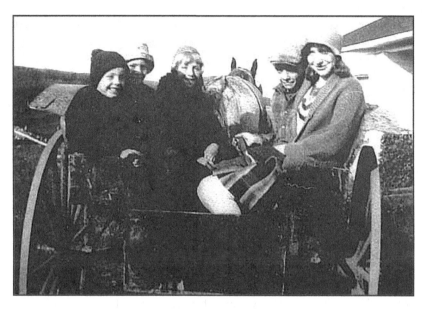

These are my 'Cyr' cousins, in 1930, sitting in their pony cart ready to ride to school in Pincher Creek. Left to right, Rita (6 years), Vera (8 years), Esther (11 years), Eugene (13 years) and Adeline (15 years). Marie Alberta is not in this photo, as she had already finished school.

When the weather was favourable, they walked to school by taking a shortcut across the fields to town. Depending on the depth of the snow, in the winter they rode in this pony cart or a sleigh. Courtesy Adeline Cyr Robbins, Author's collection.

One time when I went to visit Aunt Marion I had a special treat — my Great-aunt Bessie Vroom from Nova Scotia was visiting Aunt Marion and Uncle Dominic and family. Aunt Bessie was a fast knitter. During the time I was there she knitted me a red wool tam. I loved that little hat and wore it for years — it was almost in shreds when I finally stopped wearing it.

I remember the thrill of being big enough to call Aunt Marion on the telephone. To make the call, I had to ride to Beaver Mines, some two-and-one-half miles from the ranch. Then I asked permission from Mrs. Holmes, a friend of my mother's who owned a store there, to use her phone to make my call. I got so I would call Aunt Marion about once a week. What a thrill it was when she answered!

"Hello, Aunt Marion," I would say somewhat shyly, "this is Bessie."

"Oh, hello, dear," Aunt Marion would reply. "How are you?"

That broke the ice, and I would talk happily with my beloved Aunt Marion for a few minutes.

After a year or so of phone calls, I started trying to persuade Mom and Dad to let me ride my pony down to Aunt Marion's. Finally the happy day came; and early one morning my older brother, Don, and I started out on our ponies.

It was a hot summer day. The fastest we could travel on horseback was about three and one-half to four miles per hour. We stopped and rested our ponies in the shade a few times, so it was mid-afternoon by the time we reached Pincher Creek. As we rode along Main Street a group of curious town kids started following us. When we stopped at the City Cafe for a cold drink, the kids encircled us and started harassing us; they wanted to ride our ponies. My dad had always cautioned us not to let other children ride our saddle horses.

Reluctantly, I let one of the bigger boys, who claimed he knew my dad, ride my pony along the street. He was not a very good rider, and did not know how to handle my horse gently. I was very relieved when he brought my pony back safely. When the boy returned the bridle lines to me I mounted my pony as quickly as I could. Then Don and I headed out on the final couple of miles to Aunt Marion Cyr's.

Upon arrival, I was always really anxious to run in to say "Hello" to let them know we had arrived safely, and to get a hug and a kiss from my beloved Aunt Marion. She always seemed glad to see me, even though our coming meant extra mouths to feed. Aunt Marion had six children of her own, plus one or two hired men, making about eight to 10 people for every meal.

One arrival at Aunt Marion's that I remember very clearly was the year the Cyrs had just planted a number of small poplar trees, or "saplings," around the eastside of the lawn. Those trees are probably 30 to 40 feet tall now and eight to 10 inches in diameter, but in 1934 they were about seven feet tall and two and one-half to three inches in diameter. I probably had phoned Aunt Marion from Beaver Mines, maybe even a few days before, so I thought she would be anxious to know we had arrived safely.

At home at Beaver Mines, trees were very numerous and planting trees was unheard of. I had been taught that one of the best places to tie up my pony by the bridle lines was to the supple branch of a tree or to the trunk of a sapling. So when I saw those saplings by Aunt Marion Cyr's house I thought they were made-to-order for me for tying up my pony. My cousin Eugene, who had laboured hard to plant those precious trees, and may even have hand-watered them, had a different idea, however.

I had just tied my pony, loosely secured, to one of those supple little trees and had started across the lawn to run in and see my beloved Aunt Marion. Just then Eugene came around the corner of a granary and caught me in the act. Eugene told me, in no uncertain terms, that that little tree was not a hitching rack for my horse, and to please get it away from there. I tried to excuse myself, but Eugene came closer and repeated his demand.

So I had to untie my pony and take it over to the barn, which I would have done in the first place if I had not been so anxious to let Aunt Marion know I had arrived safely.

I do not know how long we stayed with Aunt Marion on that trek, but eventually, Don and I had to saddle up our ponies one morning, and head back to the ranch at Beaver Mines. Our return trip was made more enjoyable by the delicious lunch that Aunt Marion would have packed for us to eat along the way.

Young Aviators

My grandchildren fly often. Moreover, they started flying at a young age. Thinking about this reminded me of the first airplane I ever saw. I was probably six or seven years old and was living on the ranch at Beaver Mines. My brother Don and I were playing in the yard when we heard a droning sound overhead.

"It's an airplane!" cried Don, who had seen pictures of airplanes, and even then had a keen interest in flying.

Excitedly, we searched the sky until we spotted the airplane. We ran into the house to tell Mom the news. "Come and look at it," we urged. Mom went to the door and stood looking out. Don and I ran into the middle of the barnyard and waved frantically, hoping the pilot would see us.

The airplane was 2,000 to 3,000 feet up, I would think. We must have looked like specks on the ground. I am not sure that the pilot did see us, but we thought he did, and that was what mattered.

Every few minutes after that, a plane flew over our ranch, more evidence to us that the pilot knew we were there. Each time, we ran out into the yard and waved and hollered, "Hello! Hello!"

We learned later that it was actually a forestry airplane searching for spot fires. These are sometimes caused by lightning strikes. As soon as a spot fire was sighted, a ground crew of firefighters was sent to put out the fire. Any delay might have caused a small fire to develop into a full-scale one, like thehuge fire in the Castle River Forest Reserve during the summer of 1936.

I remember, too, my first airplane ride. Dad came riding home one summer day and said to Don and me, "Hurry up, you guys, and saddle up your horses. I'll take you down to Lees Lake for an airplane ride. Hardly believing our ears we did his bidding and soon were on our way.

Lees Lake is near Burmis, just east of the Crows Nest Pass about 10 miles from our home. At least four hours would have elapsed since Dad passed by there the first time. Since four miles an hour on horseback was the usual speed, it would take would take a good four hours to make the round trip.

The pilot was giving 15-minute rides, which were nearly over by the time we got there. Dad was short of cash and could not afford to pay for two of us. But since we were both there and he did not want to disappoint either of us, Dad persuaded the pilot to take the two of us for the price of one. "Heck, they're just small," he said persuasively.

So into the open cabin of the small, single-engine biplane Don and I clambered. I do not think we even had seat belts, but we might have. The plane roared across the grassy field, bumping along over the sun-baked "cow pies," heaps of cow manure on the grass.

Don and I had not even ridden in a car very much at that time, so a biplane ride caused us much excitement. For the first few minutes, however, we were so frightened that we huddled together in our seat. Finally, we got up our nerve and stood up, so we could peer out the side windows at the lake and trees below.

By then we didn't have our bearings and felt kind of lost, but what a thrill! The wind whistled by our ears. We could hardly hear each other talk because of the engine noise. We probably flew at about 1,000 feet, so we got a fairly close-up view of the ground. We could see a lot further into the distance than we ever had seen before.

Being up in an airplane is like climbing a mountain, only it's a lot easier! Also, you can see much further from an airplane than you can from the top of a mountain. On a clear day, the higher you go in an airplane the farther you can see. I still like to sit in a window seat whenever I fly so that I can look at the countryside. The aerial view of land always fascinates me.

In 1933, Don and I flew in a single-engine biplane, similar to this, when we went for our first airplane ride. In this picture, Jean McEwen and a friend stand beside a single engine bi-plane before taking off for a 15 minute ride. Jean paid one cent per pound for her ride.

Just like the field in this photo, the landing strip for Don and me, near Lees Lake, was a rancher's field, complete with "cow pies." Courtesy Jean McEwen Burns, Author's collection.

All too soon our fifteen-minute airplane ride was over and we were back on the ground, feeling very low down, and small, after our soaring flight. By then it was well after sunset, so we had to mount our ponies and start home. It was dark by the time we got home.

Just after we passed Gus Gamache's gate, we stopped to water our ponies in a trough Dad had made by hollowing out a big log. The trough was filled constantly with fresh, cool water running out of a pipe from a well that was fed by a spring. We never had to pump water for our ponies. Upon reaching the barn we unsaddled our ponies and tied them in their stalls. Then we climbed up into the hayloft,[4] and threw some hay down into the mangers.

When our ponies were looked after, we ran excitedly over to the house. While we ate our supper, we told Mom about our wonderful airplane ride adventure.

VISITING GRANNY AND GRANDPA TYSON

I loved my mother's parents, Granny and Grandpa Tyson, very much and was always very excited when we were going to go visit them. Mom, Dad and we children visited Granny and Grandpa once or twice a year when I was a small child. Sometimes Don or I would stay with Granny and Grandpa for a few weeks at a time.

Don felt very responsible for Granny and Grandpa Tyson, even when he was a young child, and willingly stayed for long periods of time to help out. He had no trouble finding something to do while was at Granny's. Don was quite free to visit with children on neighbouring farms, and didn't mind walking to get there.

I, on the other hand, remember periods of loneliness while I was visiting Granny and Grandpa Tyson - my only set of grandparents when I was a child. It wasn't that I longed for my parents - what I really missed was playing with the goats and other animals that we had on the ranch.

Moreover, I missed the trees that covered the hills at Beaver Mines. Granny and Grandpa lived on what I thought of as the "bald prairie," flat land with no natural trees on it. I really didn't like walking along the dusty country road in the hot summer sun.

Granny and Grandpa Tyson lived on a farm east of Pincher Creek, about 40 miles from my home at Beaver Mines. We travelled by team and wagon to visit them when I was little.

It was two days' travel by team and wagon, so it took a lot of effort for our whole family to go to see them. After the initial excitement, our trips to visit Granny and Grandpa Tyson seemed very, very long to me.

On the evening before one trip my mother said to Don and me, "You fellows will have to go to bed right after supper tonight. You'll be getting up before daylight tomorrow."

"Why?" Don and I chorused, aghast at the idea of getting up that early on a Saturday.

"We're starting out for Granny and Grandpa's as soon as we can get away in the morning," Mom replied. "We're driving as far as the Hutterites' tomorrow." Mom and Dad always had their plans firmly made before they told us anything about a change of our routine.

We could not travel the whole distance in one day, so had to stay over some place between Beaver Mines and Fishburn, Alberta. Our usual stopover place was at the Pincher Creek Hutterite Colony [5]. They were kindly, generous people who welcomed visitors cordially.

"Oh, goody!" I cut in. "May I play with the Hutterite kids?"

"Yes, you may, Bess," Mom replied, "but only for a little while. The next morning we are going to drive the rest of the way to Granny and Grandpa's."

Because a number of families live in one colony, there are lots of children to play with. Playing with the Hutterite kids was a favourite activity of mine. We would play hide-and-go-seek amongst the 100-pound sacks of ground grain in the top of a large storage building, and eat in the big dining room with the Hutterites.

I got so I really liked the Hutterites - having all those playmates was my idea of lots of fun. In addition, for a number of years, the teacher at the Pincher Creeek was Mrs. Beatrice Ankill. She was one of my mother's friends. While Mrs. Ankill was there I got to go to the Hutterite School.

That happened once, when we stopped overnight at the Hutterites' on the way home from Granny and Grandpa's. The Hutterite colony school[6] was in session. I attended class next morning while Mom and Dad were getting ready for the drive home.

We had lunch with the Hutterites and then it was time to go. But I did not want to go and leave all that fun behind. I ran up into the loft of the ground grain storage building and hid amongst the sacks of ground up grain.

It took quite a bit of persuasion to get me to come out of hiding. It took even more persuasion to get me to go home with my parents. Reluctantly I said "Good-bye" to my Hutterite friends.

One time Grandpa Tyson came up to our place to get a load of poles. While Grandpa was there Mom arranged for me to go home with him. I could then stay with him and Granny for awhile.

At first I was excited about the idea of visiting with Granny Tyson all by myself. However, I didn't realize how long it would take to go the forty miles, riding on a load of poles pulled by a team of workhorses.

It was a very hot summer day. We seemed to just creep along the parched, dusty road. I got thirstier and thirstier. So when we were passing the Pelletiers' farm, a couple of miles east of Pincher Creek, I begged Grandpa to stop so I could get a drink of water. Grandpa didn't want to bother the Pelletiers, whom he did not know very well, but I kept asking.

Secretly, I was curious to see the inside of the huge Pelletier house. We had passed the Pelletiers' house a number of times on our way to Granny and Grandpa's. Each time, I yearned to see inside what looked like a grand house to me, but I never had an excuse to ask my parents to stop. So, this time, I was very anxious to have my way about getting a drink there.

When it looked like Grandpa was not going to stop, I started to whimper a little, and Grandpa gave in. He let me run in to ask the Pelletiers for a drink, but he would not go in and impose upon them for a drink for himself.

It was so quiet in the sweltering barnyard that I feared no one was at home. Timidly, I knocked on the door, and a very beautiful young woman answered my tapping. She looked surprised to see me.

"I'm Bessie Vroom," I said quietly. "Grandpa Tyson said I could ask you for a drink of water…please."

"Bessie Vroom!" the young woman replied. "We know your mother and dad, and your Granny and Grandpa Tyson." I was very surprised at that bit of news. "Certainly, you may have a drink. Come on in."

So I went into the fragrant kitchen. I stood staring in amazement. At the kitchen table sat three beautiful young women wearing what I thought must be evening gowns. I had heard of evening gowns, but had never seen one. The gowns were made of shimmering satin of various colours. The girls were probably wearing light housecoats because it was such a hot day, but they looked like evening gowns to me.

The kitchen was dark and cool. All the shades were pulled down to keep out the heat of the sun. One of the girls gave me a cup of really cold water; I wished I could have stayed there the rest of the afternoon.

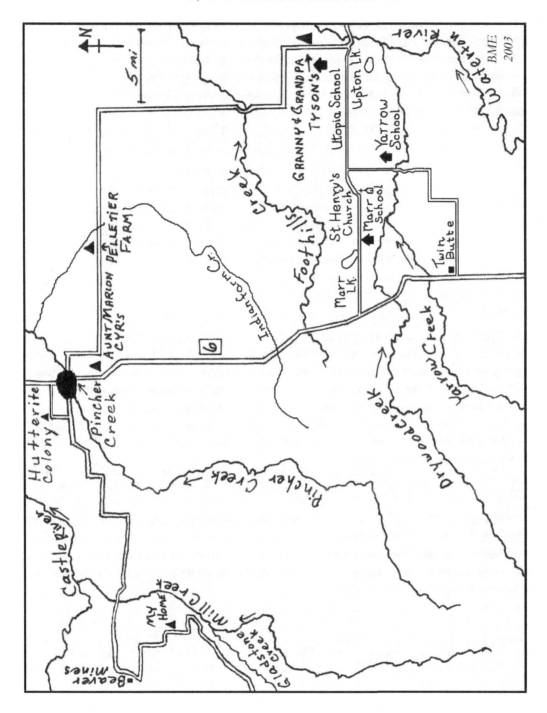

MAP 5 FORTY MILES ON A LOAD OF POLES

Map 5 *The map "Forty Miles on a Load of Poles" shows:*
- *the route from my home at Beaver Mines to the home of my Granny and Grandpa Tyson*
- *the home of Aunt Marion and Uncle Dominic Cyr, the Pincher Creek Hutterite Colony, the Pelletiers' farm*
- *Castle River, Drywood Creek, Foothills Creek, Gladstone Creek, Indianfarm Creek, Marr Lake, Mill Creek, Pincher Creek, Upton Lake, Waterton River, Yarrow Creek*
- *Marr School, St. Henry's Roman Catholic Church, Yarrow School, Utopia School. Map hand drawn by the author.*

However, I knew Grandpa was waiting for me and that he was anxious to get home before dark. Reluctantly, I said, "Thank you very much for the drink" and walked back to the wagon loaded with poles. After that brief respite, the afternoon sun seemed even hotter than before.

"Hello, darling," Granny greeted me as I ran into the house and flung my arms around her neck. "I'm very glad to see you. Did you have a good trip?"

"It seemed awfully long," I admitted. "And I got to stop at Pelletiers' for a drink of water," I added cheerily, "but I like your 'fizzy dope' better."
Granny laughed at my name for the cool drink mixture that she always made in the summertime.

The concentrate, which Granny stored in her cellar under the kitchen, was made of egg whites, sugar and cream of tartar mixed together.

When she served someone a drink of the mixture, Granny put a couple of tablespoons of the concentrate in the bottom of a glass, filled the glass with cold water, then added about one-half teaspoon of baking soda. The chemical reaction made the mixture fizz up - hence the name "fizzy dope." I thought that fizzy dope was the best summer treat of all.

By the time I was about eleven years old we got our "old Studebaker," a car, which was about a 1920-something model. It still took us about an hour to reach Pincher Creek, over bumpy, often muddy roads. Although having a car meant we no longer had to travel to Granny Tyson's by team and wagon, the ungravelled roads presented a challenge if there was a rainstorm.

We had to drive through several creek valleys on the way to Granny and Grandpa's. I remember going up out of one of these valleys during a rainstorm. Dad was trying his best to keep the car from plunging over the side of the steep grade.[7] Mom was giving him encouragement and advice.

Don and Bill and I were sitting in the back in the open homemade truck box. I remember being quite fascinated looking over the back end of the box and watching the writhing tire tracks, which looked like "snake tracks" to me.

Sometimes Granny Tyson came to visit us. On such occasions, she generally drove out with her son, Tommy, my mother's brother. Granny's visits were always a joyous occasion.

How excited we were when we saw Uncle Tommy drive into our barnyard in his Model A Ford Coupe. Don and I would dash full speed down the house yard path, fling open the gate, and race to see who could get to the car first. There were hugs and kisses all around. Then they would get out of the car and come into the house for a visit for a few hours. Sometimes they stayed over night, but often they stayed only a few hours, as Granny could not be away from the farm for too long.

One thing I remember about Uncle Tommy in those days was that he had false teeth. He was quite a tease, and loved to scare us kids by "dropping his teeth down." He would loosen his false teeth with his tongue, open his mouth, and thrust his upper plate out at us. The first few times he did this, I was quite alarmed, even frightened. Gradually, I got used to that trick, and it didn't bother me any more.

(L to R) Elizabeth Mary Tyson, George Wilson Tyson, and Tommy Tyson, June 1924, at their farm at Fishburn, Alberta.

After they came to Canada, Mom's brother, Uncle Tommy, did not continue his schooling, but became a skilled tradesman. In 1919, he worked at the Cardston Power House for Oliver Aldridge. Oliver was the son of Bill Aldridge who, guided by Indians, discovered oil in Waterton Park.

Uncle Tommy became an apprentice electrician, and worked on the wiring of the Mormon Temple, Cardston, until its completion in 1923. He was one of the electricians for the wiring the Prince of Wales Hotel, Waterton Park, during its construction 1926 - 1927. In the 1930s, he worked as an electrician in the Turner Valley Oilfields. The fields were the largest producer of oil and gas in the British Empire. Author's collection.

I remember the first time that Uncle Tommy brought his fiancee, Mary Laidlaw, to visit us. I thought that the person beside him was Granny Tyson and rushed out as usual. But, much to my surprise, a stranger was sitting beside him.

Tommy and Mary were married shortly after that. It didn't take long for us to get to know Aunt Mary. She was a very kind, loving and generous person - and a wonderful cook. All our family came to love her dearly.

Aunt Mary and Uncle Tommy lived on the farm with Granny for a few years after Grandpa Tyson died. Then they moved to Kimberley, where Uncle Tommy ran an electrical business for many years.

Grandmother Elizabeth Mary Brotherston Tyson

My grandmother Elizabeth Mary Brotherston Tyson - "Granny" I always called her - was born in Kelso, a border town in the south of Scotland. Her father, Andrew Brotherston, was a noted naturalist in the area so Granny grew up being close to nature. At an early age, she learned the names of trees and flowers near her home, and became interested in gardening. She maintained an interest in nature all her life.

After leaving school, Granny worked as a nanny in Ambleside, England, where she met and married George Wilson Tyson. They lived in a row house in Ambleside, and Granny took in summer visitors at her bed and breakfast (B&B).

Granny kept a spotless house and dressed her children, Tommy and Mary (Mollie), neatly and well. She kept Mollie's naturally curly, long brown hair in ringlets.

The children attended Sunday School regularly, and the whole family attended church services in the Ambleside Anglican Church following the Sunday School classes.

(L to R) Uncle Tommy, Grandpa Tyson and Mollie Tyson Vroom, June 1924. This picture was taken when Mom was visiting her parents on their Fishburn, Alberta farm for a few weeks in early summer, 1924. She is pregnant with her first child, Donald Ralph Vroom (born August 26, 1924 in Rossland, BC).

In the background is the "bald prairie." There were no trees on the prairies until planted by the homesteaders and settlers. Granny and Grandpa planted two windbreaks of carragana bushes, one to the northeast and one to the west. The bushes sheltered their farmhouse from wintry blasts. Author's collection.

In 1914, Granny and Grandpa Tyson moved to Canada. They crossed the Atlantic by ship and then took the train west. They came at the urging of George's brother Thomas Banks Tyson, "T.B.", as he was known affectionately by his friends.

One time when we were talking, Granny recalled how disappointed she was when the train stopped at Brocket, AB, where they disembarked. They had left the lush green, rolling hills of the Lake District in England to end up on dry, flat prairie. They settled in the Fishburn district east of Pincher Creek.

Granny was even more disappointed at their plight as far as living conditions were concerned. The situation was not quite like what "T.B." had described to them. Whereas in England Granny had her own house, in Canada she and Grandpa and their children shared someone else's home.

She and Grandpa worked for a farmer - Hector McGlenning. Granny kept house and did the cooking and Grandpa worked in the fields. Being of sturdy Scottish stock, Granny adapted very quickly to her new situation.

My mother, Mollie, attended Utopia School for two more years. She rode her white pony,

"Dick," to school until she, too, was old enough to quit school and go to work. Both Mom and Uncle Tommy continued to learn informally for the rest of their lives. Mom, especially, was always very interested in the world around her.

As soon as Granny and Grandpa Tyson were able to scrape together enough cash for a down payment, they purchased their own quarter section of land in the Fishburn district. When they first moved to their new home, there was not a bush or a tree in sight.

Though Granny had been raised in a small town and had lived in a town until she came to Canada, she made a remarkably good farmer's wife. Granny was a frugal homemaker. She was an excellent cook, could sew her own and her children's clothes, and possessed remarkable survival skills, which were sorely tested in the harsh climate of southern Alberta.

There was a small, white, house on the land. It had a kitchen and living room and two bedrooms. The house had a stone foundation and a small cellar — a partially dug out basement which was entered through a trap door in the floor at one end of the kitchen.

Most of the windows faced south, east and west, with one small window facing north. Granny always stood at the north window to watch for Grandpa coming home after collecting the mail at their rural mailbox, one-half mile away, twice a week. My mother thought that Granny worried needlessly about Grandpa.

By the time I remember Granny and Grandpa's house, a row of tall caraganas, hardy shrubs that grow well in dry climates like the Canadian prairies, formed a windbreak that protected the house from the worst blasts of the west wind. A smaller patch of caraganas protected the other side from northeast winds.

To help feed her family; Granny always grew a large garden. She was an excellent gardener and could produce a variety of vegetables without irrigation. Granny saved rainwater in a barrel by catching the runoff from the eaves during rainstorms. Some of the water was used for washing clothes, by hand on a scrub board, and some was used to water tiny, struggling new plants in her garden during long, dry spells.

Granny preserved extra vegetables - peas, green beans, broad beans, and string beans - by cutting them up and boiling them in a boiler for a specified period of time. The preserved food was carefully stored on shelves in the cellar. Large vegetables, like turnips, carrots, and potatoes were stored in heaps on the cellar floor.

My mother often recounted how she had picked saskatoons and chokecherries for her mother. A favourite berry patch was "down on the river," that is, along the Waterton River. Later in the summer, Granny, and my mother when she was living at home, walked one mile east to the Waterton River to pick saskatoons and chokecherries. Each time Granny picked fresh saskatoons she made cottage puddings with the delicious purple berries.

Granny made two kinds of cottage pudding. One kind had biscuit dough topping with lots of shortening in it, and the other had a cake batter for a topping. Granny also preserved about 50 quarts of saskatoons each summer. To bring out the flavour of the saskatoons, she added a little rhubarb from her garden.

Granny made chokecherry syrup, chokecherry jelly, and chokecherry wine with the freshly picked chokecherries. The jelly was used as a special treat on toast - homemade bread browned on a small wire rack set on top of the coal and wood range or hand held over glowing coals with a stove lid open. The syrup was a special treat on pancakes with a few spoonfuls of cream added in. Small servings of wine were offered to guests at Christmastime.

During the 1920s and 30s, wild fruit was plentiful in wooded areas of southern Alberta. Saskatoon berries were particularly abundant. Almost every family took advantage of the free food which was theirs for the picking. My brother Don and I would head out on our saddle horses to our favourite saskatoon patch. Often Mom would come with us. Because of her arthritis, Mom had a hard time mounting a horse without help from Dad, so she remained mounted on her horse and picked saskatoons into her bucket.

This photo, taken in 1920, shows the youngsters of Emil and Annie Jack of the Robert Kerr district east of Pincher Creek. They've just returned home after picking saskatoon berries in their favourite berry patch. Left to right are: Irene (Slater, Marcinko,), Edith "Toots" (Hochstein), Harvey "Buck" and Pearl (Hochstein). Each child is holding a syrup pail, standard equipment for berry picking in those days. Irene and Toots have their buckets pretty well full. Young "Buck" and Pearl have very few. Courtesy Edith Hochstein, Author's collection.

Granny used fresh cream for baking and for a treat on top of her cottage puddings. She made butter with sour cream. Granny was an excellent butter maker because she washed the fresh butter with plenty of cold water, and kneaded it diligently with a wooden paddle, until all of the buttermilk was worked out of it. Getting all the buttermilk out ensured a pure, sweet taste to the butter, as opposed to a sour, stale taste if all the buttermilk were not removed.

Granny used the butter for table use and for baking, and sold the extra butter if she could find a customer. "One time," Granny told me one day, "I had just got a steady customer who would take a few pounds a week when the cow went dry." That was another disappointment.

Granny also raised chickens for eggs and meat. Granny carefully packed the eggs in cartons for Grandpa to take with him to sell for a few cents cash at the grocery store in Hillspring. He always went to the store after taking a wagon load of wheat to the Hillspring elevator by team and wagon. The wheat also sold for cash, or credit. Whenever a hen stopped laying eggs, it was a candidate for chicken and dumplings. Granny soon learned to butcher chickens, and could dress a hen in short order. She preserved chicken by "bottling the meat." She did this by cutting it into small pieces and putting it into jars. She then boiled the jars for three hours in an oblong boiler full of water on the cook stove.

Granny Tyson was an excellent cook. She made hearty meals on a daily basis. Oatmeal porridge made in a stovetop pot was a staple for breakfast. She always had vegetables from her large garden. Often Granny bottled some of the meat that they got from the "beef ring." This was a cooperative whereby the farmers of the district took turns contributing a steer once a month. The meat was then divided amongst the contributors. There were no deep freezers, so the women bottled the meat.

Granny and Grandpa Tyson were generous and kind towards their neighbours. During World War I, Grandpa drove Granny to monthly meetings and work bees of the Canadian Red Cross, which were held in various homes in the Fishburn district. "Work bees" were social get-togethers of women held for a specific purpose. In Granny's case, the purpose was to spend a day quilting.

The women made quilts by putting a layer of warm material - often big oblong pieces of cotton batting or, better still, sheep's wool - in between two large pieces of cotton, or other, material. The top layer was then stitched to the bottom two layers by hand using small running stitches. This stitching process was called "quilting." The stitching was done in various patterns, which added to the beauty and value of the quilts.

The top layer of a quilt was often made of scraps of various kinds and colours of material, which were cut in a particular design and sewn together using a sewing machine.

This is the type of wagon that Grandpa Tyson used to haul grain from his farm at Fishburn, Alberta to the grain elevator at Hillspring, AB, in the 1930s. Drawing by Edith Annand Smithies.

Granny's kind-heartedness extended well beyond her family. She used her skills to help her neighbours in many ways. Granny owned a treadle Singer sewing machine, one of the few sewing machines in the district. Grandpa would load it in the back of their democrat and take it to wherever a quilting bee was being held on a particular day. At the end of the day he called back and took Granny and the sewing machine home again.

Granny was also skilled at hand knitting. She seldom sat down without her knitting in her hands. She knitted sweaters, scarves, hats, and mitts for the soldiers who were Overseas in WWII. Each month she, and other knitters, took their finished items to the Red Cross meeting. Their creations were bundled up and sent to Red Cross headquarters for eventual shipment to Canada's troops.

One neighbour's baby was allergic to milk, and was on the verge of starving. When Granny Tyson saw the little fellow, she pleaded, "Let me take the poor little tyke. I think I can do something for him."

Granny drew on knowledge she had gained as a nanny in England. She fed baby Laurie Blackburn barley water. Sure enough! The baby thrived and Laurie grew to be a strong man. I often wondered why Laurie, a jeweller in Pincher Creek, always regarded me with kindly interest. Years later I found out - my grandmother Tyson had saved his life!

Granny Tyson also raised roosters for eating and for selling. Each year she sent us two for Christmas. The weather was so cold that the dressed roosters could be transported to Beaver Mines, via the mailman, without refrigeration. Grandpa took the freshly butchered roosters to catch the rural mailman who serviced the Fishburn, Alberta district. In Pincher Creek the roosters were transferred to the sleigh of the Beaver Mines mailman, who brought them to Beaver Mines the next day. We picked them up when we got our mail.

Granny's Christmas cooking was legendary. In early October she always made rich dark fruit cakes, which would be stored in the cellar "to ripen." By Christmas, the flavours of the various fruits permeated the cake and blended with each other. Just before Christmas, Granny also made Scottish shortbread, using her own delicious homemade butter.

Along with the roosters Granny would send a layer of fruitcake and a round of shortbread. We children were always happy to see Granny's Christmas parcels arrive. It was a signal Christmas was near.

My mother did not open Granny's parcels right away, however. But always on Christmas morning, nestled amongst the branches of our Christmas tree, there were soft parcels wrapped in white tissue paper and tied with bright ribbons. In these parcels were new hand knit sweaters and mittens for each of us children - welcome additions to our meagre wardrobes. Granny Tyson was a skilled and prolific hand knitter.

Grandfather George Wilson Tyson

Granny Tyson did all the inside-the-house work, with one exception - Grandpa was always first up in the morning, and lit the kitchen stove. Then he would go outside to start his morning chores. Granny got up shortly afterwards and put the porridge on the stove so it would be cooked and breakfast ready when Grandpa came in from the barn.

Wood was used in the summer time for quick fires, and in wintertime to start the fire in the morning. The cookhouse fire was kept burning all day in wintertime to help keep the house warm. Coal was also used in a heater in the living room for warmth in the wintertime. Each fall, Grandpa used his team and wagon to haul a load of lignite coal home from a boxcar, which had been shunted onto a siding at Hillspring.

Grandpa did the major outside work. The morning chores included milking the cows when they were "fresh," that is, when they had recently had a calf and were producing milk night and morning. The cows were kept in the barn and fed hay over night so that Grandpa could milk them first thing in the morning and then turn them out to pasture for the rest of the day.

Grandpa threw down hay from the hayloft to feed his team of workhorses when he went out to the barn in the morning. On his way out to the field, if he were working that day, Grandpa drove the team past the water tank, which he filled by pumping water from the well, and let his team drink as much as they wanted.

Fortunately, Grandpa had a well with an abundance of water. However, the water had a lot of soda in it. Their water was not considered very good drinking water. But it was all they had, except for hauling water by the barrel from the Waterton River, a distance of about a mile. On the plus side: the soft water was very good for washing clothes, as it required very little soap.

When Grandpa came into the house after milking the cows, he separated the milk into cream and skim milk by putting it through a "cream separator." A cream separator had a large metal bowl on top, into which Grandpa poured the fresh milk. Then he turned the handle of the separator at a steady pace. In the separator, the milk ran through a series of metal discs - cream came out one spout, and skim milk out the other. When we kids got big enough, turning the separator handle became our job morning and night.

Washing the cream separator was a daily chore which had to be done before the milk went sour and gummed up the insides of the separator. To delay the souring process, and save water, cold water was poured through the separator as soon as the milk had all gone through. Cleaning the separator was a hard task. It had to be taken apart and the discs washed, first in hot soapy water, and then scalded with boiling water from the teakettle. Cleaning a separator which had sour milk stuck on the insides was an onerous task, to be avoided if at all possible.

The separating done, Grandpa sat down to a hearty breakfast of porridge and toast, made with Granny's homemade bread, and, when the chickens were laying, eggs. Grandpa generally sat and read the paper awhile before he went back out to the barn. He had to give the horses time to finish their feed.

About two-thirds of Grandpa's quarter section was planted to wheat or hay; the rest of the quarter section was taken up with the barnyard and out-buildings, the house yard, which included the garden, and pastureland.

Grandpa never had a tractor. He always farmed with horse drawn machinery - plough, harrow, seed drill, binder, hay mower, and hay rake. Like most farmers in the district, Grandpa hired someone with a threshing machine that was powered by a huge tractor to thresh the grain he harvested.

The threshing crew moved from farm to farm until everyone's harvesting was done. Often, they were paid with a share of the threshed wheat. Grandpa grew just enough hay to feed his few horses and cattle for the winter. He saved enough wheat to feed the chickens for the winter and took the rest of his grain to the Wheat Pool elevator in Hillspring, a small town about eight miles away, to get what cash he could. Some of the wheat he took to have ground into meal for the animals.

Grandpa Tyson was "a man of honour." Once he signed a contract, he stuck to it. The most notable time that he demonstrated total honesty was during World War I. Just prior to the War, Grandpa, and a number of farmers in western Canada, had signed a contract to take their grain to a Wheat Pool elevator for a certain price.

World War I dragged on past the time when it was expected to end. A shortage of food in Europe loomed; the price of grain soared. Farmers then had a choice. They could break their contract with the Wheat Pool, sell their grain on the open market, and probably become very wealthy, or they could honour their Wheat Pool contract.

According to my mother, some of Grandpa's neighbours broke their contract, and urged Grandpa to do likewise, but he steadfastly refused. Grandpa would not commit an act that he considered dishonest. As a result, many of Grandpa's neighbours indeed did become wealthy and bought out smaller farmers, eventually amassing large tracts of land. Grandpa, on the other hand, was never wealthy in dollar terms, but his honour was intact.

Grandpa passed on his belief in total honesty to my mother. One time the people in the Fishburn, Alberta district noticed that some of their mail seemed to be missing; the rural deliveryman was the chief suspect. An inquiry was held to try to find proof of the mailman's guilt or innocence. No one except my mother, no doubt out riding on her pony, Dick, had actually seen the mailman do anything untoward with the mail.

Throughout the inquiry the mailman insisted that he was delivering all the mail. He tried to debunk my mother's statement to the contrary. Mom, at the time only sixteen years old, took the stand. The trial dragged on. My mother was threatened if she did not "tell the truth," which was actually not the truth.

Finally, my mother offered to show the court where the mailman was stashing the mail. Still not believing my mother, the people followed her to a certain culvert, where, indeed, the mailman had been hiding some of the mail intended for local farmers. Interfering with mail delivery is a serious offence. The delinquent mailman was charged, convicted and punished accordingly.

Grandpa Tyson was a very mild-mannered person, though he remained stern, in my eyes, throughout his life. Whenever I was out visiting him and Granny and did or said something of which Grandpa disapproved, he said what I for the longest time thought was, "Cush! Cush, Bess!" I discovered years later that Grandpa was actually saying, "Gosh! Gosh, Bess!" According to my brother, Don, Grandpa Tyson never used a harsh expletive.

Grandpa Tyson always had a pipe of tobacco after lunch, but he did not drink any kind of liquor, except maybe a taste of Granny's chokecherry wine at Christmastime. Many years later Granny told me how embarrassed Grandpa was one time when he went into Pincher Creek on business and some men on the street called out to him, "Hey, Tommy! Have you got over Saturday night yet?" Grandpa did not know what they were laughing about, and ignored them.

It turned out that his brother, my great-uncle Tom, had been on a tear in Pincher Creek the previous Saturday, and the men had mistaken Grandpa for him.

Grandpa died in 1937 when I was 10 years old. I remember going to Grandpa's funeral by team and wagon, in June. It had rained all week and the wet muddy road was very slippery, even for the horses.

Everything was bright and green. Wild roses were blooming in profusion. As we drove along what we called "the grade,"[8] Mom had Dad stop the team and pick a bouquet of wild roses.

When we entered St. John's Anglican Church in Pincher Creek, Mom laid her humble bouquet gently on Grandpa's casket; a final tribute to her beloved father.   •

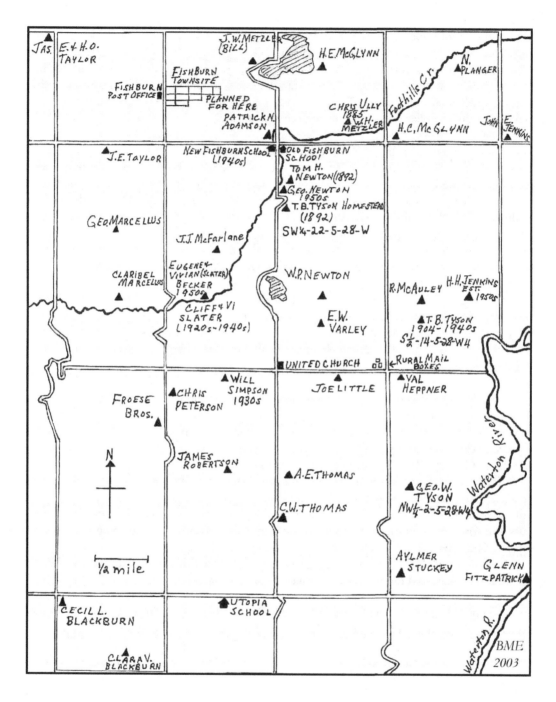

MAP 6 FISHBURN DISTRICT NEIGHBOURS, 1920s – 1950s

MAP 6 *The map, "Fishburn District Neighbours, 1920s – 1950s," shows the general location of:*

- *the homes of some of Granny and Grandpa Tyson's neighbours at that time. Shown on this map are the homes of: Patrick N. Adamson, Eugene and Vivian (Slater) Becker, Cecil L. Blackburn, Clara V. Blackburn, Glenn Fitzpatrick, Froese Brothers, Val Heppner, H.H. Jenkins estate, John E. Jenkins, Joe Little, Claribel Marcellus, George Marcellus, Robert McAuley, J.J. McFarlane, H.C. McGlynn, H.E. McGlynn, J.W. (Bill) Metzler, George Newton, H. Newton, W. P. Newton, Chris Peterson, N. Planger, James Robertson, Will Simpson, Cliff and Vi Slater, Aylmer Stuckey, H.O. (Harry) Taylor, James E. Taylor, J.E. Taylor, A. E. (Art) Thomas, C.W. (Wes) Thomas, George W. Tyson, T. B. (Tom) Tyson, Chris Ully, and E.W. Varley.*
- *Fishburn, Post Office, Fishburn Townsite (Proposed), the old Fishburn, School, the new Fishburn, School, Fishburn United Church, rural mailboxes at Val Heppner's corner, Utopia School, and Waterton River and Foothills Creek. Map hand drawn by the author.*

I can remember sitting in the church during Grandpa's funeral service. The first pew was full of family members. I was the last one in and had to sit in the second pew. Sitting there by myself, wearing my navy blue serge dress, I felt quite alone in my grief.

After Grandpa died, Granny stayed on the farm, finally leaving in the 1940s during the Second World War. At the time, there were very few retirement homes where people in small towns and rural areas could remain living near their friends and families. So, Granny lived with George and me, and our family, in Waterton Park the winter 1949-50, and with Uncle Tommy and Aunt Mary Tyson in Kimberley, BC, for a number of years. Granny then lived with my brother, Don, and his wife Jacquie and their children in their Department of Transport home at the Kimberley Airport. She remained with them until her death in 1957 at the age of 83 years.

When Grandpa Tyson died I had no more grandfathers, so my mother's uncle, Thomas Banks Tyson, or "T.B." assumed the role of grandfather in my life. I'm with "Old Uncle Tom" in this 1940 photo. We called him this to distinguish him from my mother's brother, Uncle Tommy Tyson.

"Old Uncle Tom" was one of the early settlers in the Fishburn district. When he was 16 years old, in March 1885, "T.B." sailed to Montreal from Liverpool. In 1889, he moved to the Fishburn District.

In 1892, T.B. Tyson took up homestead rights on NW 1/4-22-5-28-W4, adjacent to Tom Newton's homestead. Tom Newton was a childhood friend from Ambleside, a small village in the Lake District of England. "T.B." had persuaded Tom to join him in Fishburn.

Old Uncle Tom was fond of my mother, and was very good to our family. When I was teaching school near Drumheller, AB, during WWII, I always visited Uncle Tom as I passed through Calgary on my way home to Pincher Creek at school vacation.

Here, Granny Tyson is standing beside her house on her farm at Fishburn, Alberta in 1938. Granny kept a lovely house. Her linoleum floors were always clean and shiny, although not overly so. Her freshly starched, frilly, curtains and a houseplant, lovingly cared for, are at the window.

I remember the house was cold in the wintertime, but was delightfully cool in the summertime. Coal for the heater, which warmed the house in wintertime, was stored in the cellar.

Granny never forgot her love of flowers. She always had one section of her garden reserved for flowers - phlox, bachelor's buttons, cosmos, and a patch of baby's breath. Author's collection.

[1] A shortcut is a trail that is used to cut distance off of a regular route.

[2] A halter shank is the lead rope from a horse's halter. It is a piece of tack specially designed for leading or tying up horses. Tack means equipment for horseback riding, such as saddles and bridles.

[3] A quarter section is an area of land that is ½- by ½-mile. Alberta was divided into parcels of land with each one called a "section." Each section had four ¼-sections for a total of 640 acres per section.

[4] The hayloft was the top part of the barn where sufficient hay to last the animals all winter was stored.

[5] Hutterites are a religious sect whose members live communally in what are called "Hutterite Colonies" communal farms have large tracts of land and a cluster of farm buildings - apartments, barns, machine sheds, granaries, and a cookhouse and dining room. From 150 to 300 Hutterites may live and work co-operatively in each colony. In addition, they have their own schoolhouse.

[6] A Hutterite colony school is a one-room school with a multi-graded classroom, where one teacher teaches grades one to eight and where English is a second language for the children, who speak German at home.

[7] This steep grade was a steeply sloped road, which had been cut out of the side of the hill, using a horse-pulled road grader, as it climbed out of the bottom of the creek valley.

[8] The grade was what our family called a flat, straight stretch of road about one-half mile long and about one mile from our home. The grade was cut out of the end of a short range of hills, using a horse-pulled road grader, on the way to Beaver Mines.

EATING MINNOWS, AND OTHER CHILDHOOD ADVENTURES

An Unusual Summer - Mom Goes Down East

One day in 1934, the summer Bill was nearly three years old, my mother remarked rather casually to my dad, "I think I'll 'go down East,'[1] Ralph, and get some treatments from Dr. Locke in Oshawa. I have heard he is really good at helping people with arthritis. I will be gone about six weeks. I can stay with Jack Kelly's[2] sisters in Oshawa while I am there. Don can go out to stay with my parents at Fishburn. I have arranged for Bess to stay with Frank and Mrs. Holmes at Beaver Mines. Bill can stay with the Truitts up Gladstone Valley."

Mom's arthritis had steadily worsened since the first symptoms had shown up in about 1925, just before Don was born in Rossland, BC. Dr. Locke had a reputation for being able to manipulate the bones of arthritic patients so that their pain was relieved. Dad agreed that it was a good idea for Mom to go. To get enough money for Mom's train ticket to Oshawa., Dad took one of his best horses and rode until he found a buyer who would pay the necessary amount.

About the first of August we children were taken to the homes of the families who we would stay with for a few weeks. Mom travelled by train to Oshawa and had her arthritis treatments as planned. However, the arrangements she made for us children didn't go exactly as she planned.

Like all two-year-olds, my brother Bill was a lively child, full of curiosity and not wanting to be left out of anything. Bill stayed with Lawrence Truitt, brother of Cy and Adam Truitt, for the summer. Lawrence could barely walk because of his rheumatoid arthritis. He spent a lot of time just sitting in his rocking chair reading, and looking out across the valley.

The summer that Bill was stayed with the Truitts, Lawrence amused himself by extending Bill's vocabulary, mainly by teaching him a number of swear words. Mom always said that Bill was her sweetest baby. "Before that summer," my mother often lamented, "Bill was the sweetest little boy." Indeed, childhood pictures show Bill with an angelic expression. However, after several weeks under the tutelage of kind-hearted Lawrence, Bill's speech patterns were anything but angelic.

One day Bill wandered away from the Truitts' watchful eyes and made his way about one-quarter of a mile along a trail down the hill to a neighbour's place. The neighbours were new to the district and had never seen Bill before. They did not know where he had come from; he just suddenly appeared at their kitchen door.

"What's your name?" asked Christie Kyllo, not knowing what else to say to a small child who seemed to come out of nowhere.

In July 1934, Mom went to Dr. Locke's clinic in Oshawa, ON, to get treatments for her rheumatoid arthritis. Dr. Locke's famous "twist" brought temporary relief to hundreds of people. Mom is just to the right of the right-hand pole, with her long hair in ringlets. Her auburn hair was naturally curly, and just had to be brushed around her finger to make ringlets. Mom was gone a whole month. We kids stayed with neighbours and relatives. Author's collection.

"I'm George Willum," Bill announced proudly.

"George Willum who?" Christie inquired kindly.

"George Willum," said Bill resolutely.

"But who are you and where do you live?" asked Christie, her impatience showing in her voice.

"I'm George Willum. I live in that dod-damned house," Bill responded pointing up the hill, and showing his impatience with adults.

Christie tried a new tactic. "Art," she called to her husband who was sitting in the front room reading, "come here."

Reluctantly Art left his comfortable chair and went out to the kitchen. "Do you know who this child is?" queried Christie in a tone of voice that implied Art had better know. "He just came to the door out of nowhere. He says he's 'George Willum', and lives in 'that dod-damned house'," she said, making a wide sweep with her arm.

"I've heard the Truitts have Billy Vroom staying with them for the summer," Art replied in a helpful tone of voice. "Perhaps this little fellow is Billy."

Christie was not amused. But she walked Bill back up the hill to the Truitts' home.

"Here's a little fellow who came to visit me," she said to Lawrence.

Bill ran to Lawrence and started talking excitedly, telling Lawrence about his visit.

Bessie Runs Away

In the meantime, I was not very happy staying with Mrs. Holmes. In the first place, to my way of thinking, there was "nothing to do" because I could do none of my usual activities. There were no other children to play with and there were no animals, either. I missed my Mom and Dad and brothers. To add to my distress, Mrs. Holmes " made me stay in bed long after my usual early-rising hour.

To pass away the time I would lie on my back and examine the boards in the ceiling, finding imperfections in the varnish - a hair that had fallen out of the paint brush used to varnish the ceiling or a variation in grain or colour. I also looked for any other flaws I could detect.

The Holmes had a teen-age daughter, Betty, but she did not seem to be around very much. I remember one time when Betty was home, the two Ballantyne girls, Alma and Elva came to visit Betty. I was demonstrating how I could run on all fours, in various gaits - walking, trotting, single-footing, and galloping. The big girls, who were long-legged teenagers, tried to imitate, but their hind legs were too long. I thought they looked quite funny. Eventually, the girls collapsed on the floor, laughing and giggling at themselves and each other.

Mr. Holmes owned the Number One Coal Mine, and would walk over there to examine the workings every few days. One day I volunteered to go along. But instead of going into the mine I made some excuse to stay down on the road. I actually had made up my mind to run away and go home to Dad at the ranch, which was about a mile and a half further on.

As soon as Mr. Holmes disappeared into the mine, I headed up the road toward home. I scurried along as fast as I could go, watching the dust puff out as I hurried along the hot, dusty road. I was just congratulating myself on having made my getaway when I happened to glance backwards. And there, not twenty feet away, was Mr. Holmes. He was following my tracks in the dust. When I saw Mr. Holmes I started to run, but he could keep up with me.

"Where are you going, Bessie?" Mr. Holmes asked.

"I want to visit Daddy," I pouted stubbornly.

"All right," Mr. Holmes agreed. "We'll go and see your dad."

To my surprise when we got to the ranch house, it was empty. No one was there. "I'll look upstairs," Mr. Holmes volunteered.

As soon as Mr. Holmes went upstairs I ran out the kitchen door, around to the back of the shack and into the icehouse. There I hid under a platform of boards, but again Mr. Holmes found me. "The shack" was a small building that attached to the house with a board walkway and was once used for a summer kitchen and. We just used the shack to store a lot of household furnishings that were not in use when I was a child.

"Let's go back and see Mrs. Holmes," he said persuasively. Seeing no other alternative, I reluctantly agreed.

The upshot of that occasion was that I got to leave the Holmes's, but I still did not go home. Instead, Dad arranged for me to stay with some friends of the family, Alfie and Alice Primeau. They lived about three miles southeast of Beauvais Lake, Alberta, and northwest of Twin Butte, a hamlet about fifteen miles, as the crow flies, southeast of our ranch.

"We'll go over to the Spread Eagle Stampede," my dad said cheerfully, a couple of days after I had arrived home unannounced from the Holmes's. "Will there be lots of kids there?" I asked hopefully.

"I'm sure there will be," Dad answered with a knowing smile.

We got up bright and early the next morning and headed out. We rode along the forestry trail that skirted the eastern slopes of the Rockies.

I discovered that the Spread Eagle Stampede was much like the Castle River Stampede. The stampede was put on by the local people, and was held on a flat area just west of Yarrow Creek, which is west of Twin Butte. Events included saddle bronc riding, steer riding, and calf roping put on by local cowboys. There was a racetrack, and the local people raced their best horses.

At the stampede, I got to know some of the children in the Spread Eagle-Drywood-Twin Butte area, such as the Bruders, Therriaults, Bechtals, Holroyds, Hilliers, and a number of others. I rode my pony in the children's pony race. Years later, I met many of those young people again at dances at Twin Butte and at high school in Pincher Creek.

Dad and I joined up with Alfie and Alice Riviere Primeau, whose ranch was about ten miles north of the Spread Eagle Stampede grounds. We shared their picnic lunches at noon and at suppertime.

In the evening, an open-air dance was held on a makeshift board dance floor laid out on the grass. All the young people had a wonderful time.

A heavy downpour of rain cut the dance short. People loaded their families into wagons and buggies and headed for home. I went home with Alfie and Alice Primeau, and Dad went back to our ranch. I couldn't keep my pony at Primeau's, so Dad took my pony home with him. Unbeknown to me, plans for school that year were for me to stay with my Aunt Marion Cyr in September, while my mother settled back into ranch life after her trip down East.

I liked being at Alfie and Alice Primeau's. I stayed with them for a few weeks. Alice was friendly and kind, and gave me quite a bit of freedom. They also got up early in the morning, which I liked to do. They had cats and dogs that I could play with, and there were horses and cattle around their ranch.

Just before I got to Primeau's, Alice's brother, James Riviere, came down with an attack of acute appendicitis and had to be rushed to St. Vincent's Hospital in Pincher Creek for emergency surgery. After spending 10 days in hospital, James came out to Primeau's and stayed with them for another couple of weeks until he was well enough to go home.

I was very fond of James. He was great friends with my mother and dad and often visited us at our ranch near Beaver Mines.

The Primeau's had a son, Jimmy, about my age. James used to have a lot of fun watching Jimmy and me play together, quite happily, making up our own games. One of our favourite games was "Moses with His Eyes Knocked Out."

At a given signal, we would race out the door onto the front porch and see who could be the first one to sit down in a pail that always seemed to be sitting beside the door. James would watch us by the hour. One day, he got an especially big kick out of our game.

When Mom was around she would assign Don or me to look after Bill. If she and Dad went away for a day or two, they took Bill with them, much to the chagrin of Don and me. We wanted to go, too, but had to stay home to go to school. If Mom rode to Beaver Mines to a meeting, she took Bill with her on her saddle horse leaving Don and me at home looking after each other.

Mom took this charming picture of Bill in 1934, shortly before she left for Dr. Locke's Clinic in Ottawa. In this picture, three-year-old Bill was sitting by the shack holding a fluffy cat. My mother always said, "Bill was my sweetest baby." Author's collection.

Jimmy and I raced to sit down in the bucket, which turned out to be Alice's scrub bucket. As quite often happened, Jimmy won. He got to the bucket first, and plunked himself down in it.

"Nyah! Nyah! You're a fat potato," he called out to me. Disappointed, I turned away.

Jimmy, however, got the surprise of his life. "A-a-rgh!" he cried in alarm.

Alice had scrubbed the floor that day, but had not dumped the scrub water yet. Jimmy's shout of glee at beating me to the bucket turned to a wail of hurt feelings and indignation. He had landed in a bucket of cold scrub water and got his pants soaking wet.

More children to play with sounded like a wonderful idea to me.

"Please let me go home with James," I begged Alice.

James interceded on my behalf. "Bess'll be all right," he assured Alice. "Mama and George and Maggie and Frances and Babe are there, and she'll like playing with Nellie and Henry." His words were music to my ears. The upshot was I went along when Primeaus took James home.

At the time I was at George and Maggie's, *Nichemoos* was living in a little cabin near the main house. She did not come to George's house for all of her meals, so the privilege of taking *Nichemoos*'s meals to her fell to my friend Nellie and me.

The Riviere children and grandchildren called *Nichemoos* "*Kookem* Mrs. Brown. *Kookem* is a Cree word meaning "Grandmother."

"Please take *Kookem* Mrs. Brown's breakfast to her," Mrs. Riviere would say to Nellie and me. "She doesn't like to get up early and come to breakfast in the house." Nellie and I would carry *Kookem* Mrs. Brown's breakfast carefully along the path to the little cabin, and knock timidly on her door. "Come," *Kookem* Mrs. Brown would say in Cree. She spoke very little English, and it was hard to get her to understand what we said to her. Nellie knew quite a few Cree words, and I gradually learned a few.

At the Rivieres, *Kookem* Mrs. Brown was treated like one of the family. When she felt like it, she went over to the Riviere home and had dinner and supper with the family. Otherwise, Mrs. Riviere made up a dinner plate for *Kookem* Mrs. Brown, and we children delivered it.

This is Nellie Gladstone (Mrs. Frenchy) Riviere and Isabella Brown sitting in the sun beside Nellie's cabin in 1929. The cabin was on the homestead of Nellie's brother, George, on the south side of Drywood Creek on SW1/4-S13 -T4 -R30-W4. I stayed with Nellie for a few weeks in the summer of 1934 while my mother was down east in Oshawa, ON, receiving treatments for her rheumatoid arthritis.

Also living with Nellie that summer were two of Nellie's grandchildren, "little" Nellie and "little" Henry Riviere, and her daughter-in-law Maggie Clark (Mrs. George) Riviere. Two of Nellie's daughters Inez (Mrs. Orin Rae) and Frances (Mrs. Bill McWhirter) also visited Nellie for part of the summer. Frenchy, who spent much of his time at his little cabin near the north boundary of Waterton Lakes National Park, sometimes came to visit.

At that time Mrs. Brown was living in her own little cabin just up the path from Nellie's. We children respectfully called her "Kookum," a Cree word meaning Grandmother. At mealtime, Nellie and I carried Kookum's steaming food up the little path leading to her cabin. We often sat and visited with her while she ate. Courtesy Frances Riviere McWhirter, Author's collection.

We often stayed with Mrs. Brown while she ate her meals. I was fascinated by the dark-colored fur coat and hat, which hung beside Mrs. Brown's bed, even in summertime. "Where did she get her fur coat," I asked. "Oh, my grandmother bought it for her," Nellie replied casually.

Mrs. Brown had seen the fur coat in the catalogue and said to Mrs. Riviere, "I want that coat. Will you buy it for me?" So Mrs. Riviere got cash from Mrs. Brown and bought a money order to send away for the fur coat. Mrs. Brown had a widow's pension from the federal government because Kootenai had worked for the Parks Service. In due time, the coat arrived. It became one of Mrs. Brown's greatest treasures.

"*Kookem* Mrs. Brown loved to get dressed up in her fur coat and hat and go out for rides with my mother in the sleigh or buggy," remembers Frances Riviere McWhirter. "They would go to visit various neighbours."

Sometimes George R. "Joe" Annand would drive all the way out to Mrs. Riviere's home to pick up *Nichemoos* and take her back to Waterton to visit with his wife, Betsy, for an afternoon. The Annands had proved up on a homestead near Drywood School, west of Twin Butte, from 1916 to 1920, and had been neighbours of the Rivieres and George Gladstone.

Floyd Riviere remembers stories from his childhood that his father, James, told about *Nichemoos*. While she lived beside Mrs. Riviere, *Nichemoos* was the "doctor" of the whole neighbourhood.

"Whenever she heard of illness in a neighbour's family," Floyd recalled, "*Nichemoos* would pick up her buckskin bag filled with native medicinal herbs, and head out by team and buggy. One well-known native Indian medicine used by *Nichemoos* was wild strawberrry root to cure diarrhea. To relieve the pain of stuffed up sinuses, *Nichemoos* made a fine powder out of dried root of wild cabbage. 'Snuff this up your nose,' she admonished the sufferer, and shortly thereafter the sinuses were cleared."

When it came time for school to start, the Rivieres took me back up to Alice Primeau's. The Primeaus took me to church at St. Michael's Roman Catholic Church in Pincher Creek on Sunday, and I went home with Aunt Marion Cyr. I stayed with Aunt Marion and attended St. Michael's School for the month of September.

Nichemoos lived several years after the summer I stayed with the Rivieres. She was a strong Roman Catholic, and her sister had been a good friend of Father Lacombe, the famous missionary to the Blackfoot nations.

Nichemoos died at the home of Mrs. Riviere on April 1, 1935. There had been a heavy spring snowstorm, and the road to the ranch was impassable by car. Billy Gladstone, Mrs. Nellie Riviere's brother, drove *Nichemoos*'s remains out to the Pincher Creek-Waterton highway in a sleigh pulled by a team of fine black horses.

At the highway, *Nichemoos*'s body was transferred to a vehicle supplied by the Parks Service and driven by Joe Annand of Waterton Park — Mr. Annand and his wife, Betsy, had been friends of *Nichemoos* since their homestead days near Twin Butte. The funeral service was held in the old log Roman Catholic Church in Waterton Park.

A hearse also came out from Pincher Creek. Unfortunately, as recalled by Betty Annand Baker, the hearse had two flat tires. The funeral director asked George Baker, owner of Park Transport Company, to change the tires. "This delay caused George to miss the funeral," said his wife, Betty Annand Baker.

When the service was over, the pallbearers, headed by Joe Annand, placed *Nichemoos*'s coffin in the hearse. Then the hearse, followed by the mourners, took *Nichemoos*'s body to its final resting-place, a grave on the hillside overlooking Lower Waterton Lake beside her late husband, Kootenai Brown.

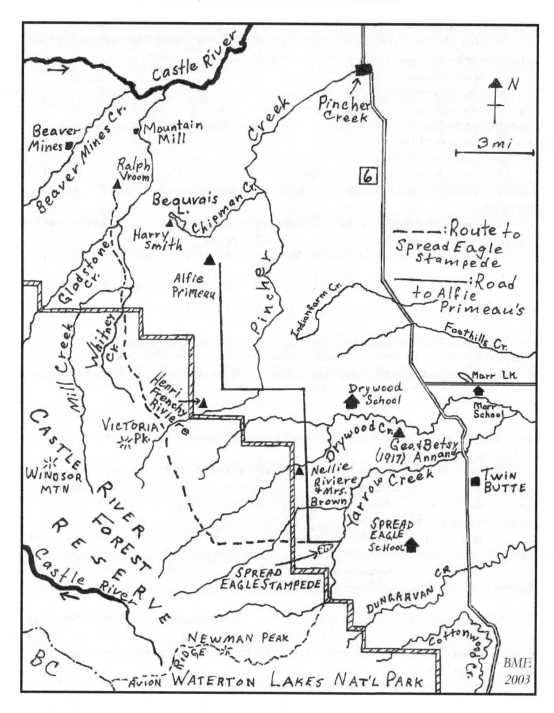

MAP 7 VROOM RANCH TO SPREAD EAGLE STAMPEDE, 1934

MAP 7 *The map "Vroom Ranch to Spread Eagle Stampede, 1934" shows the location of Spread Eagle School in relation to our ranch. It also shows the approximate route of the trail we rode on horseback to get to the Spread Eagle Stampede.*

On this map is shown the location of:

- *Drywood School, Marr School, and Spread Eagle School*
- *the homes of Alfie and Alice Primeau, Henri "Frenchy" Riviere,, Nellie (Mrs. Frenchy) Riviere, Mrs. Isabella Brown (Nichemoos), Harry and Anna Smith, Ralph and Mollie Vroom*
- *the (1917) homestead of George and Betsy Annand*
- *Mountain Mill, Pincher Creek, Twin Butte, and Waterton Lakes National Park*
- *Avion Ridge, Newman Peak Victoria Peak and Windsor (Castle) Mountain.*
- *Beaver Mines Creek, Beauvais Lake, Castle River, Chipman Creek, Drywood Creek, Dungarvan Creek, Foothills Creek, Gladstone Creek, Indianfarm Creek, Marr Lake, Mill Creek, Whitney Creek, Yarrow Creek. Map hand drawn by the author.*

Mom Returns from Down East

Mom felt much better when she returned from down East after her treatments at Dr. Locke's clinic, but she had been away a month and had not had to do housework like she did at home. To give Mom a bit more of a rest, and to let her get accustomed to looking after Bill, as well as doing housework, I stayed on at Primeau's until school started. Then I was given a choice.

"Your dad says you can stay with your Aunt Marion Cyr for awhile this fall," Alice informed me one day.

"Goody! Goody!" I exclaimed, totally delighted by the idea. I was seven and one-half years old at the time and was in grade three.

However, at Aunt Marion's, I had to walk to school, which was the only part of staying at Aunt Marion's that I did not really love. At home at Beaver Mines I always had my pony to ride, so walking seemed slow and boring to me. But, when I walked with Aunt Marion when she was on her way to early Mass at St. Michael's Church, I had to go much faster or get left behind.

Aunt Marion wanted to take me home before a September rain or snowstorm made our road impassable for a car. So, about the third week in September, home I went. By then I was very glad to be home, and was content for quite some time to enjoy the freedom no one but my parents ever allowed me.

For instance, I loved going barefoot, and neither Mrs. Holmes, nor Alice Primeau, nor Aunt Marion, had allowed me to go barefoot while I was staying with them. So the first thing I did when I got home was sit down on the kitchen floor and take off my shoes, exclaiming, "Well! At least I won't have to wear my shoes any more!" Mom knew I was happy to be home.

I was truly glad to be home after my summer adventures. I was confident that at home I could ride off on another adventure whenever the opportunity arose.

Once we children were all safely home, we settled back to the usual routine - almost! Mom was shocked when she heard Bill punctuate nearly every sentence with one swear word or another. "What will I do with him on Women's Institute day?" she wondered half to herself. "I can't take him to the meeting with him swearing like that."

"Why don't you wash his mouth out with soap?" I asked helpfully. "That's what you do with kids that swear."

"Hush, Bess," Mom said quietly. "I'll think of something."

During the summer holidays, we children sometimes caught and rode our ponies just for fun. In this 1934 picture, we are in the house yard. I am on "Rex" and Don is on "Pickles." Bill is standing between us. Author's collection.

By the day of the next meeting Mom had hit on a solution to the problem. "You take Bill to the far end of Beaver Mines," she said to Don and me, "and don't come back until the meeting is over." It was a warm sunny afternoon, but the time dragged for us.

"There's nothing to do here," we complained to Mom when the meeting was finally over. We got on our horses and rode home, not too happy with our afternoon chore of looking after Bill.

Bill Eats Minnows and His Other Adventures

"Don, you take Bill with you today," said Mom one morning when Don was "going out to play," a loose term which could mean almost any kind of adventure, ranging from very safe to very risky.

By then Bill was going on seven years old. My sister, Marion, was nearly a year old and Mom wanted me to spend some time with her. Usually Don was Mom's helper, and I had a lot more time outdoors.

"What if he gets hungry?" asked Don.

Mom replied with her usual comment in answering such a question. "He won't get hungry. He ate a good breakfast," Mom assured Don cheerfully.

"But what if he does?" Don repeated, trying to make his point.

"Don, you're old enough to know better than ask me that," Mom responded. "Please take Bill with you, like I asked you."

At seven years old, Bill was a very good rider and easily kept up with his older brother. Don discovered to his surprise that Bill was pretty good company. They rode happily along on that warm summer day.

"We'll stop here," said Don after a couple of hours. They had just crossed the steel bridge on the Castle River several miles south of Cowley, Alberta.

"What are we going to do here?" queried Bill.

"I'll show you," answered Don. "Let's tie up our horses."

They got off their horses, took off their saddles so the horses would cool down, and started to play on the flat rocks beside the water. The river, a deep turquoise blue because of its depth of several feet at that point, swirled and eddied beside them.

"I'm tired," complained Bill after a short time.

"Watch me climb over the top of the bridge," Don coaxed Bill. "I've practiced before." So saying, Don ran over to the steel bridge and scampered up the bridge abutments and walked upright along the top of the superstructure of the bridge. He had wonderful balance!

"I'm still tired," mumbled Bill half-heartedly.

"Let's try to catch some of those minnows," suggested Don brightly, ignoring Bill's complaint of tiredness.

For the next hour or so the two boys happily tried to catch minnows with their hands. They caught about fifty of the tiny fish and put them in a small pool of water. It was probably rainwater caught in a depression in the huge, flat granite rocks worn smooth by glaciers some 10,000 years ago and by the flowing of river water over them when the river was in flood condition.

Finally, Bill wailed, "I'm hungry!"

"There's no food," answered Don. Hoping to divert Bill's attention away from his hunger, Don added. "Look at all these minnows chasing each other around!"

"I don't care," sobbed Bill. "I'm hungry."

"There's nothing to eat," Don retorted. "You'll have to wait until we get home," he added firmly. There were no berries on the shrubs beside the river, and they had no sandwiches.

"But I'm hungry!" insisted Bill, starting to cry again.

"That's okay, Bill," Don said kindly, trying to console his young brother. "We'll think of something."

"What will we eat, though?" cried Bill, trying to hide his tears by wiping them away on his shirtsleeve.

"I know!" said Don cheerfully. "We'll eat some fish."

"We don't have any fish, do we?" whimpered Bill, feeling a little hopeful.

"Minnows are fish," explained Don. "We'll eat them."

"I don't like fish," protested Bill.

"You'll like these ones," Don assured him. "They're little ones."

"But they're not cooked," objected Bill.

"You don't have to cook little fish," declared Don. "Here! Watch me!" And with that Don swallowed a raw minnow whole. "Now it's your turn, Bill," asserted Don.

Not wanting to appear "chicken," that is, to be a poor sport, in front of his big brother Bill took the proffered minnow and swallowed it.

"We're taking turns," stated Don swallowing another minnow. "Now it's your turn again."

They continued taking turns eating minnows for several minutes. Finally, Bill declared stubbornly, "I'm full!" He would eat no more.

"That's okay, Bill," said Don. "We'll go home soon." It was almost sundown by then, so a few minutes later the boys saddled up their horses and headed for home, with another adventure to remember.

For the October Women's Institute meeting Mom made Don and me stay home with Bill. We liked that even less, and the time dragged worse than before. The afternoon seemed so long that after awhile I suggested, "Something must have happened to Mom. Let's go and meet her." So the three of us set off walking down the road towards Beaver Mines.

We got nearly a mile from home when we spied Mom on her saddle horse at the other end of the grade.

Again I had a bright idea. "Let's hide and surprise her," I proposed. So all three of us scurried into the bushes beside the road, and waited for what seemed an eternity.

By the time Mom rode alongside where we were hiding we felt a little guilty about our actions, so we came out of the bushes fairly quietly. "Hi, Mom," we said hopefully. "We came to meet you."

"I thought I saw some kids duck into the bushes," Mom said, disbelief ringing in her voice. "I didn't think they could possibly be mine."

By this time Bill was pretty tired and didn't want to walk home. He started to cry a little. "Hoist him up behind me, you guys," Mom said to Don and me in her no-nonsense voice.

"What about us? Why should Bill ride and not us?" I cried, realizing what a predicament I had gotten us into.

"You two can walk," Mom answered firmly, nudging her horse to start along the road for home.

Disgruntled, Don and I trudged along behind Mom and Bill. To amuse ourselves we started throwing little pebbles at the horse's heels to make it kick up and scare Bill.

"Mommy! Mommy!" Bill would cry, grabbing onto Mom's blouse tightly and hanging on for dear life each time the horse kicked up.

"What are you two doing?" Mom queried, realizing that something unusual was going on.

"Nothing. Nothing," we declared innocently.

The horse still kept kicking up a little bit every once in awhile, but Mom did not say any more — she knew what was going on. She just nudged her horse into a slow jog and got about 100 feet in front of us, well out of range of our pebbles. Then Don and I had only each other to talk to and commiserate with the rest of the way home.

I don't remember how Mom punished us when we got home; she may have mentioned our behaviour to Dad when he came home and he gave us a talking to. His talk must have sunken in; we never behaved like that again.

"Yow-w-w! Yow-w-w! Ou-ou-ou-ouch!" Bill wailed. "You dod-damned hornets!" Three-year-old Bill stepped higher and higher as he ran back and forth past a pile of scrap metal and tires in front of the carpenter shop one hot September day.

Dad, just coming out of the barn, stood and watched the procedure for a few minutes — Bill was always onto something new. "What are you doing, Bill?" Dad finally asked, unable to contain his curiosity any longer.

Not missing a step, Bill howled, "I'm trying to kill all these dod-damned hornets!"

Dad was puzzled for a minute, then he remembered the folklore that if a bee or a hornet stings a person it will die. Some hornets had made a nest in one of the old tires.

Every time Bill went past the carpenter shop on his way to or from the barn one of the hornets flew out and stung him. Bill had believed the old story and was trying in his own way to get rid of the insect pests all at once! There were no chemical insect repellants or insect killers in those days, except for what we called "Paris green."[3]

Bill had used his ingenuity to make up his own method for killing hornets!

Sometimes, on a hot summer afternoon, Mom had us fill a tub with cold water so we could "go swimming" in it. In this 1932 picture Don, Bill and I are getting cooled off.

The ladder in the background is leaning against the eaves of the second storey of our house. Dad was using it so that he could get up on the roof to clean the chimney, a fire prevention measure. Author's collection.

Other Play Activities on the Ranch

The years of my childhood, especially the summers, passed quickly and happily. We were constantly busy with tasks, into which both of my parents injected a spirit of fun and adventure, often regaling us with stories from their youth in southern Alberta in the early 1900s.

My parents really did have a pretty ranch. The land is set in a wide valley, half encircled by high hills to the west and north. To the east and south, lower hills open up to a view of foothills leading right up to the Rocky Mountains. Although many of the hills were open, short-grass pastureland, and the flatter areas were hay fields, a lot of our ranch was covered in mixed forest. This included deciduous trees of the poplar family, such as willows, aspen and balm of Gilead, and evergreens like pine and fir trees.

Just enough of the land was cleared to provide fields for growing feed for the animals, and gardens for food for our family. We children could not spend all of our playtime visiting or playing with the animals, but we had lots of other exciting activities to keep us occupied when the animals were not available. We enjoyed many of the simple pleasures of childhood.

In the springtime, the open hills were covered with a succession of delicate wild flowers. Mom learned the names of all these flowers from her mother, and taught them to us children. While the last snowbanks of winter still lingered in the woodland, we children searched for signs of spring.

"Mom! The crocuses are out!" we cried excitedly, as we burst into the kitchen carrying our first mauve bouquets clutched in our hands.

When the crocuses started to fade, fuchsia-coloured shooting stars sprang up, and we picked bouquets of them for Mom. By then the wooded areas in the pasture were dry enough that we could start walking our favourite trails searching for elusive violets and bright yellow lemon lilies. In succession, purple larkspurs and lupins, and finally bright yellow sunflowers covered the open hillsides.

This 1931 picture shows the Ralph and Mollie Vroom ranch home in winter. In the foreground is the hayfield across the road from, and west of, the barnyard and house yard.

Beyond this is the original corral, the barn, the goat house, the gate into the big corral, the blacksmith shop without its high gambrel roof, the root house without its high gambrel roof, the shack, the house. Grandpa Oscar Vroom helped build the gambrel roofs on the blacksmith shop and root house about 1931. The rest of the pole corrals and the pole fence around the house yard were built about 1935. The house, now over 100 years old, is still standing. Author's collection.

Skunk cabbages and cow parsnip sprouted up along the banks of the little creek as it meandered through the willows that divided the west quarter into two distinct hay fields.

In mid-August, elegant tiger lilies peeked out from amongst the tall grass in the west quarter on a hillside that was not completely cleared of underbrush.

For Mom, spring arrived when a pair of bluebirds returned to build their nest in a birdhouse under the eaves of the shack. Mom watched for them attentively as the grey of winter changed to the verdant green of spring. "I saw the bluebirds today," she told us happily one day when we came home from school. Together we watched the nest-building activities of the bluebirds, and saw the first faltering flights of the young ones.

We children spent many happy hours just playing in the house yard and around the ranch buildings. It was a glorious time!

Years later, I was struck by how the hills of the Lake District surrounding Ambleside, England, resembled the hills surrounding our ranch. Ofttimes, Mom must have stood at the kitchen door and gazed up at those open hills, and thought of her childhood home. Interestingly, old-timers referred to Lees Lake, that body of water of sweeping beauty where Don and I took our biplane ride, as "The Killarney of the Foothills."

The main buildings on our ranch, the barn, the blacksmith shop and the root cellar, also called the root house, were made of about ten-inch logs, overlapping and notched together at the ends. Parts of those log buildings, built in the early 1900s, have stood for nearly 100 years. The house was two stories high, the bottom half was covered with narrow boards and painted white; the top half was shingled and painted brown. The house, which is still standing, is over 100 years old.

The house yard was spacious and covered with tall, sweet-smelling grass. After a heavy rainstorm we used to swan dive off the front verandah railings, and then pretend to swim in the soggy, wet grass.

"The little garden," located right beside the house and ringed by a row of low red currant bushes, set the house off from the road.

By 1936, three sides of the house yard fence were made of poles; the barnyard opened to the road; several pole corrals set off the barnyard. The house yard had a number of tall poplar trees in it, which Don and I climbed on a regular basis.

"Ouch! Ouch!" I yelped, as I lay on the kitchen table with my trousers down.

"Lie still," my mother said gently, but firmly. "Let me get these slivers out before they start to fester. You know that you should not be sliding down the root cellar roof."

Earlier in the day Don and I had been sliding down the rough boards that made the roof of our root house. The "root house" straddled the little creek in the northeast corner of the house yard. It was a specially constructed building with controlled-temperature year round to keep vegetables from decaying during storage.

The sides of the creek underneath the root house were lined with rocks to make retaining walls. Cool air from the "rocked-up" creek was drawn into the root house through a hole left between the rocks. A wooden ventilator shaft ran from inside the root house and up through the roof. It drew stale air to the outside of the building, kept down the interior humidity, and kept the vegetables from moulding. Thick log walls, and two heavy doors, kept heat out during the summer and cold out during the winter.

The original roof of the root house was a "gable roof," that is, a roof with a single ridgepole and two sloping sides, looking somewhat like an inverted V. A couple of the boards were smoother than the rest of the boards and we kids used them as a slide.

We frequently got some slivers in our bums. Then we would run yelping to the house for solace from our mother. Mom would make us lie down on the kitchen table, and warn us to lie very still. Then she would patiently remove the slivers, which fortunately were generally just under the skin.

We stayed off the roof until the sliver wounds healed, and then we would be out there again.

Dad used the largest trees in our house yard to hang thick ropes to make two swings. The seat of the "big swing" was a two and one-half-foot-long plank. Two children could sit side by side on that swing, but you needed someone to push you, which was a disadvantage.

The "little swing" was made for just one small child at a time. I often stood up on the seat and pumped with my legs until I was going so high that the ropes would go slack. When the ropes jerked taut again, I got a thrill, and a bit of a scare, so I did not go up that high very often.

When we tired of pushing each other in the swings, we cast about for something else to do.

"I bet I can walk further along the corral rails than you can," Don challenged me one summer day.

"What do you mean 'walk the corral rails'?" I asked, my ears perking up.

"We can climb up on them and walk along the top rail and see who can go the farthest without falling off," explained Don, who always did like heights. I did not especially like heights, but, not to be outdone by Don, I went along with most of his ideas.

Dad had built several miles of pole fences out of logs about five inches in diameter. All our pole fences were a fair height. The fences around the big corral, the stack yards, and the house yard were five or six poles high. The little corral and the corral behind the barn, however, were eight or nine poles high.

"I just fall off," I said downheartedly after a few tries. Don seemed to be able to walk the rails with no difficulty.

"You'll get practiced at it," Don encouraged me. "Just spread your arms out like I do for balance."

"Okay, I'll try," I conceded.

And thus began one of the best games that Don and I ever made up for ourselves. It wasn't long until I was enthralled by the competition of pole walking. We would spend hours and hours walking the corral rails. First I tried just to beat Don, but after awhile I would go out, practice by myself, and compete with my own record. My aim was to walk all around the corrals without touching the ground, except if there were a wire or a metal gate.

Most of our corral gates were made of poles, but getting past a gate was always tricky because gates were not so firm as the main corral rails were. We often would make it all the way around a corral only to fall off when trying to navigate a gate. We passed from corral to corral where the sides met. Once we turned the corner we would start along the adjoining corral's rails. We also tried not to retrace our steps, but that was not always possible.

Walking the corrals in summer time was generally quite easy, we thought, but other times of year posed a greater challenge.

I loved to be pushed on a swing when I was a young child. In this picture, Mrs. Bruce caught me sitting on the "big swing" pretending to be shy in this 1934 photo. Mrs. Mabel (Edward) Bruce photo, Author's collection.

One of my favourite poems when I was a child was "The Swing" by Robert Louis Stevenson. Here is what I can remember of it.

THE SWING
By Robert Louis Stevenson

Oh, how I love to go up in a swing
Up in the air so blue
Oh, I do think it the pleasantest thing
Ever a child can do.

Up in the air and over the wall
'Til I can see so wide
Rivers and trees and cattle and all
Over the countryside.
. . . .
. . . .
Up in the air I go flying again
Up in the air and down.

Wintertime was another difficult time for walking the corrals. When the days were consistently cold we could manage all right. However, the poles often had patches of snow and ice on them, and when we tried to walk along them we slipped off. Other times the poles would be covered with frost, which was even more slippery than snow and covered the whole pole.

When a Chinook had partly warmed the railings, walking them was treacherous. During a Chinook some of the poles would be all right to walk on, but some would thaw a bit and have frost on them and be very slippery. Our rubber boots wood slide right off, so we had to be very nimble to land on our feet and not be hurt. Luckily, in the winter there were often snow banks beside the corrals, so when we fell we didn't always hit the hard ground some five or six feet down.

If there were deep snow or snow banks on the ground we often made extra fun of our falls by turning a somersault and landing in a snow bank at the base of the corral. To make our falling off seem to be deliberate, we would "turn a somersault," that is, flip over in the air before we hit the snow bank.

Once we were covered with snow we would often lie in the deep, fluffy snow making snow angels. To make "snow angels" we lay on our backs and flapped our outstretched arms to make wing patterns in the soft snow. We could play in the snow for hours, eventually straggling into Mom's warm kitchen, hungry and soaking wet!

The little corral was eight or nine poles high. In the winter, Don and I could do somersaults off the top rail into the snowbanks.

At other times of the year, when the poles were wet after a rainstorm they were very slippery, so walking at that time was fairly risky. When we lost our footing, we would try to land in the deep, wet grass growing on the outside of the corral rails. However, after a few harder bumps we would call it a day, and would go into the house to warm up. Courtesy of Don Vroom, Author's collection.

One bright, sunny, hot summer day when I was about 10 years old, my brother Don and I walked about one mile along the little creek, following the small, barely moving stream as it wound through swamp and muskeg and thick willows in a neighbour's field. We were hunting magpie eggs.. Magpies, in those days, were considered to be "nuisance birds," that is, they were unwelcome around farmers' buildings as no use could be seen for them. The rural municipality offered a reward of one cent for each egg that was collected and turned in to the district councillor.

For our afternoon's labours, we collected twenty magpie eggs at most for a total of twenty cents. That seems like very little money nowadays, but it was a lot to us and, what's more, it was ours to spend as we wished. However, in doing so, we probably tore our clothing in a number of places, much to Mom's disappointment, I am sure.

But, in order to get paid, we had to take the eggs to Mr. Spellman, who lived on the other side of Beaver Mines, about four miles from home near Coalfields School. We probably walked home by way of the store and bought candy with our treasure. We must not have felt too good about our magpie-egg expedition, as I cannot remember gathering magpie eggs ever again, though I can remember climbing trees to get crows' eggs. Since crows ate the eggs of other birds, we felt no remorse at gathering crows' eggs.

The crows' nests were in tall trees that were on the edge of a grove of trees in the west quarter just across the road from our barnyard. Don was really good at scrambling up trees that had no low branches, and liked to climb to the very top of them.

James Riviere lent my dad the wonderful horse "Silver" for me to ride to school. Silver was the horse that James had trained to lie down. In 1935, James called by our place with his bride, Gay De Meester. They stayed overnight and in the morning Gay offered to cook the pancakes.

I was intrigued when she used the last few spoonfuls of batter in the bowl to make "cats" with long tails, "bears" with fuzzy ears, and "puppies" with big feet. For a year or so after that, I always coaxed, "Daddy, please make us some animals like Gay did." When he had time, Dad obliged me, but his pancake animals were never as good as Gay's.

Here Gay is on "Snip". James is wearing the beaded black velvet vest that his mother, Mrs. Nellie Gladstone Riviere, made for him. Mrs. Riviere made a beaded vest for each of her sons. She drew the design, such as floweres, on the vest freehand. She then sat on the floor while she stitched on the tiny coloured beads to make colourful designs. Courtesy Lorraine Riviere Pommier, Author's collection.

Learning to Ride a Bicycle

I don't know where I got the idea that I wanted a bicycle. Maybe I saw one in the Eaton's or Simpson's catalogue. But one day when I was about ten years old I said to Don, "Wouldn't it be fun if we had a bicycle?"

"Why?" asked Don.

I had my answer all ready, and replied, "Oh, we could ride it along the road and across the field. It would be fun."

"Well, I don't know," answered Don thoughtfully. "The road is pretty hard and rough, and it gets awfully muddy sometimes."

"We could ride in the field," I persisted. "It's soft."

Don didn't answer, so I continued. "Let's order one from the catalogue. "I'll write it out," I volunteered.

"Okay," said Don with a worried look, "but I don't know what we'll use for money to send with the order."

When we were children, there wasn't money for luxuries. Once during the "Dirty Thirties", Mom sent the only dollar bill she had seen in years to the Alberta Registrar of Brands, to re-register her horse brand.

My mother made my underwear from bleached cotton obtained from 100-pound cotton flour sacks. She got these sacks when she bought staple foods, such as flour and sugar, in large quantities from McRoberts Store in Pincher Creek. The short, short panties I wore with my fairy costume in "The Sleeping Beauty" in Coalfields School Christmas concert were made from a bleached 100-pound sugar sack.

Our pets were animals common to ranches and farms, and exotic pets were rare. Whenever I visited Mrs. Bruce, I was fascinated by her small green parrot. Sometimes the bird was in its cage, and sometimes it was sitting on a perch somewhere in the room.

The parrot paid little heed to me, but would sit on Mrs. Bruce's outstretched finger when she whistled softly to it. A skilled photographer, here Mrs. Bruce holds the parrot silhouetted against a white cloth so her treasured pet shows up better. Courtesy Katherine Bruce, Author's collection.

I really hadn't thought about needing cash to send with the order to Eaton's. All I knew about catalogue ordering was that every once in awhile, maybe before the Castle River Stampede and once again before school started, I was allowed to choose one item, usually a pair of shoes or a pair of cotton slacks, to buy from the catalogue. Mom sewed all the rest of my clothes - dresses, coats, and even my underwear - on her old Raymond sewing machine. When we were small, a number of our coats were made from material obtained by cutting down adults' coats.

Mom also bought large quantities of staples, such as prunes and raisins, from the Neale Brothers. They were travelling salesmen who came to our ranch every fall to take an order.

I am sure we wore hand-me-down clothes, but I was not really aware of them; all I knew was that magically some more clothes would come in a bundle from somewhere.

Most of the clothes were wearable, but I remember one frilly, pink organza dress that looked completely useless. However, next Christmas it became a costume for a play in the Gladstone Valley School Christmas concert. My parents never wasted anything.

I didn't want Mom to know that I was ordering a bicycle, so I took the catalogue out to the shack and carefully wrote out my order. I checked to make sure I had put down the right item number, used the name exactly as in the catalogue, and put down the page and the price - something like twelve dollars.

I proudly showed my effort to Don. "See, I have it ordered," I announced. "All I need is the money."

"Where are you going to get that much money, Bess?" Don asked, sounding as kind as he could.

"I'll ask Mom," I replied cheerfully.

"Well, I don't know, Bess," responded Don patiently. "That's a lot of money, and Mom doesn't have much."

I started thinking about what Don said, and wondering what I could say to my mother to convince her to give me the money for a bicycle. It took about a week for me to get up the nerve to show my order to Mom. In the meantime, I kept my precious order hidden in the root cellar.

But summer holidays didn't last very long and soon summer would be over. I knew that if I didn't get that bicycle right away I would have to wait until next summer before the road was dry enough to ride on with my bicycle. So I gathered up my courage, took the catalogue and my order, so neatly made out, and stood beside my mother. By then my order sheet was kind of rumpled from being checked so many times, and from being in the dampness of the root cellar.

"What is it, Bess?" Mom asked quietly.

"I want a bicycle," I blurted out, as I held out the catalogue already turned to the right page. "See, here it is. And I've got the order all made out."

My mother never immediately refused any of my requests, no matter how impossible they might have seemed. "Well, we'll have to ask your father," Mom answered, hedging for time while she tried to figure out how to refuse my request without hurting my feelings too badly.

"Oh! Oh!" I thought to myself. This is not going to be as fast as I thought." Out loud I asked, "When will Daddy be home?" Dad was away with our team and wagon helping some neighbours.

"It won't be long, Bess," answered Mom.

There was nothing I could do but wait. I tried to busy myself playing with the goats, but that didn't seem very interesting compared with the possibility of having a bicycle to ride. All I could think of was how I would ride my new bicycle when I got it.

Unbeknown to me, Don must have told Mom how much I wanted a bicycle, and how I was ordering one. We did not tattletale on each other about our escapades, but this seemed different to Don, so he talked to Mom about it. Mom must have talked to Dad, who started looking around for a second-hand bicycle.

When Dad drove into the barnyard a couple of days later, I ran out to greet. "Daddy! Daddy!" I cried. "Mommy said to ask you if I could have a bicycle!"

"Did she?" Dad answered, trying to keep a straight face. "What kind of bicycle?"

"Like the one in the catalogue," I replied quickly.

"Well, how about this one?" Dad asked looking in the back of the wagon.

I climbed up on a wheel to look in; I could hardly believe my eyes! There in the back of the wagon was a bicycle. "Try it out, Bess," Dad suggested. "See if it fits you." He lifted the bicycle out of the wagon box and set it on the ground.

Disappointment welled up inside of me. The bicycle was not like the one in the catalogue. The handlebars were kind of bent and had no rubber handles on them. The tires were flat and the wheels had no fenders, and that wasn't all! The bicycle was nearly as tall as I was and had a crossbar. Most of the padding was gone from the seat. When I looked at the front wheel it looked awfully crooked.

It was a bicycle though. I didn't say anything, so Dad said encouragingly, "Try it out, Bess."

"It's broken," I protested.

"Oh, pshaw, Bess! The wheel's just a little bent," Dad countered, knowing ahead of time what I would say.

"I can't get on it," I continued in a discouraged tone of voice.

"Sure you can," Dad persisted. "Take it over to the barn doorstep and climb on there."

So I pushed the rickety bicycle over to the foot-high front doorstep of the barn.

As the bicycle rolled along, the warped front wheel made a kind of zigzag track in the barnyard dust and rubbed against the bicycle frame. Getting on that bicycle was like climbing back on a horse that had just bucked me off. I had to get on that horse and I had to get on that bicycle. So I lined the bicycle up beside the barn doorstep.

I knew I could not reach the pedals, and wondered how I could make the bicycle go. However, the barnyard sloped gently from the barn to the road, so all I had to do was get on the bicycle, balance myself and roll down the slope.

But that was easier said than done. As well as being way too big for me, because of the position of the barn step and the slope of the land, I had to mount the bicycle from "the wrong side." I had to get on the right-hand side instead of the left-hand side as in getting on a horse; that was a complication.

The first few tries I rolled only ten or twenty feet before I lost my balance, causing the bicycle to fall over sending me sprawling on the grass. Nothing was hurt but my feelings, so up I got each time and tried again and again. By dark, I could get almost to the road before falling over. I was pretty proud of myself, and walked back pushing the bike, feeling kind of tired.

"You'd better come for supper, Bess," Dad said after he got his team put away. "Try again tomorrow."

In the morning I rushed with my chores, cheerfully hauling in armfuls of wood, and doing whatever else I had to do. Finally, I was finished, and back out I went to the bicycle.

"I'll help you today," offered Don. So Don came with me, and we took turns riding the bike. Being bigger and older, he learned faster that I had done.

"I'll never learn," I said dejectedly after several more tries.

"Sure you will," encouraged Don, "just sit up straight and balance like you did on the corral rails." To make the bicycle riding practice more interesting, we made it a little competitive by making a game of it.

"You're a cow pie," we'd call out to each other whenever we fell over before we got to the road. Of course, I did not want to be a cow pie, and I did not want Don to beat me at anything, so I tried even harder. Whoever fell the most often before we reached the road was the most cow pies.

It wasn't too long before I could ride as far as the road without falling over. Then Don showed me how to stand up, straddling the crossbar, and pedal. That way I could reach the pedals. That was something new to learn, so I tried and tried.

The gate to the hay field across the road was open. I knew that I would be well away if I could get across the bumpy road with its wagon wheel ruts made when the road was muddy after a rain. I was sure that I could pedal even farther along the tracks made by the hayrack when we brought loads of hay in from the fields.

The land continued to slope until it reached the little creek that meandered through the hay field about three hundred yards from the road. Eventually, I could pedal further than the shallow creek, splashing myself as I peddled as hard as I could, and go about one hundred yards beyond it before I hit land too rough for me to navigate.

So, if I could stay on the bicycle, I could get quite a ride out of it. The only trouble was that I could not pedal the bicycle back up the slope, so I had to push it back to the barn doorstep for another start. Eventually, I got so that I could pedal it part way back, but I always got tired and had to walk.

The road that ran by our place was rutted from wagons going along when it was muddy, but by the middle of summer the ruts had worn down somewhat. Only a few people in our area had cars at that time. Motorists seldom came up our road in a rainy weather, as the road was just too slippery. Cars were sure to have trouble, especially where the little creek crossed the road between our water trough at the spring and Gus's gate about one-quarter mile from our house. Until the road was bone dry, people in cars went around by Hamilton's, on the other side of the big hill, to get up Gladstone Valley.

In the summertime after a long dry spell, however, a few cars would go by our place. Gradually, the ruts got worn down, and I ventured along the road on the bicycle, even though I had to pedal all the time.

The zigzag track from the warped front wheel of the bicycle looked like a snake had wriggled along in the deep dust of that dry clay soil. I tried to follow my same track each time I went along the road.

I practiced on that old bicycle for a couple of summers and got so I could ride it fairly well. One time I rode my bicycle up to see Mr. and Mrs. Robert Stillman, neighbours who lived one-half mile south of us, to show it to them. When I got there they were not home, so I had to turn around and ride home. There were two fairly long hills in that one-half mile of road, so I thought I would have a little rest from pedalling and get a good ride home.

It was lucky I had learned to use the brakes on the short hill by our spring and water trough, or I would have got going too fast. I could have hit a rut, too, which would have sent me flying so that I would have been badly injured. I did get going too fast for comfort a couple of times, but managed to stop safely.

I never did own a bicycle that was the right size for me. About four or five years later when we were living in Waterton Park, Alberta, for one year, most of the kids had bicycles. Every once awhile, someone else would lend me a bike to go for a ride. One time I went up the Akamina Highway past the first two switchbacks with some other kids.

The highway was only gravel then. Coming back down to the town site I got going a little too fast and swung out into the deep gravel on the outer edge of the curve.

Down to my left were trees and rocks and bushes. The kids behind me saw my situation, and one of them yelled, "Pedal hard, Bessie!" and pedal hard I did. I got out of the gravel okay and back down to the town site. That was a close call. I was much less adventurous on a bicycle after that.

But I wanted to prove to myself that I was not afraid of fast bike riding. When I was in grade eleven in Pincher Creek, I borrowed a bicycle from one of the other kids and pushed it all the way to the top of the hill on the old Number Six highway south of Pincher Creek. Number Six had very thin blacktop at the time. I intended to ride all the way down those hills, about a mile in all, without using the brakes. Part way down, however, I said to myself, "Discretion is the better part of valour." Carefully, I applied the brakes and slowed down a few times so that I got back to town safely.

(Above left) Pat Kelly of Oshawa, ON, on "Chief" at Beaver Mines, about 1936. He has a revolver in his holster. Pat was the younger brother of Jack Kelly who worked for dad in the early 1930s. In 1934, Mom stayed with the Kelly family in Oshawa when she went to the Dr. Locke Clinic for her rheumatoid arthritis.

(Above right) Pat Kelly standing in front of our large log barn on the ranch. Pat is dressed in his "Sunday best", complete with a pair of black and white pinto goatskin chaps. Author's collection.

---

[1] Go down East means go to Ontario in eastern Canada.

[2] Jack Kelly was one of our hired men during the 1930s. He was one of the thousands of young men who travelled across Canada looking for work during the Great Depression.

[3] Paris green was a green powder that was mixed with water and sprinkled by hand on the leaves of the garden potato plants to kill the potato bugs.

A SAVAGE FOREST FIRE, AND
BUILDING A CART

During the 1930s the Canadian prairies suffered from a drought with so little rainfall that crops burned up from the heat of the sun. Many families moved up into the Gladstone Valley area where their cattle could feed on the grassy hillsides, and they could cut a little hay for feed for the winter.

By the summer of 1936, however, even the foothills and the Rocky Mountain area of southern Alberta were affected by the drought. The grass and the forests were tinder dry.

One dark night in mid-July, during a "dry lightning storm" - a storm during which no, or only very little, rain falls - a particularly powerful bolt of lightning hit a dry spruce tree high on a mountainside. The tree lit up like a torch.

The burning tree became as hot as a blast furnace. It exploded into a shower of sparks and flying pieces of burning wood. Helped by a brisk wind, the fire jumped from tree to tree. It became a wild fire as each succeeding tree "topped," exploding into a shower of red-hot embers, which landed on adjacent trees and the sere grass of the forest floor. Soon, the entire mountainside was enveloped in roaring flames.

The smoke and ashes billowed up into the atmosphere and drifted hundreds of miles. One day a glowing ember, still so hot that it singed that grass where it alit, landed in our barnyard.

In the 1930s, Dad was a licensed Alberta guide. He took out fishing and hunting parties during the summer and fall to make much needed extra cash for our livelihood.

During the summer of 1936, Dad took Milt Condon from Blairmore, AB, and some of his cronies, on a 10-day fishing trip in the Castle River Forest Reserve.

Twelve-year-old Don helped Dad take his pack outfit as far as Castle River Ranger Station. By previous arrangement, Milt had taken his food and gear for the trip to the ranger station by truck. When all of the equipment was loaded on the packhorses, Don returned to the ranch by himself, a distance of about 15 miles. As events turned, he became the "man of the family" until nearly the end of September.

We kids knew something was wrong when Dad did not return at the end of ten days.

"I heard on the radio that a forest fire has broken out in the forest reserve," Mom told us. "Maybe Daddy had to fight fire."

Our fears were confirmed when, a few days later, the Mill Creek forest ranger, Mr. Prigge, rode into our yard with an anxious look on his face. He spoke to my mother with deep concern in his voice.

"Get ready to move, Mrs. Vroom, "he said, emphasizing every word. "We can't control the forest fire. Pack up your most essential items of clothing and belongings and be ready to move out on short notice."

Dad held a Class 'A' Alberta guide and outfitter's license for many years. One of his regular clients was Milt Condon (on the left) of Blairmore, AB. Dad, Milt and a couple of friends were on a ten-day fishing trip in the Castle River Forest Reserve. They camped close to the Castle River, directly west of Castle Mountain (now called Windsor Ridge).

While on this trip in mid-July 1936, a lightning strike started a forest fire. Dad's pack horse outfit was commandeered to carry supplies for the fire fighters. Dad was put to work cooking. They fought the blaze for more than two months, often endangering their own lives in the process. Though the men fought valiantly, the fire raged into autumn.

Dad was an old time raconteur who used his story telling ability to entertain guests. When told in the twilight around a flickering campfire, or after a hearty meal, Dad's stories were mesmerizing. Each time Dad told a story, he did so in a slightly different way, changing a few details here and there, depending on his audience.

Charlie Barclay and Adam "Dutch" Truitt of Gladstone Valley often stopped at our place at mealtime en route home from Beaver Mines. Their eyes always sparkled and glowed as they listened to Dad recount yet another adventure from his youth. Author's collection.

Sweeping his arm over the range of hills to the south of our ranch, Mr. Prigge continued, "We've had no rain for a long time. We're afraid that if a strong wind comes up the fire will sweep right down over those hills and burn out this whole valley."

"Have you heard of Ralph?" my mother asked.

"Only that he's cooking for a fire crew away up the Castle River," replied Mr. Prigge.

"Thank you," answered my mother, "We'll pack a few things right away."

Turning to Don and me, Mom spoke to us in a calm, firm voice, "This is serious. There is no telling what a forest fire will do." Mom was remembering how in the summer of 1925 their lumber camp near Rossland, BC, had been burned out by a forest fire.

Continuing speaking, she said, "You guys help me get some stuff out of the house." We hastened to comply.

For the next few days Mom had we three children - Don, who was twelve years old going on thirteen, me, nine and one-half years old, and even Bill who was only four - pack essential items out of the house. The items made only a small heap in the barnyard.

Covered in a tarp, our small pile of belongings sat there all summer long, ready to be picked up easily if we had to move out in a hurry. In the meantime, Mom and we children had to manage as best we could.

Two riders, one of Bert Riggall's guides (right) and a guest, stop to rest their saddle horses after a steep climb to the summit of the Clarke Range of the Rocky Mountains near the Hawk's Nest lodge at Twin Butte, AB. The view in this photo shows the head of Castle River, the Great Divide, which is the backbone of the North American continent, and some of the high mountains in south east British Columbia. All this country was burned or threatened by the Castle River Fire in the summer and fall of 1936.

Bert Riggall, whom my dad knew and admired, was one of the best known, most highly esteemed outdoorsmen in North America. He made a living for himself and his family by taking wealthy tourists, mostly Americans, on personally guided tours of the Rocky Mountains, often through the vast wilderness area seen in this picture.

Mr. Riggall's guests rode on sturdy saddle horses. Their food and sleeping equipment was carried by pack horses. Each party of tourist stayed out on the trail for a period of time ranging from several days up to three weeks. Gourmet meals were cooked in the open air, often by his wife Dora Williams Riggall. Meals were served out of doors and the guests slept in tents. Bert Riggall photo, courtesy Katherine Bruce, Author's collection.

This photo was taken by Michael Bruce in 1931. Five summers later, all this country was burned out by the intense heat of the Castle River fire. You are looking south, from the atop the 7096-foot flat-topped ridge that extends eastward from Table Mountain. In the distance, Castle Peak (8394 ft.) is a turret- shaped pillar of rock perched on top of Windsor Ridge, just north of the peak of Windsor Mountain (8346 ft.). The headwaters of Mill Creek start southeast of Windsor Mountain.

From left to right, the mountains are: part of Prairie Bluff (which oldtimers refer to as Corner Mountain), located straight south of Beauvais Lake; Mount Gladstone (8068 ft.) between the headwaters of Gladstone Creek and Mill Creek; Victoria Peak (8400 ft.); Drywood Mountain (7800 ft.), between Drywood Creek and South Drywood Creek; Castle Peak and Windsor Ridge.

My dad, my two brothers, Don and Bill, and my cousin Vera Cyr (Gingras) and I climbed Windsor Mountain in the summer of 1938. We were on a three-day pack trip starting out from our ranch near Beaver Mines. We camped beside Castle River at the base of Castle Mountain.

We left home really early and arrived at our campsite by noon. We then left our saddle and pack horses and climbed Windsor Mountain on foot. The first part of the climb was through the forest which had been burned out in the Castle River fire of 1936. When we came to the steeper part of the climb, we traversed big boulders. Nearer the top was a band of shale. The afternoon got hotter and hotter, but we forced on.

When we reached the base of the turret, a vertical pillar of rock which was nearly 100 feet high, we could climb no further. We had no rock-climbing equipment. In fact, we were climbing in running shoes, which were worn out by the time we got back to our campsite.

The biggest thrill of the climb for all of us youngsters was when Dad took one us at a time and held our hand while we stepped out onto what seemed like a big chunk of earth clinging to the top of Windsor Mountain at the base of Castle Peak. By bending forward, ever so carefully, we could peer down and see the basin near the head of Mill Creek nearly 2000 feet below us. When each of us had a chance to peer over the edge from that dizzying height, we once more gazed up at the insurmountable turret and then started the tiring climb back down the mountain. Michael Bruce photo, courtesy Katherine Bruce, Author's collection.

Dad had learned of the forest fire when Forest Ranger Jack Frankish, rode into his camp early one morning. Jack was the ranger stationed at the Elk Lodge Ranger Station.

"A fire has started away back in the mountains, Ralph," he told my dad. "It looks like it will be a big one. You'll have to get your party out of here as fast as you can. Then come right back in. We need you and your outfit to help fight it."

When a forest fire breaks out, "martial law" goes into effect. It is an emergency situation where men and equipment can be commandeered to fight the fire.

Dad knew he had no choice. There were no ifs, buts or maybes. All his horses were needed to pack fire-fighting equipment and supplies to the firefighters.

This is my cousin, Mae Vroom, 16 years old, at the time of her "coming out," 1932. The daughter of Harold and Ruby Vroom, Mae was an adventurous young woman, who leaped into the breach while her dad was away fighting the fire. Besides doing the chores at home, Mae drove a ½-ton truck to take food and other supplies as far as the Castle River Ranger Station at the end of the forestry road. There she met Dad's pack train that carried the urgently needed supplies further into the mountains.

Unfortunately, the "fire had its way," burning furiously until heavy rains in late August finally drenched the tinder dry forest and undergrowth. The fire fizzled out, and the weary men headed home. The fire had devastated some 300 square miles of prime timberland in the Castle River Forest Reserve and killed much of the defenseless wildlife in its path. Courtesy of Ruby Peters Jaggernath, Author's collection.

So Dad packed up his outfit and accompanied the fishing party as far as the Castle River Ranger Station, which was about five miles south of Elk Lodge. Once there, the fishermen put their gear in their truck and headed for home down the narrow forestry road. Dad, his pack outfit and several saddle horses were commandeered on the spot.

Because he was an experienced camp cook, Dad was hired initially to cook in one of the mobile campsites set up to feed the hundreds of men who laboured to extinguish the fire. Dad's string of packhorses was put to work carrying supplies and equipment to the firefighters.

The firefighters were greatly hindered in their efforts because the only access to the area was by narrow trails, the only mode of transportation was on foot or horseback, and goods were carried in backpacks or by packhorses. There were no helicopters, water bombers, or two-way radios. The firefighters used puny, by today's standards, hand held equipment. But it was the best there was in those days.

As noted in the *Crowsnest Pass and Its People*, the fire was not completely extinguished until November 18, 1936. The story further recounts how valiantly Senior Forestry Officer Joe Kovatch and his firefighters worked, even though their lives were endangered.

When Dad returned, he told us of some of the bravery of the firefighters. Only later did we learn that my dad was one of the men who performed heroic deeds.

A fast-burning arm of the fire had cut off a crew of firefighters from the base camp. Word spread quickly and it was feared the lost men were injured or disoriented. Someone had to find the men and lead them safety.

Dad was so anxious that he instantly volunteered. Riding his bravest saddle horse, he travelled for many miles through blinding smoke and hot cinders, while the fire crackled and burned around him.

Finally, he reached the area where they were last known to have been and located the cave where the marooned men had taken refuge. It was only then he discovered that his older brother, Harold, Mae's father, was among them.

With Dad leading the way, the men walked the many miles out to the Castle River Ranger Station, and went on to fight the fire again.

This picture, taken in the 1925, shows Uncle Harold and Aunt Ruby Vroom in front of the old cabin on their ranch in the Beaver Mines Creek Valley.

Uncle Harold is dressed in his gumboots and overalls, his usual attire for cleaning out the chicken coop which housed his flock of White Leghorn chickens. They sold fresh eggs and butchered chickens to regular customers in the Crows Nest Pass.

Uncle Harold and Aunt Ruby also had adventurous childhoods. Uncle Harold, in 1904 when he was 15 years, had come west with his parents to this valley from Nova Scotia on a CPR settler's train.

In 1906, Aunt Ruby came by covered wagon with her parents, Washington and Belle Mitchell, and three siblings, from Meridian, Idaho, to a homestead in Gladstone Valley. Their stories are told in my volume 2, "Pioneer Adventurers". Courtesy Ruby Peters Jaggernath, Author's collection.

The Cart

The extra money that Dad earned as a guide was welcome, as dollars were very scarce in the mid-1930s, the decade of the Great Depression. The onslaught of the forest fire meant, though, that Dad, along with his horses, saddles and bridles, was away from the home ranch for about six weeks, instead of ten days as originally planned.

The days dragged on into weeks. Don and I were concerned that our dad might be away for the whole summer. What was worse, Dad had much of our riding tack with him, all the saddles and our best bridles and martingales. We children were left with only our ponies, no saddles, and not our favourite bridles.

We understood, however, that it was an emergency situation. A forest fire was very serious. We knew we had no choice but to adapt to the situation.

With our favourite saddles gone, we had to ride bareback. Since we were used to riding with a saddle, we felt rather insulted to have to ride bareback. Besides that, early in the summer, I had jumped off my horse into Beaver Mines Creek and hit my tailbone on a rock at the bottom of the creek. Hence, riding was very painful, and I had to go slowly, which also irked me. But Mom, whose saddle was also away on the camping trip, and who was pain-ridden by her rheumatoid arthritis, could not ride bareback at all.

Mom was prepared to stay right at home for the duration of Dad's ten-day camping trip, as originally planned. However, as the days dragged into weeks, Mom really needed to get at least as far as the Beaver Mines General Store, where she could use a telephone to do some business in Pincher Creek.

Our ponies could not pull the regular wagon, and the work teams were too big, and their harnesses too heavy, for Don or me to handle. Dad had the "light team," the team that was used for pulling only light loads such as buggies, and small wagons, away on the fishing trip where they were doubling as packhorses. So we had to figure out something else.

Don, the inventive one of the two of us, figured out that if we made a cart that the ponies could pull, we could take Mom to the store.

The Castle River Ranger Station, shown here in the 1920s, was located about five miles south of Elk Lodge Ranger Station, in the Castle River Forest Reserve. Elk Lodge was located beside a tall pole gate at the main entrance to the Forest Reserve. The road to both ranger stations ran past Uncle Harold's ranch and Grandpa Oscar Vroom's cabin. Trails ran off in various directions from Castle River Ranger Station. Courtesy of Ruby Peters Jaggernath, Author's collection.

"What we really need," Don declared early one morning, "is a cart."

"How can we get one with no money?" I asked hopelessly.

Don was ready with an answer. "Maybe we can use some of the parts of those old cars that are standing at the bottom of the side hill," he conjectured.

The cart that Don and I made in the summer of 1936 was actually a "Bennett Buggy."[1] Don might have heard about Bennett Buggies, but I certainly never had.

"I think I can make a cart out of these wheels," conjectured Don, as he looked at the front axle of an old Model T Ford. "We'll haul these wheels down behind the goat house and work on the cart there." So together, we pushed and pulled until we had the unwieldy contraption where we wanted it.

"What will we use for a team?" I asked hopelessly. "We can't harness the big team."

Again, Don was ready with an answer. "You know those buggy harnesses that we found?" Don reminded me. "We can use them. You can train a couple of our ponies to drive."

Don and I rummaged around amongst the harnesses in the barn one day, and found two buggy-horse harnesses. When we shortened all of the straps, the harnesses fitted our half-Shetland ponies fairly well.

We had discovered the solution to our problem! While Don set about hammering and sawing on the cart box, I trained the ponies as a team.

I had often driven our work team for Dad when he was doing various chores around the ranch, such as when using the stone boat or the manure boat. Moreover, I had trained Smokey and Baby Darling to pull my hand sleigh in winter and toy wagon in summer. I was confident that I could train the ponies.

The "stone boat" was a conveyance that Dad had made by nailing several four-foot-long planks across two runners made of small logs, which were peeled of bark and then flattened on the bottom and chopped slanted at one end. "Planks" are heavy boards which are about two inches thick and eight inches wide, The stone boat pulled along like a low sleigh, going across bare ground in the summer and sliding along on the snow in wintertime.

The "manure boat", like the stone boat, had flattened logs for runners. However, the manure boat had board sides about three feet high. During the winter Dad shovelled the manure from the "barn manure pile" into the manure boat and took the manure out to spread on the fields as fertilizer. The barn manure pile was a heap of manure, which accumulated over several months, as horse and cow manure was shovelled out of the barn each morning. When the manure had sat in the pile long enough to deteriorate it made excellent fertilizer.

We didn't tell Mom all of our plans, but she knew something was going on. Her painful arthritis kept her from walking out behind the goat shed to investigate the hammering. When she queried us, we just answered, "Oh, nothing, nothing" or "Oh, we're just playing." Mom didn't press the matter. . She was confident that eventually "the truth would out," and we would have to tell her exactly what we were doing.

Don and I were able to keep our plans secret from her until the cart was finished. But Mom knew I was training the ponies to drive, and her curiosity was growing. She had heard the daily pounding behind the goat house, and had watched, no doubt with trepidation, as I trained my team in the barnyard.

The Prigge family on the front porch of their cabin at the Castle River forest ranger station in 1935. The cabin was located about five miles inside the Castle River Forest Reserve, near where West Castle River joins the Castle River. Standing in the back are Mrs. Prigge, Mr. Prigge. Left to right on the railing are three of the Prigges' children: Alan, Billie, and Dennis. Brian, between Billie and Dennis in age, is not in the picture.

The Prigges lived so far from a school that Mrs. Prigge home-schooled all four children while they lived there. As the children passed out of grade school, they went "to town" for high school.

The tranquil nature of this picture denies the peril the Prigges were in the next summer. In 1936, the Prigges were stationed at Mill Creek ranger station when the forest fire burst out in the Castle River Forest Reserve. The fire fighters thought the fire was going to get away on them and that it would spread into Gladstone Valley. Dad and his pack horses had been commandeered to work with fire-fighting crews in the Castle River valley. One day Mr. Prigge rode by our place on his saddle horse and told my mother to prepare to evacuate.

My mother was no stranger to forest fires. Ten years earlier, in 1925 when Don was a baby and Dad and his brother Alfred were operating a logging camp near Paulson, BC, a forest fire swept through and threatened to engulf their camp. They dug a big hole and buried what valuables they had, then stood beside the railway track and waited until a freight train stopped for them, taking them to safety at Christina Lake.

In 1936, after Mr. Prigge's warning, Mom had us children get ready for us to be picked up and taken to safety, if necessary. We carried bedding, clothing and other items needed for survival out of the house and stacked them in a pile in the barn yard. Fortunately, although a few burning pieces of log landed in our barn yard, we were never in critical danger and didn't have to move out. Courtesy Katherine Bruce, Author's collection.

I drove the ponies around the corral to get them used to the harness with its blinders and croup strap[2] and its other buckles and straps. Those were fancy harnesses!

Then I drove the ponies around the barnyard, first pulling a set of doubletrees and then pulling a small hand sled.

When I figured the ponies were ready to show off, I called Mom to look out the door to inspect my team, while I drove them around the barnyard pulling a small hand sled.

Unfortunately, as we were making a rather sharp turn, the sleigh pulled out to the side. The ponies, glancing back, caught sight of the sled following them. They ran terrified toward the barn and squeezed in though the half open door, smashing the sled in the process, but doing no other damage.

It took me awhile to get the ponies settled down after that fright.

While I was training the ponies to be a team, Don was busy building the cart. He had found the front axle and wheels of an old Model T or Model A car, up where several old cars were "parked." They were left standing there, as possible spare parts for another car. Don had fashioned a box about three feet wide and five feet long to fit the axle.

Don surveyed his creation with satisfaction, and then declared, "It's finished except for a tongue."

A "tongue" is a pole affixed to the axle of a cart and suspended in the team's neck yoke. A "neck yoke" is a short wooden pole that is suspended between the two horses of a team driven abreast. It is held in place by straps on the horses' harnesses and holds the tongue of a wagon or cart up off the ground. The neck yoke enables the teamster to steer and stop the vehicle safely. It also keeps the cart from "running up," that is, coming forward, onto the horses' heels when stopping or going down a hill, and thus precipitating a runaway.

"What'll we do?" I asked, my voice full of concern.

"There are some little jack pines over in those woods," Don stated, motioning to the wooded are about one-quarter mile east of our house. "Now if we just had some way to get one home, we'd be okay."

Suddenly I felt very important. "I know!" I volunteered excitedly, "My team and I can bring one home."

Don looked a little doubtful, but he didn't argue with me. So we set off to look for a suitable pole.

"This one will be just fine," asserted when we found a tall, straight jack pine about four inches in diameter at the base. So saying, Don chopped down the small tree, and cut the limbs off it.

Then we wound a 20-foot logging chain around the fallen, de-limbed tree and hooked the traces of the ponies' harnesses onto the chain. My team of ponies and I proudly hauled the tree home without mishap. We had passed the first test!

"Now all I have to do," declared Don, "is to attach the tongue onto the chassis and we'll be ready for a test run." My excitement was growing by the minute.

We wired the pole to the axle, attached the doubletrees to our cart, and attached the singletrees to the doubletree.[3]

We positioned the harnessed ponies astride the cart tongue, and attached the neck yoke to the strap at the bottom of the harness collars. Then we placed the small end of the pine tree wagon tongue into the strap fixed to the centre of the neck yoke, and hitched the ponies' traces up to the singletrees. We were ready for our maiden trip!

170

We presented our cart, in glowing terms, to Mom. She must have conceded that it looked roadworthy, so the next mail day we happily set off for Beaver Mines in our cart. We were to get the mail, and bring back heavier grocery items, which were difficult to carry while riding bareback on our ponies.

This dramatic picture shows a plume of white smoke from the 1936 forest fire in the Castle River Forest Reserve. The smoke is billowing up over Crandell Mountain just north of Waterton town site. Although the fire was some 25 miles north, on the opposite side of the Castle River divide, Waterton residents were nervous lest a change of wind direction send the fire south, down the Pass Creek Valley, and into the town.

The residents had good reason to be nervous. Radio communication with the Castle River fire fighters was non-existent, so the Waterton residents had no idea what was happening on the fire-fighting front. Moreover, the previous year, Waterton residents were in real danger from a forest fire that originated in Glacier Park, Montana.

As that inferno was sweeping north along the Upper Waterton Lake valley, heading straight for the town site, people were ready to evacuate at a moment's notice. By a great stroke of good luck, just as the fire was poised to sweep north past Bertha Creek, a change in wind direction stopped the fire. Waterton town site was saved.

Adelle Rackette photo, courtesy of Frank Goble, Author's collection.

Our buggy, however, had a flaw. It went along fine as long as we were going slowly, and the dirt road was smooth. However, as I gained confidence I went a little faster, finally going at a smart trot.

We were going along fine, until the wheels hit a deep rut in the dried mud of the dirt road of our ungravelled road. This jarred the car-buggy wheels loose from their straight position, and they flew into a diagonal position. Then, instead of turning, the wheels just dragged along, and the ponies could hardly move our marvellous invention.

"What'll we do now," I moaned.

"I know," replied Don. "I'll get a stick out of the bush and straighten the wheels out. So Don, ever the creative problem solver, went off into the bush to look for a strong stick, while I, the teamster, stayed with the ponies and kept them calm.

A few minutes later Don came back with a piece of willow about three feet long. He used the stick as a lever and pried the wheels into position. Then he wedged the stick into the front axle to keep the wheels straight, and tied it with bailing wire. We proceeded, very cautiously, the rest of the way to Beaver Mines, and home again, without further delays. We probably did not mention that little event to Mom.

We drove the cart like that for a week or so. If the wheels went diagonal, we repeated our repair process, a fairly simple operation when Don and I were both with our buggy. But one day, I was alone when the wheels went squeegee.

I knew how dangerous it would be to try to make the repairs without someone holding the team. Moreover, the ponies were not strong enough to drag the cart off the road. So I just had to sit there and wait until a neighbour on his way to the post office came along and helped me get straightened out again.

When I got home, Don modified his cart design, and stabilized the wheels of our two-wheeled cart.

The threat of the forest fire hung over us all summer, and we were very aware of the danger. The sun was obscured for days on end by thick, black smoke, and blackened cinders and ashes often fell in the house yard and barnyard, depending on wind conditions. At one time, the fire was within 12 miles of our home. Mr. Prigge called on us occasionally to check that we were still ready to move out if necessary.

In spite of the forest fire threat, the next few weeks were quite blissful for Don and me. We could travel much more comfortably, though more slowly in our cart than when riding bareback, and we could more easily bring home the mail and groceries from Beaver Mines, two and one-half miles away.

Travelling by cart all the time was slow and boring, and we missed our Dad. So one day, Don and I decided that we would go to see if we could find him. We packed a lunch, but did not tell Mom our real intentions. Then, riding bareback on our ponies, we headed for the fire-ravaged forest reserve.

We never got near to where Dad was working. But, by following the graded dirt road as far as Elk Lodge, at the entrance forest reserve, we did get into the midst of the forest fire. At that point, about ten miles from home, one of the firefighters spotted us, and turned us around for home again.

It was lucky for us that he did. The road allowance up to Elk Lodge was fairly wide with cleared out ditches. Trees on either side of the ditches were burning as we went along. Every now and again another one would "top," sending a burning cone or branch flying toward a nearby tree and setting the tinder-dry needles underneath it on fire. The flames would immediately rush to the top, and suddenly the whole tree would be ablaze, giving off a fierce heat.

But, beyond the gate into the Forest Reserve, the road was just a trail, with very little brush cut back on either side. The heat from the nearby burning trees would have been very uncomfortable, it not downright harmful, to the ponies and us.

So, disappointed, Don and I rode slowly home, stopping at the post office to check for mail, so that when Mom inquired where were had been, we could rather vaguely reply, "Oh, down at the store."

Mom evidently did not want to make us excessively timid with seeming to worry unduly about us. I suppose she thought, and rightly so, that if we got home safely from and escapade we would not do that again.

As the summer passed along, Don and I became more and more confident about travelling in our cart. Our team of ponies was behaving beautifully, and we had worked all the bugs out of our cart.

We had invited Mom to go with us as soon as we put the cart on the road, but she declined our invitation. As the weeks went on, however, her resistance to our persuasion weakened.

"I really should get down to Beaver to phone into Pincher about some business," Mom mused one day.

"You can go in our cart," I said brightly. "We'll put a seat in the back for you to sit on." Mom didn't accept our invitation right away.

This picture, taken in the 1920s, shows Elk Lodge Ranger Station, at the northern boundary of the Castle River Forest Reserve. Forest ranger Jack Frankish was stationed here at the time. Courtesy of Ruby Peters Jaggernath, Author's collection.

As we had made several uneventful trips to Beaver Mines with our cart, we finally convinced Mom that our cart was safe. Finally, after six weeks of not being out of the barnyard, Mom consented to go to Beaver with Don and me.

So that Mom would be more comfortable, we put an old car seat in the back end of the cart box. We positioned the seat so Mom faced backwards, and thus could not see where we were going or if anything went wrong.

We tied the ponies to the hitching rail, and carefully helped Mom into the cart. We were very proud of ourselves for our accomplishment. We had made a reliable cart and had trained our saddle ponies to work as a team for the cart.

With our brother Bill, who was by then nearly five years old, seated between Don and me on the plank seat, we set off toward Beaver Mines. We knew this was the "acid test," the most crucial test of our invention.

We were more than a little nervous, because we knew there was always a chance that something else would go wrong. We had coached/coerced Bill into silence about all of Don's and my ventures, so Mom did not know the details of many of our escapades.

This 1928 photo is of Jack Frankish, the forest ranger stationed at Elk Lodge at the entrance to the Castle River forest reserve, and his dog team. You can see the upsweep of the front of the toboggan-like sled immediately behind the tail of the rear dog. This dog is the "wheeler" and is a very important dog in any sled team.

Alma "Jo" Ballantyne Johnson knew Jack's "wheeler", named Padua. Padua was exceptionally well trained. Jo also remembered that Jack's lead dog was so vicious that no one would go near it.

The picture is taken in front of Ballantyne's Store and Post Office. Mrs. Ballantyne's pots of geraniums are on her windowsills. The small shed to the right was used for storing boxes for customer's groceries.

At the back left is an old livery stable, with its many horse stalls, built about 1911 when Beaver Mines was a thriving mining town. Courtesy Katherine Bruce, Author's collection.

Because we had Mom along, I drove extra careful.

The trip was uneventful for about a mile and a half, and we were beginning to loosen up and relax a bit. We began to think we were "home free," that is, that all our problems were over. Gradually, our confidence in the success of our venture increased. Mom seemed to be comfortable, and did not appear to be worrying about our safety.

Then, disaster almost struck!

Just at the "Number One Coal Mine hill," about one and one-half miles from home, a never-before-or-after incident occurred. Just before the mine there was a short, slightly sloping grade, after which the road turned and went down a fairly steep, though short, hill. Somehow, as we were coming up the little grade, the cart tongue worked out of the thick strap that attached it to the neck yoke. The cart tongue suddenly slipped out of the neck yoke strap and fell to the ground between my team!

The purpose of the tongue and neck yoke is to steer a wagon or cart, and to hold the vehicle back when going down a hill, generally with the help of a hand brake applied to a wheel. Our crude cart, however, did not have a hand brake, and depended entirely upon the tongue and neck yoke to hold it back and keep it from running up on our team's hind legs when going downhill.

I still remember the sinking feeling in my stomach when the cart tongue dropped to the road. Thinking quickly, as people on lonely ranches in the early days had to do, and even today must do, I quietly said, "Whoa," to the ponies. I pulled back on the reins firmly but gently so as not to frighten my team. My quick thinking in the face of imminent disaster probably saved our lives.

"What's the matter?" Mom asked, somewhat anxiously, from her backward-facing position.

"Oh, we're just stopping for a minute to give the ponies a little rest," I answered as nonchalantly as I could. "We'll be going right away again."

Don, meanwhile, quietly got down from the cart seat and walked swiftly but softly to the ponies' heads.

"Whoa, fellows," he cautioned in a friendly tone of voice.

"There's nothing to be afraid of. Steady, fellows," Don said softly to the ponies who were becoming nervous about the mishap. "You're all right, Babe. Don't move now, Rex."

With a deft movement, Don lifted the tongue and pushed it back into the thick leather strap of the neck yoke. He secured it by wrapping a lariat rope around and around the neck yoke and tongue, giving more than enough security.

In the meantime, I was holding fast to the reins and talking quietly to Mom and Bill. "Everything's fine," I said reassuringly. "Keep sitting down, Bill. Don't scare the ponies. It's okay, Mom."

If Bill had any idea what was going on, or what might have happened if we had gone over the brow of the hill, he never let on.

"Easy, fellows," I said to the ponies. "Just rest a few minutes. You've a long way to go yet. What are you doing, Don? Can we go now?" I kept up the patter until Don climbed back into the cart.

Then I clucked my tongue and relaxed my hold on the reins as a signal for the ponies to start. "Come on, Rex, don't drag behind and let Babe do all the pulling," I said in my best teamster's voice. The moment of danger had passed and we were on our way again.

However, Mom was not fully convinced that everything was okay. "Why did we stop?" she asked after a few minutes.

"Oh, just to rest the ponies," Don and I repeated, so Mom did not ask again.

I am not sure if we ever did tell her what actually happened.

Mom, bless her courageous heart, never said another word, and never queried us afterwards about what really happened to cause that five-minute delay. I fancy that she had a pretty good idea what had gone wrong, but actually did not want to know for sure.

Nor did Mom tell Dad, I am sure, or he would have said something. At the time Don and I thought, and I still think, that we handled the emergency quite well.

I have often thought that a Guardian Angel was watching over our family on that day. Had we been but ten feet further along the road when the tongue dropped, we would have been just over the crest of the hill. The momentum of the cart and the pull of the traces before we got the ponies stopped, would have kept the cart going. The slope of the hill would have increased the cart's speed so that it ran up on the ponies' hind legs.

The frightened ponies would have started to run, causing the tongue to jab into the dirt road. The cart would have upset throwing all of us out, possibly in the pathway of the careening vehicle. We children would have been injured or killed, and Mom would have been caused dreadful pain and injury, it not killed.

The ponies by this time terrified and running wildly would have been further frightened by the cart dragging behind them. They would have continued running with the doubletrees dragging behind them, until the traces broke or the ponies were so exhausted they could run no more.

The ponies could have been injured, too, either by the wreck they were pulling or by a barbed wire fence they might have crashed through as they ran in terror. However, none of these terrible things happened and, after minor repairs, we proceeded quietly on toward Beaver Mines.

As it was, surely the Lord was with us; and we had less than a five-minute delay before we proceeded onward along that dusty country road on that calm, hot day, looking as if butter would not melt in our mouths

After that delay, Mom was somewhat nervous again and the cart ride started to seem very, very long to her.

Then suddenly, as it by pre-arrangement, Mom was delivered from her plight.

There ahead of us was Dad's string of horses — his pack and saddle horse outfit. The forest fire had been quelled, and the weary firefighters were heading home.

Imagine the excitement of our little family group at the prospect of being reunited after a nearly six-week separation!

We kids were disappointed, however. Dad was not with the horses. Archie Gamble, one of the firefighters and a stranger to Don and me at the time, was leading the horses. Dad had stopped by the Beaver Mines General Store for a long denied "package of 'baccy," some pipe tobacco.

Mom, on the other hand, was very pleased to see the horses, even without Dad. She asked Archie to help her out of the cart and onto one of the saddle horses. Archie helped Mom onto a big grey horse, called "Ted."

We tried to persuade her to come on with us up to the store to see Dad, but she insisted on riding back home. We couldn't understand why!

In this picture, taken in 1937, we three children are ready to go riding with Dad on a summer day. Here Dad is on "Fly", I am on "Rex", Don is on "Laddie," and Bill is on "Pickles."

I am wearing the red tam that my Great-aunt Bessie Vroom knitted for me when she was visiting. Aunt Marion Cyr in 1934. That was the year that Mom went down East to Dr. Locke's Clinic. I spent the month of September at Aunt Marion's and attended St. Michael's Roman Catholic School in Pincher Creek. Author's collection.

We were very anxious to see our dad after what seemed like an eternity. Without Mom to worry about, we could travel faster. So, with Bill clinging to the makeshift seat between Don and me, I whipped up my team. We raced to the Beaver Mines Store as if the devil were after us.

The nearer we got to the store, the more excited we became and the faster we went. We arrived at the store at a full gallop, even though we had to turn off the road and into a rocky ditch to let a car go by.

Dad was amazed when he saw our team racing along the flats by Beaver Mines Creek, and bouncing over the rocks up the hill to the Beaver Mines Store and Post Office. "That must be 'a couple of wild men' to be driving like that," he thought to himself.

From that distance he did not recognize that it was his own children, though he probably had a good idea that Don and I were the culprits.

Dad had watched our reckless progress for more than a half-mile. After our initial happy greetings and hugs - he pretended not to recognize us - he gave us a talking to about not running our ponies. We had thought he would overlook our behaviour on such a special occasion, but he did not. Rules for behaviour were rules for behaviour, and Dad was always a strict parent, especially where such matters as care of our ponies was concerned, and hence his comment about the "wild men."

After a short visit with people at the store, we headed home. The return journey, safe and uneventful, seemed rather long after the exciting events of the journey from home to Beaver Mines. We rather envied Mom who had gone home by saddle horse instead of in our cart.

Dad did not mention what he thought of our cart, which disappointed us somewhat, but we soon forgot about it. With Dad and the horses, and consequently our tack, home again we soon lost interest in our team and cart. Moreover, the summer work on the ranch had to be finished, the potatoes had to be picked, and school was starting in a few days. So we had lots of things to keep us busy and out of further mischief for a while.

All was right with our world and we went happily onward, as only children, and a very few fortunate adults, can do. Occasionally, on a weekend I would harness up my ponies and drive the cart a short distance. But after a couple of months I parked the cart behind the goat house where it had been created, and left it. There the cart sat for many years, a silent reminder of that hot, dry, fiery summer.

Archie and another firefighter, Vic Kemble, stayed on as Dad's hired hands on the ranch for a few months. Later Archie ran Gus Gamache's place near our ranch.

------

[1] Bennett Buggies were an ingenious adaptation by prairie farmers who could not afford gasoline for their Model T or Model A Ford cars, or whatever kind of cars they owned in the Dirty Thirties. Many farmers took the motors out of their cars, hitched farm teams to them, and drove along in style in their Bennett Buggies. The lines for the team were run out under the windshield, which was hinged for hot-weather ventilation. In wintertime, sleigh runners were used in place of wheels. Bennett Buggies were named after the Rt. Hon. R.B. Bennett, who was the Prime Minister of Canada during the Great Depression, the so-called Dirty Thirties.

The name Dirty Thirties was coined because of the many dust storms that occurred on the prairies and the terrible economic conditions that existed during the decade of the 1930s. At times, we could see the dust from dust storms in Saskatchewan hanging in the sky over the top of the big hill, north of our ranch.

[2] Blinders are heavy flaps of leather which prevent a harness horse from looking backwards and being frightened by whatever contraption it is pulling. A croupstrap, also called a crupper, is a part of a fancy buggy harness. It is a strap that is attached to the back strap, which is attached to the collar. The croup strap has a loop on the end that goes under the horse's tail to help hold the harness in place.

[3] Singletrees are pieces of wood which swing in the middle and to which the traces of a horse's harness are fastened. A doubletree is a crossbar made of wood, which swings in the middle, to which singletrees are attached when a team is driven abreast.

KILLING A GRIZZLY BEAR

During the hot, dry summer of 1936 a forest fire killed many wild animals in the mountains of the Castle River Forest Reserve and caused the dislocation of many others.

One of the dislocated animals was a huge grizzly bear. Because of the widespread devastation the forest fire caused, the grizzly was unable to get sufficient food from its usual sources. So the grizzly bear had taken to foraging in garbage sites. The garbage was left hastily covered as the firefighters' mobile field kitchens were moved from place to place as needed, during the fire-fighting operation.

Dad's Pack Train Spooked by the Grizzly Bear

One dark night, in early August, Dad's pack train came unexpectedly upon the grizzly bear in one of these buried garbage sites.

There were two men working with Dad's pack train, one riding in front leading the lead packhorse by the halter shank, and one riding in the rear to make sure the packhorses kept moving along. They both were aware of the grizzly's habits. Momentarily, however, they had forgotten about the dangerous bear.

Suddenly, one of the packhorses got a whiff of the bear's scent and let out a snort. This spooked the rest of the horses, which were "tailed together," the halter shank of one horse was tied to the tail of the horse in front of it. All the packhorses then started to snort, rear, and pull back, creating general confusion. The lead horse pulled the halter shank out of the lead man's hand and veered off the trail into the timber, creating more havoc. The bear took off in the other direction.

In the bedlam that followed, several of the horses were seriously injured as they plunged in frenzy through the trees that were still standing. In their terrorized flight to escape the dreaded grizzly, the horses jumped over "deadfalls," or dead trees that the wind had blown over, and which had accumulated on the forest floor over the years.

One mare, "Blackie," had her "tail pulled down." Her tailbone was broken, when another horse pulled back and yanked on it. Never again could Blackie raise her tail in a normal manner.

The rest of the packhorses managed to tear loose from each other, and plunged wildly across the mountainside, crashing through the green timber north of the forest fire's devastation. In this terrified dash from a fearsome assailant another packhorse, "Whitey," was injured so badly that she had to be destroyed.

Whitey had a long whipsaw tied across the top of her pack. As she fled through the timber, knocking her pack against trees as she ran, one end of the saw came loose and swung under her belly. The saw lashed back and forth, and cut the horse's hind legs. As Whitey, now driven by pain as well as fear of the unknown, raced blindly onward, the loose end of the saw whipped back and forth, slashing the tendons of her hind legs.

Killing Whitey on the spot was the merciful thing to do.

This photo, taken in 1917, is of a pack train of nine horses - plus the suckling colt of one of the pack mares - on a big game hunting trip in the Rocky Mountains. The riders are on a grassy ridge looking toward Wall Lake, just north of Waterton Lakes National Park, on the Alberta/British Columbia border.

Leading the pack train is A. H. "Pop" Harwood, long time postmaster at Waterton Park and a friend of Kootenai Brown. The middle rider is Logan McWhirter, while Bill Terrill brings up the rear. All three men were homesteaders in the Twin Butte area. "Pop" and Bill were partners in a guide and outfitting business for a time.

"Pop's" son, Steve, took this striking photo, capturing some of the grandeur of the Rocky Mountains. Steve's saddle horse is the third horse from the lead. Steve had only one arm, having lost the other when he was taking a loaded shotgun out from under a buggy seat. The gun went off accidentally and sheared off one of Steve's arms. "It never slowed him down," said Essie Cox.

This photo was taken the year Essie was born. On this trip her father, Logan, shot a mountain goat that had one horn turned ahead - the result of a fight with another goat. Bill and Frances Riviere McWhirter had the mounted head for many years. Steve Harwood photo, courtesy Essie McWhirter Cox, Author's collection.

The other packhorses banged into trees in their headlong flight. The packs, which normally extended some twelve to eighteen inches on either side of the horse, were ripped off. Some packhorses were carrying two panniers,[1] one pannier on either side of the packsaddles.

During the horses' flight, the contents of the panniers, including canned goods and other foodstuffs, such as flour and sugar, for the firefighters, were scattered far and wide over the mountainside.

The terrified packhorses ran until they were exhausted. Then they stopped and stood in their tracks, drenched in sweat, and shaking with fear.

The next day, the two packers spent many valuable hours rounding up the horses, picking up the scattered items as they could find, and going back to base camp for more supplies and equipment.

The grizzly bear had been sighted, on occasion, during the summer, but never before had he caused the confusion and uproar of that night, albeit unwittingly, because he was merely hunting for food. During the commotion of the pack train he had caused by his sudden appearance, the grizzly took off into the forest from whence he had come. The grizzly was not encountered by the firefighters again, though signs of his foraging in the buried garbage heaps of the deserted firefighter camps were seen regularly.

By mid-September, as a result of a fortuitous rainfall in late summer, the main forest fire had been extinguished. Meanwhile, the grizzly bear, displaced and disoriented by the forest fire, continued his ravaging ways when the fire was over.

Deprived of his usual food supply of small wild animals, roots, nuts and berries, and seeking enough food to fatten up for the winter, the grizzly became more and more aggressive in his search for enough to eat.

During the summer, he had become less wary of people. At last, in his search for food, the grizzly started attacking the ranchers' cattle near the edge of the forest reserve. This earned him the reputation of being a "nuisance grizzly bear."

A grizzly bear is a very large, very fierce bear. Grizzly bear colours range from dark brown to a pale cream. This was a silvertip grizzly bear[2] that stood six feet tall at the shoulders and had claws six inches long.

Forestry officials decided that the bear had to be eliminated. This was in the days before grizzly bears were considered an endangered species. Once in a marauding state of mind, grizzlies were considered to be just plain dangerous.

Nowadays forest rangers, and National Park wardens, tranquilize nuisance grizzlies and airlift them by helicopter to a more remote area of the mountains. Transferred bears are tagged, and their movements monitored by forest rangers or park wardens, depending on the bear's location. But in the 1930s, nuisance grizzly bears were destroyed.

Because my dad was a very experienced hunter and trapper, he was hired to trap and kill the menacing grizzly bear. Dad, accompanied by the forest rangers, rode back into the mountains up the main branch of the Castle River to a point about 15 miles beyond the Buckhorn .

Dad set the grizzly bear trap, and baited it, in the middle of what had once been a shallow slough, but which had dried up over the years. At one time, huge trees nearly three feet in diameter had stood there. Most of these trees had fallen over, and in the fall of 1936 lay criss-crossed in a jumbled mass in the knee-high grass.

The bear trap weighed some seventy-five pounds. When opened out flat, it was about two and one-half feet in diameter. The bear trap looked like a huge gopher trap with a row of sharp teeth around the outside rim.

Dad wired the thick chain of the bear trap to a sixteen-foot log about ten inches in diameter, making a movable anchor. This ensured that the bear, with its titanic strength, would not break the trap chain by pulling and jerking on it.

If the trap had been secured to a solid anchor, the bear could have easily snapped even the heavy beartrap chain. The wounded bear would then have been loose in the forest, more dangerous than before.

In the 1930s, grizzly bears were attacking and killing livestock that ranged just north of Waterton Lakes National Park. This became a real problem for ranchers. The bears were short of food after the huge forest fire of 1936 ruined their feeding grounds along the Castle River Valley, the headwaters of which were just over the summit north of Red Rock Canyon. The roots, berries and small rodents which the bears normally ate were destroyed or killed by the fire.

Just like the starved, gigantic grizzly Dad killed in 1936, the bears at this south, or upper, end of the Castle River watershed turned to their closest source of food - cattle owned by nearby ranchers. These bears were hunted by ranchers from the Twin Butte area, about 25 miles southeast of Beaver Mines, AB

This mid-1910s photo shows a huge grizzly bear killed by Bert Riggall. The inscription of the back of the photo says: "The end of a cattle killing grizzly near Hawk's Nest." Hawk's Nest was a hunting lodge on Bert's ranch just north of Waterton Lakes. Bert Riggall photo, courtesy Katherine Bruce, Author's collection.

After setting the trap, Dad returned to the ranch to carry on with the fall work. The forest ranger promised to inform Dad as soon as Pete LaGrandeur, the stock rider for the Castle River Forest Reserve, found the bear in the trap. About ten days passed before there was any word of the trapped grizzly.

Then one day, forest ranger Frankish rode into our barnyard, and told Dad that the bear was in the trap. A trapped bear suffers great pain. If the bear were left in the trap more than a day or two, it would either chew or tear its paw out of the trap. Then it would escape into the wilds to become more dangerous than ever. Hence, haste in killing the bear and putting it out of its misery was of the utmost importance.

Mom and we kids did not want to miss out on the excitement of the trip. So it was agreed that we would go as far as the Buckhorn Ranch, a guest ranch about 10 miles from our house, and stay there while Dad went to get the bear.

Dad and Mom got everything ready, as much as they could, before dark the night before we were to make our trek. Then, by lantern light, Dad fed the team that we were going to use to drive in the wagon to the Buckhorn and the other animals that were in the barn, and milked the cow. By lamplight, Mom washed up the supper dishes, and got us kids off to bed so we would be up for an early start in the morning. Dad had arranged for neighbours to do the evening chores the next day, and had to take word to them, too.

We were all up well before dawn the next morning. Getting three young children, ages twelve, nine and five years, loaded into a horse drawn wagon and headed out on the road before daylight took a tremendous effort. But my mother, hardy soul, persevered. The same chores as in the evening were again repeated by lantern light.

Looking south, the Buckhorn Ranch is nestled below the hill. Table Mountain looms in the background. Taken when the sun was low in the west, this view shows that Table Mountain is not a rectangular block but has at least one deep ravine cutting into its northwest side.

Mom, Don and Bill stayed at the Buckhorn while Dad and I went to kill the marauding grizzly bear. Courtesy Ruby Peters Jaggernath, Author's collection.

We kids, especially Don and I, were very anxious to go, so of course we helped all we could. Don helped Mom in the house, and I helped Dad feed the animals out in the barn. We each had to saddle our own horse.

Long before daylight, the light wagon was loaded, and we set out. The gray light of dawn was barely showing in the sky as we headed down the road towards Beaver Mines. The turn-off to the Buckhorn was about a half mile south of the Beaver Mines Store and Post Office.

In this 1931 photo, snow still clings to Table Mountain making ravines and ledges show up clearly. This was the view I saw in late September 1936 when riding with my dad to get the trapped grizzly bear.

Dad told me that around 1910, when he was about 19 years old, he and a friend raced their saddle horses "on the top of Table Mountain." The venue of Dad's horse race was along the ½-mile stretch on top of the relatively flat 7096-foot high ridge that run eastward on the southeast side of the mountain.

The view from the top is magnificent. Ranch hands at the Buckhorn Guest Ranch, such as my brother Bill and his friend Dave Harder, have accompanied hundreds of guests on saddle horse rides up this monotlith which dominates the Beaver Mines Creek Valley.

Michael and Anthony Bruce, sons of Edward and Mabel Bruce of Beaver Mines, climbed the mountain a number of times in the 1930s. In his memoirs, Anthony wrote, "We climbed and what a view there was from the top! Of course, the golden eagles were flying all around us and what magnificent birds they were. I am quite sure that the largest of them would have had a wing-span of close to 11 feet and could likely have packed up and carried away a new born fawn or lamb. We were far above the timber line, but on looking down towards the north-east, there was Beaver Lake about a mile away." Michael Bruce photo, courtesy Katherine Bruce, Author's collection.

MAP 8 *The map, "Vroom Ranch to Killing the Grizzly Bear, 1936," shows:*
- *the Buckhorn Ranch, Elk Lodge, Harry and Bessie Truitt's home, the Ralph and Mollie Vroom Ranch,and Grandpa Oscar Vroom's home.*
- *Avion Ridge, Bauerman Brook, Beaver Mines, Beaver Mines Creek, Beaver Mines Lake, the BC boundary, the Castle River, Castle River Forest Reserve, North Castle (Mtn.), Waterton Lakes National Park, and Windsor Ridge (formerly Castle Mtn.)*
- *"X" marks where Pete LaGrandeur joined Dad and me.*
- *"XX" marks the approximate area of the Castle River Forest Reserve where Dad, Pete LaGrandeur and I were, when Dad shot and killed the grizzly bear he had trapped. Map hand drawn by the author.*

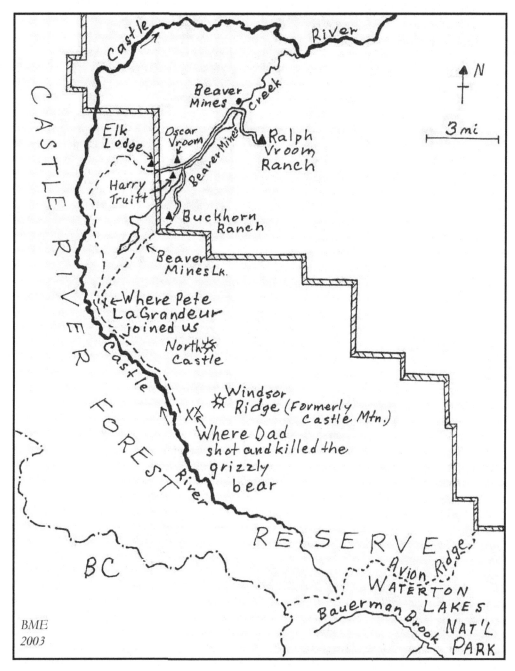

MAP 8 VROOM RANCH TO KILLING THE GRIZZLY BEAR, 1936

Taken in August 1938, Pete LaGrandeur (left) and Hugh McLaughlin are at the Castle River Forest Reserve stock riders' cow camp. The cow camp was used by the stock riders who were tending cattle which had been driven from prairie ranches to the forest reserve for summer range. The packhorse is carrying food and camp equipment for their fishing trip.

Pete, who had a special way with horses, is riding a bronc he was breaking at the time. That Pete would ride a bronc on a fishing trip in the mountains is evidence he was an excellent horseman. Hugh, a good rider but not in Pete's class, is on a well trained saddle horse.

While on that trip, a grizzly bear chasing an elk came roaring through Pete and Hugh's campsite and knocked over their tent. The next day Pete and Hugh found the remains of the elk about ¼ mile from their camp. The grizzly had cunningly chased the elk into an area littered with deadfalls. There the grizzly attacked and killed the elk, ate some of the meat and then left the site, continuing its search for food elsewhere.

Pete and Edith Vliet LaGrandeur and their seven children lived at the stock riders' camp the summers of 1933 to 1943. The cow camp was located a few miles inside the forest reserve between Elk Lodge and the Castle River ranger station (which had previously been the site of Kelly's Camp). The Castle River station was on the east bank of the Castle River, about ½ mile south of the confluence of the West Castle and the Castle Rivers.

The cow camp was reached by a very winding road which partly followed a low ridge to avoid swampy areas of the forest reserve. In recent years, having been straightened, it leads to the West Castle Ski Resort. The site where Elk Lodge station was situated in the 1930s is now a scenic campground for forest reserve visitors.

During the years Pete was the stock rider on the forest reserve, the LaGrandeur family spent the winters on various ranches. One year they lived in a small log cabin located beside Harold Vroom's house on his Sunny Vale Ranche, southwest of Beaver Mines. During the Castle River forest fire in the summer of 1936, the family was evacuated from the forest reserve, and lived in the Women's Institute hall in Beaver Mines. Later, Pete and Edith built a new log house for their family on a hill to the west of the Beaver Mines Creek Valley road, just south of the junction that leads to the Buckhorn Ranch. Memories and photo courtesy Robin LaGrandeur, Author's collection.

Dad drove the team, and Mom and Bill rode with him in the wagon. Don and I rode our ponies alongside, pretending to be chuck wagon outriders. Behind the wagon, Dad trailed a small string of horses which included his own saddle horse and three packhorses. The packsaddles and panniers were in the wagon. Dad was going to cut blubber off the grizzly bear's carcass. He was to bring back all the blubber that he could carry in the panniers, as well as the grizzly's skin, as his payment for trapping and killing the grizzly.

We got to the Buckhorn well before noon. Phyllis Smith, the cook, insisted that we all have a meal before Dad headed out on his saddle horse, leading the packhorses, for his rendezvous with Pete LaGrandeur. They had planned to approach the trapped grizzly bear together.

What they had not planned was that I would persuade my dad to let nine-year old me go along with him.

How did a nine-year old child get into such a situation? It was not easy, but it seemed natural for me to be with my dad. I trusted him completely, and he was pretty sure of my behaviour.

I was a very good rider, having ridden horseback four miles to school for about three years. I also often accompanied Dad on his horse-chasing expeditions, so he knew that I had lots of stamina. Besides, Dad thought there would be practically no danger, as the grizzly was securely trapped.

This view of Table Mountain was illuminated by a brilliant sunrise as our family travelled to the Buckhorn Ranch by team and wagon the morning of the day Dad and I went to kill the grizzly bear.

Whenever I rode Paddy to visit Grandpa Vroom, I saw this view at a distance as Paddy walked southwestward along the road in Beaver Mines Creek Valley. Grandpa's cabin was about one mile north the Castle River Forest Reserve boundary.

This 1931 photo was taken just south of Grandpa's, from a trail running straight south of Elk Lodge forest ranger station, which was located at the northern entrance to the Castle River Forest Reserve. Our friends, Ranger and Mrs. Prigge, and their four children, Alan, Billie, Dennis and Brian, were stationed at Elk Lodge for a few years in the 1930s. Also stationed there in the 1920s & 1930s was forest warden Jack and Mrs. Alice (Jenkins) Frankish. Michael Bruce photo, courtesy Katherine Bruce, Author's collection.

Perhaps my mother was relieved not to have to look after me for just one day, after being alone with the three of us all summer.

For whatever reason, Dad decided I could go with him, assuring my mother, "We'll be safe. There'll be nothing to worry about, Mommy." Don stayed to help Mom look after Bill

So Dad set off up the trail, whistling a cheery melody and leading the two packhorses. I brought up the rear on my sturdy Dartmoor pony, Jackie. The hot September sun beat down on us as we rode along the trail, which traversed mountainsides denuded of shade trees by the summer's Castle River forest fire. Here and there on the valley floor was a patch of trees that the fire had missed, clothed in bright autumn orange and gold. The rest of the landscape in that beautiful mountain valley was seared and black.

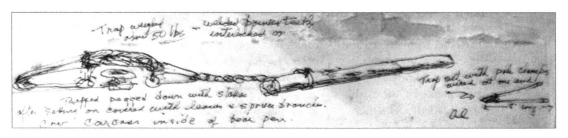

This diagram by Robin LaGrandeur illustrates how his father, Pete and "Bear Grease John" Stiebertz set a grizzly bear trap. Robin's notes read, "Trap weighed over 50 lbs. - welded pointed teeth interlocked. Trap pegged down with stakes; covered with leaves and spruce branches; cow carcass inside of bear pen; trap set with pole clamps (8' long) wired at one end."

This trap was similar to my dad's, which weighed some seventy-five pounds. When opened out flat, it was about two and one-half feet in diameter. The bear trap looked like a huge gopher trap with a row of sharp teeth around the outside rim. Dad wired the thick chain of the bear trap to a sixteen-foot log about ten inches in diameter, making a movable anchor. This ensured that the bear, with its titanic strength, would not break the trap chain by pulling and jerking on it. Diagram by Robin LaGrandeur, Author's collection.

At a prearranged place at a fork in the trail, we met Pete LaGrandeur, who came along as a back-up rifleman. Pete would also help Dad skin the bear and load the blubber into the panniers.

Pete LaGrandeur was a long time friend of my dad. They had known each other since the heyday of their cowboy years in the early 1900s. Pete was an excellent horseman - at the 1924 Calgary Stampede, Pete was the Canadian Bucking Horse Champion and the Canadian All-Around Champion.

Dad knew that Pete could handle the horses if they got "spooked" by the smell of the grizzly bear. Moreover, Pete was a true frontiersman, and Dad trusted him completely. An excellent marksman, Pete made an unbeatable backup man for Dad's grizzly bear shooting

The three of us rode along together toward where the grizzly was trapped. Dad and Pete were swapping stories to help pass the time.

Even before we reached the bear I was tired and hungry, but I dared not mention my tiredness or my hunger, lest I could not go on future trips with Dad. I had been allowed to go on this dangerous expedition only if I was "no trouble," if I did not complain about anything and did not get in the way of my dad.

A couple of hours later we were near enough to the bear that the horses picked up his scent, and began to snort and prance. So we dismounted, and tied up our horses in the shade of some green willow trees, where they could rest up for the return trip. Moreover, they would not be panicked by the strong smell of the bear. We walked the last 300 yards across the log-strewn meadow, to where the grizzly bear was trapped.

By then it was nearly dusk. The sun had set behind the mountain peaks. Dad, an amateur photographer, wanted to get a snapshot of the grizzly. Darkness falls early and swiftly on short September days in the Rocky Mountains, so time was of the essence.

The bear, a huge male, was lying motionless behind a big log when we reached it. Dad wanted to get as close as he could, hoping to get a better picture in the fast-fading light. To get the best picture possible, Dad handed his rifle, a .30-06-calibre Winchester, to Pete to carry. He thought that the bear was exhausted, and was still chained to the heavy toggle.

Dad then opened up his folding camera and stepped nearer to the trapped grizzly. Just as Dad had the camera focussed, and was about to snap the picture, the bear reared up on its hind legs and waved the trap and toggle in the air, letting out an angry, pain-filled roar as it did so.

At that moment, Dad realized that the bear no longer was chained to the 16-foot toggle. In its pain and rage, the grizzly had chewed the toggle in half, and now had less than eight feet of log attached to the bear trap chain.

"Get out of here!" Dad admonished. Though we were in imminent danger, Dad spoke calmly, but with an urgency that left no doubt what we had to do. We turned and ran, scrambling over the deadfalls.

He still wanted to get a snapshot of the huge grizzly, the largest one he had ever seen in all his years in the mountain.

Roaring with pain and fury, the grizzly bear chased us. Over the deadfalls we scrambled. Glancing back, I saw the grizzly running along on all fours, dragging the trap and toggle. Every few minutes the bear stood up and swung the trap and toggle in the air, a testament to its great strength.

Though we were in grave danger, I was not particularly afraid at that time. I was running because I had been told to run, and because Dad and Pete were running.

Just as we were beginning to gain ground on the bear, and it seemed to be tiring, I got a bright idea, an almost a fatal idea I realize in retrospect.

I spied a skinny jack pine about fifteen feet tall, standing alone. I had heard that when chased by a bear, a person should get behind a tree, so I veered off to the left and got behind that jack pine. I stood facing the oncoming grizzly and watched, mesmerized, as the enraged bear lunged painfully after us.

Dad did not miss me for a minute or so, and the bear did not slow down. By the time Dad noticed that I was not right behind him, the bear was almost even with me.

Looking around for me, Dad saw me, now about 25 yards away from him, behind my small tree, with the trapped bear advancing up the middle.

"Come on, Bess!" he shouted. By then I had realized that we were all in danger. Terrified, I would not budge.

"Bess! Come on!" Dad yelled again. Still I would not move.

At that moment he made a decision that, I heard him tell often in later years, was the most difficult decision he ever made. He decided to go back and get me. Dad handed the camera to Pete, grabbed his rifle, and ran back across the path of the pain-maddened grizzly.

I had not been frightened in the beginning, but by then I was scared half to death. Dad literally had to grab me by the hand and half pull, half drag me over the fallen tree trunks right across the path of the grizzly, and over to where Pete was standing.

Pete, in the meantime, was standing with his rifle trained on the grizzly ready to kill it if it came too close to us.

Dad grabbed me by the hand and, pulling me along on the high run, re-crossed the bear's path to rejoin Pete.

"Now don't you leave my side again, Bess!" Dad spoke softly, but sternly. He need not have worried. I had no intention of going off on my own again.

After about one hundred yards the bear stopped chasing us and slumped down to the ground. "I think he's played out now," Dad conjectured, but again he was wrong, as it turned out.

Dad still was not satisfied, and wanted to try for another snapshot. That was a huge grizzly, and he wanted a record of it for posterity.

"Give me that camera again, Pete, I think I can get him now," said Dad.

"I don't like the looks of him, Ralph," remarked Pete, reluctantly handing the camera to Dad again.

Dad leaned his rifle against a nearby tree. Pete stood back several yards with his own rifle cocked and ready. By then it was getting quite dusk.

Dad readjusted the camera lens and approached the bear, determined to get that priceless close-up snapshot. True to my promise, and now thoroughly frightened to leave my dad, I followed at his heels, putting my hands on his hips when he stopped.

Again the grizzly reared up on his hind legs, towering over us like a mountain, it seemed to me. Dad snapped a picture, rolled the film, and took another picture for good measure. Then with a careful, deliberate motion, he set the camera on a nearby log and calmly took his rifle from Pete, confident that he could drop the bear with one shot at that close range.

I, following Dad's first instructions, still hung on.

"Let go, Bess!" Dad ordered, but I wasn't about to leave his side again.

"All right, then," he said firmly, realizing that I would not leave, "Don't joggle my aim."

I held my breath for what seemed an eternity, and Dad fired at the bear, confident that he would break its neck and bring it down with his first shot.

In the fast-falling dusk, however, Dad missed his mark by a hair's breadth. Bright red blood gushed from the wound. He had cut the grizzly's jugular vein, but that was not enough to stop the powerful, frenzied beast. The bear still lunged forward.

Dad quickly pulled the bolt of his rifle, flipped out the empty shell, and reloaded. He stood his ground, with me holding on behind him, and fired a second shot. This time the bullet found its mark, and broke the bear's neck. The grizzly fell to the ground, stone dead.

This picture of a rearing grizzly bear, with its long, razor-sharp claws, shows how big and fierce these huge animals are.

My brother Bill took this impressive wildlife photograph. Bill was a park warden in Banff National Park for 34 years prior to his retirement in 1988, and was a renowned expert on grizzly bears. For the last number of years of his service, Bill was on the National Parks mountain-rescue team. Bill Vroom photo, courtesy Moe Vroom.

The bear fell so close to Dad and me that without stepping forward, and holding his rifle with his right hand at the trigger, Dad leaned forward and touched the grizzly's nose with the end of the rifle barrel. The bear had fallen about one yard from us, literally at our feet. That was a close call!

I was still standing with my hands resting on Dad's hips, certain that behind him I was surely safe.

Pete LaGrandeur, as back-up man, had his rifle trained on the bear, and would have killed the bear himself had Dad missed his second shot.

All three of us had a narrow escape, barely missing a terrible mauling, and perhaps even death. And all because my Dad tried, without the benefit of a telephoto lens, to get a picture of that trapped bear.

To top it all off, the pictures, with low light, and film and camera limitations, did not turn out. They were just a blur when the film was developed! It was lucky we were spared.

The rest of the night was almost anti-climactic. In the deepening dusk, Dad skinned the bear and removed the blubber from its carcass, while I sat and watched.

A little bit of excitement occurred when Pete brought the horses up near the site of the kill, so that the panniers could be filled with blubber, and loaded onto the packsaddles.

The horses still remembered the encounter with the grizzly during the forest fire, and snorted and pulled back on the reins, as their nostrils caught the bear's scent. They almost got away from Pete. To calm the horses, Dad walked up to them and rubbed some bear grease on their noses. In a few minutes they were used to the smell did not notice the bear odour.

Dad and Pete carried the panniers over beside the bear's carcass and filled them with blubber. By the time the panniers were filled, it was getting quite dark. Dad and Pete lifted the heavy boxes up on each side of the packhorses and tied them on securely.

Dad rolled the bearskin up in a piece of canvas and secured the bundle on the top of one packhorse. For this, he used a diamond hitch, a favourite knot of outfitters. The detached head was rolled in another piece of canvas and tied on the other packhorse. Then we mounted our saddle horses and started off down the trail.

Two men from the Twin Butte area, Bert Riggall and Henri "Frenchy" Riviere, became renowned as grizzly bear hunters. This photo, taken in the 1930s, shows Bert holding one of his favourite grizzly bear-hunting rifles. According to his note on the reverse, Bert is kneeling beside a grizzly bear he "shot at the head of Castle River". Over several decades Bert took hunting and sight-seeing parties out into the mountains, eventually using a string of over 40 pack and saddle horses.

Notice the bear's long, white claws. Grizzly bears cannot retract their five- to six-inch long claws. These formidable weapons, plus the bear's strong, sharp teeth, are always at the ready whenever the bear attacks an animal or a human. Bert Riggall photo, courtesy Katherine Bruce, Author's collection.

By the time we left the site of the kill, it was really dark. The packhorses were loaded quite heavily, and because burned timber had fallen across the trail, travelling was very slow. The packhorses could barely get over some of the fallen trees, and Jackie had a hard time, too. The trip seemed endless.

To make it a little more exciting for myself, I would hold Jackie back for a few minutes and then trot him along to catch up. By then, it was so dark that I could hardly see the rump of the last packhorse, even when I was only a few yards behind.

A few miles down the trail, at the fork where he had first joined us, Pete left us, and went back to his stockman's cabin. Dad and I and the horses continued on toward the Buckhorn Ranch.

While Pete was with us, there had been story telling and laughter, which I quite enjoyed. When Pete left us, however, there was only an almost-overwhelming silence, broken occasionally by Dad's cheery whistling.

As Dad and I rode quietly along the trail, I became aware of the eerie night sounds of the mountains.

To make it scary, it was rutting season and the elk were bugling to one another. The first time that I heard an elk's whistle followed by a loud grunt, I nearly screamed with fear. I did not scream, however, lest I frighten the already spooky horses.

Every once in awhile, an owl hooted his querulous cry, "Who-oo? Who-oo?" Then another elk bugled about a quarter mile away. The mournful whistle echoed along the valley. I was scared of the dark to begin with and these strange night noises increased my fear, but I dared not complain. Going with Dad on that expedition was a rare privilege and I felt that I had already caused enough trouble, so I tried to be brave.

Before long, I was so tired that I nearly fell asleep as Jackie plodded along behind the heavily-laden packhorses, which could travel no faster than a walk. I had been up since 4:30 a.m., so was exhausted. To break the monotony, I would sometimes stop Jackie for awhile, and then trot him to catch up, listening for Dad's whistle to make sure I was going in the right direction.

After a few miles, I again became more confident. I was very tired of poking along at a slow walk behind the packhorses, so I again held my pony back. On one occasion, I stopped a little longer than I figured on. In the meantime, Dad had come to a smoother part of the trail, and had started jogging along.

When I went to catch up, Dad wasn't where I thought he was. I couldn't hear Dad's whistle nor the horses' hooves thudding on the hard trail, and I couldn't see Ted's white rump.

Panic-stricken, I tried to make my pony go the way I thought he should. I had no idea which way to go, but Jackie seemed determined that he knew. I had no choice but to let my pony have his head. Eventually, I caught up with Dad. I was very happy and relieved when I sighted the white rump of Ted, the rear packhorse.

Dad seemed quite unconcerned about my having been missing, which kind of disappointed me. He no doubt knew that my pony could smell the other horses and could easily find his way along the trail.

I breathed a sigh of relief, and rode quietly onward. After that bit of a scare, I was glad to poke along behind the slow-moving packhorses. For the rest of that moonless ride, I stayed close on the packhorses' heels. I kept myself amused by watching the stars in the cloudless sky on that crisp autumn night, and tried to find the various constellations that Mom had pointed out to me from the back porch of our ranch house.

At last, well past midnight, we reached the Buckhorn. Of course, we had to unsaddle the horses and put them in the barn before we could go into the cookhouse dining room ourselves. A thoughtful ranch hand had put hay in the mangers for our horses.

Mom and Phyllis were waiting up for us. After a delicious meal, I tumbled into bed for a dreamless sleep, not awakening until nearly noon the next day, which was very late for me to get up.

By the time I arose, Dad had already told the story of his picture-taking attempts and the chase by the grizzly bear. Mom questioned me about the experience.

Feeling that I was really on centre stage, I talked expansively about meeting the grizzly bear. "You know, Mom," I said exuberantly, "that bear sat right up and smiled at me."

"How big was he?" asked Don, feeling somewhat left out, as he had not been allowed to go.

"Oh, about as big as a mountain," I replied casually.

Taken in 1926, this photo shows the family of Henri "Frenchy" & Nellie Gladstone Riviere with a huge grizzly bear that Frenchy shot on his Victoria Peak Ranch at the head of Pincher Creek. Frenchy propped the bear up so everyone could have their photos taken with it. Left to right: Frances (McWhirter), Charlie, Nellie "Babe" (Murphy), Inez (Rae), James and Alice (Primeau) Riviere.

One of the rounded foothills of the Twin Butte area shows in the background. Courtesy Frances Riviere McWhirter, Author's collection.

By mid-afternoon, Mom and Bill the bearskin and the panniers full of blubber were all packed into the wagon and ready for the trip home. Mom and Bill climbed up on the seat again. Don had saddled our ponies, and we mounted up.

Thus readied, our entourage set off for the home ranch. Dad again drove the team. The packhorses and Dad's saddle horse were tied to the back of the wagon. Don and I brought up the rear.

The next few days were very busy for Mom and Dad. The bearskin was rubbed with salt, then nailed to the side of the carpenter shop to dry.

Mom rendered down the blubber on the kitchen stove. What a stink! For weeks the whole house reeked of the strong bear smell, but it was worth it. The resulting oil was stored in five-gallon cans.

Taken about 1926, this photo gives some idea of the size of the grizzly bears that roamed in the foothills of southwestern Alberta.

Henri "Frenchy" Riviere, a strong, well-built man who stood over six feet tall, is standing in front of the tanned hide of a huge grizzly bear he shot on his Victoria Peak Ranch. The Riviere ranch nestled right up against the main range of the Rocky Mountain at the head of Pincher Creek.

Courtesy Frances Riviere McWhirter, Author's collection.

For years afterwards, Dad used that oil to keep our tack in top condition. Early each spring Dad brought our saddles, bridles and harnesses into the house so he could clean and grease the leather. First he took the tack apart and washed and dried the leather. Then he carefully kneaded the grizzly bear grease into the clean leather and reassembled the gear.

Having our saddles, bridles and harnesses spread all over the dining room floor for weeks on end each spring was quite a sight, but it was too cold to work outside. My mother endured the inconvenience with typical good humour. Don and I were always proud to ride our well cared for horses with their glistening tack.

The grizzly bear's head was sent to a taxidermist to be mounted. It was sold to a collector for much needed cash for our livelihood. The bearskin, after drying, and a certain amount of stretching, measured nine feet eleven inches from left front claw tip to right front claw tip. Indeed a huge grizzly!

For years, the grizzly bear skin, with its six-inch long claws, hung under the chimney in the living room of our house, reaching from the ceiling to the floor. Dad estimated that the grizzly was eight feet tall when it stood on its hind legs. I would estimate a similar standing height as the bear was much taller than my dad, who was five feet and six inches tall.

"Playing Bear" in the living room in the dark was a favourite game of Don and me, and eventually of Bill, for several years. We would take turns riding around on Dad, shrieking with delight, while he crawled on all fours, and snarled and "G-r-r-rd-d!"

The trip was not soon forgotten, either. Our grizzly bear-hunting expedition made good story telling for my dad, and me, for years afterwards.

Rancher Kills Mate Of Trapped Grizzly

Calgary, Alta., Oct. 26.—Guests of Clifton C. Cross, president of Clifton C. Cross and company, limited, Calgary, and owner of the Buckhorn ranch at Pincher Creek, recently enjoyed grizzly steak for dinner.

The rancher shot and killed the mate of a grizzly which had been caught in a trap a few days previously.

The two bears, during the preceding fortnight, attacked and killed 16 head of cattle on the ranch which lies in the foothills between Pincher Creek and the Rocky Mountain forest reserve.

As a consequence, Mr. Cross has almost 2,000 pounds of grizzly meat on hand at the ranch.

In the past two months, Mr. Cross and his ranch hands have killed 14 bears of the cinnamon variety.

This news clipping, from the fall of 1936, is a follow-up story to my grizzly bear adventure. After the male grizzly was killed, a female took over his territory. The sow grizzly met the same fate as her male counterpart.

Dad carried this clipping, and other precious personal belongings, in a brown leather pouch, even keeping it with him throughout his time in the Canadian Army Overseas during World War II. Author's collection.

---

[1] Panniers are sturdy wooden pack boxes, lashed with special rope hitches to the packhorses.

[2] A silver tip grizzly bear is dark brown with light-coloured tips on its hair.

EPILOGUE

This book, *The Vrooms of the Foothills: Adventures of My Childhood*, set in the 1930s, is the first of a series of books I have planned. The books are my memoirs, but the stories are representative of everyone whose families immigrated to western Canada in the late 1890s and early 1900s. When completed, the series will give a broad picture of what everyday life was like for ordinary people in a kinder, gentler era, when everyone looked out for and helped everyone else.

In Volume I, "Adventures of My Childhood," I tell of some of my experiences and as a young child living on my parents' remote ranch in the foothills of southwestern Alberta.

I tell how I rode more than eight miles round trip to school when I was only six years old; how my early playmates were sheep and goats; how I chased herds of horses over the foothills; and how I learned to break my own saddle horses.

I also tell of the savage forest of 1936 fire that ravaged the Castle River Forest Reserve near my home; and the story of how my brother and I built a cart and trained our saddle ponies to be buggy horses.

The most exciting chapter, I think, is the one in which I tell about accompanying my dad when he went to kill a marauding grizzly bear. He had trapped the grizzly back in the Rocky Mountains, some 30 miles by saddle horse from our ranch.

Volume 2, "Pioneer Adventurers" goes back to a time before I was born—when my grandparents were young, and how they worked to survive. I tell the story about my paternal grandparents, and my dad and his siblings, moving to western Canada from Nova Scotia at the turn of the 20th century, and about my maternal grandparents and my mother moving from England in the early 1900s.

The subtitle of another volume will be "Songs My Mother Sang," which suggests how important homegrown entertainment was to keeping up a high morale, and thus its importance to the very survival of early settlers in the west. People were concerned not only about the wellbeing of their own family, but also about keeping up the spirits of people in the broader community.

I will tell about some of the adventures my parents had in their young married life in the 1920s — stories my dad used to tell visitors to our ranch when I was a young child, and that my mother told. Dad told breath-taking stories about chasing wild horses in the interior of British Columbia and of riding a bronc across a high railway trestle — and being stranded in the middle of the trestle just as a train came along.

Another book in the series will tell how I worked as a child, but still thought that work was fun. I will also tell how our family fared during World War II when Dad joined the Canadian Army, leaving my mother, brothers, sister and I to look after each other and our herd of horses for nearly four years.

Subsequent volumes will also contain the pioneer stories of some of the ranch families who were our neighbours, and long-time friends of my parents and grandparents. Everyone knew everyone else for a radius of 25 to 40 miles in those days, and some people knew others much further away. Their remembrances will give added richness to the story of the settling of the foothills of southwestern Alberta.

MAPS

MAP 1 House yard, barnyard and corrals, 1936   11

MAP 2 Beaver Mines – Castle River, circa 1935   30

MAP 3 Gladstone Valley and Beaver Mines Creek Valley, 1930s   58

MAP 4 Trails in the Little Pasture and over the Big Hill, 1936   73

MAP 5 Forty Miles on a Load of Poles   124

MAP 6 Fishburn District Neighbours, 1920s – 1950s   134

MAP 7 Vroom Ranch to Spread Eagle Stampede, 1934   144

MAP 8 Vroom Ranch to Killing the Grizzly Bear, 1936   185

REFERENCES AND SOURCES OF INFORMATION

Brooks, Alessina Bruce, *Dad's Memories - Happy 80th Birthday Dad,* unpublished memoirs of Anthony Bruce, undated (circa 1994).

Department of the Secretary of State. *The Canadian Style: A Guide to Writing and Editing.* Dundurn Press Limited, Toronto, Ontario, 1985.

Friesen, D.W. & Sons Ltd., printers. *"prairie grass to mountain pass": History of the Pioneers of Pincher Creek and District.* Published by Pincher Creek Historical Society, Pincher Creek, Alberta, 1974.

George, James L., *There's a Church in the Valley: A history of Mountain Mill Church.* Privately published, undated (circa 1995).

Guralnik, David B., Editor in Chief. *Webster's New World Dictionary, Second College Edition.* The World Publishing Company. New York and Cleveland. 1970.

Hacker, Diana. *A Canadian Writer's Reference.* Nelson Canada, 1989.

Huddleston, Fred. *A Hisstory of the Settlement and Building Up of the Area in S.W. Alberta Bordering Waterton Park on the North From 1889.* Privately published, undated (circa 1969).

Crowsnest Pass Historical Society. *Crowsnest and Its People.* Published by Crowsnest Pass Historical Society, Coleman, AB. 1979.

Land Office, Municipal District of Pincher Creek, Pincher Creek, Alberta, 1934 and 1950 maps.

Lynch-Staunton, Mrs. C. *A History of the Early Days of Pincher Creek: of the District and of the Southern Mountains.* Published by the Members of the Women's Institute of Alberta. Undated (circa 1920).

MacFarlane, Winnifred. *An incomplete genealogy of first known VROOMS in Holland.* Ottawa, ON. Undated (circa 1970). *

Pincher Creek Echo, The. Pincher Creek, Alberta.

Pincher Creek and District School Division #29. *Unfolding the Pages.* Pincher Creek: Gorman & Gorman Ltd., 1992.

Russell, Andy. *The Canadian Cowboy: Stories of Cows, Cowboys, and Cayuses.* Toronto: McClelland & Stewart, 1993.

Webster's New World Dictionary, Second College Edition. The World Publishing Company. 1970.

www.collectionscanada.ca, Library and Archives Canada, *ArchiviaNet: On-line Research Tool, Western Land Grants (1870-1930)* website.

---

* Material for this undated genealogy was compiled by Winnifred MacFarlane of Ottawa, ON. Based on the date of the most recent entry, which was the date of death of Ralph Ernst Vroom in Pincher Creek, Alberta, July 26, 1969, I approximate the date of the completion of this compilation to be 1970.

Appendix I

GLOSSARY

"Babe" *"Babe"* was "a smaller-sized, half-Shetland black mare with a blaze in her face." *"Babe" belonged to my brother Don.*

"Baby Darling" *"Baby Darling"* was "a light brown goat with a white stripe on his face." *Bill rode Smokey and led Baby Darling as a pack goat in the Castle River Stampede parade.*

"Dandy" *"Dandy"* was "a bright bay, pure-bred Morgan stallion that my dad owned." *Dandy, a stallion that Dad got from Joe Kovatch, was reputed to be the best Morgan stallion west of Winnipeg; he was used to sire many of our finest saddle horses.*

"Dickie" *"Dickie"* was "a Shetland stallion, owned by Dick Smith of Pincher Creek, that we had on loan for a while." *I was happy when Dad brought Dickie home for me to ride.*

"Ginger" *"Ginger"* was "a sorrel, part-thoroughbred, gelding that I broke all by myself when I was about ten years old." *Ginger had to be topped off every morning for about a week when we first brought him in from the winter range.*

"Henry" *"Henry"* was "our very fastest male goat." *Henry would go careening around the goat house at breakneck speed.*

"Jackie" *"Jackie"* was "a sturdy, dark bay Dartmoor pony with a wavy black mane and tail that Dad brought home for me the summer I was seven years old." *Jackie carried his neck in a proud bow when he walked.*

"Kokie" Bosley stallion The *"Kokie" Bosley stallion* was "a brown part thoroughbred that had belonged to man called 'Kokie' Bosley. The *"Kokie" Bosley stallion sired some very fine saddle horses.*

"Laddie" *"Laddie"* was "Leaf's first colt, he was a bright bay half-Shetland sired by Dickie." *Don named Leaf's first colt "Laddie."* (See also "Leaf.")

"Leaf" *"Leaf"* was "a lovely bright bay mare with a white star on her forehead and a small white stripe on her nose and was Don's second brood mare." *Leaf had one colt that I remember — a bright bay half-Shetland pony, sired by "Dickie," and named "Laddie."*

"Moonshine" *"Moonshine"* was "a buckskin outlaw that only Dad could ride." *Dad always rode his fanciest horse — often a buckskin outlaw that he called "Moonshine" — to the Castle River Stampede.*

"Moses with His Eyes Knocked Out" means "a made-up children's singing game where two of us raced to see who could sit in a bucket the fastest." *When we went to play "Moses with His Eyes Knocked Out" later, we didn't know that Jimmy's mother had left scrub water in the bucket in the meantime.*

"Nickle" "Nickle" was "Babe's first colt. He was a brown male colt that Dad named "Nickle." *Nickle was just the right size for Bill.* (See also "Pickles.")

"Paddy" *"Paddy"* was "a full-sized, well broken, very steady saddle horse that I rode when I was two and one-half years old." *"Paddy" stood about 15 hands tall.*

"Pickles" "Pickles" was "the first colt of Don's mare, Babe, and was a brown male colt that Don named "Nickle." "Nickle" got the name "Pickles" because my younger brother, Bill, could not pronounce an 'n', so Nickle became known as "Pickles."

"Rainbow" *"Rainbow"* was "a bay and white pinto, part Morgan, mare. She was my first brood mare." *Rainbow was gentle and quiet and easy to ride.*

"Red Cloud" *"Red Cloud"* was "a sorrel saddle horse standing over 17 hands tall." *Red cloud was a gallant saddle horse that my dad owned.*

"Rex" *"Rex"* was "a clear bay half-Shetland with a white blaze in his face; he was sired by Dickie and was Rainbow's second colt." *Rex became one of my favourite ponies.*

"Ribbons" *"Ribbons"* was "a brown filly and was my second horse." *"Ribbons" was Rainbow's first, and only, colt; she was sired by "Dandy."*

"Silver" *"Silver"* was "a regular-sized, palomino horse." *I discovered that Silver was trained to lie down.*

"Smokey" "Smokey" was "the name of a tall, placid smoky buckskin goat that my parents owned and that I played with when I was little." *I rode on Smokey when I was a small child.*

"T.B." "T.B." stands for "Thomas Banks." *My Great-uncle Tom Tyson was known affectionately by his friends as "T.B."*

"Ted" *"Ted"* was "a big grey horse that my dad owned." *Mom had no trouble deciding that she would get out of our cart and ride "Ted" back to the ranch.*

"Tippy" *"Tippy"* was "a sort of slate blue and white pinto dog, and was probably part Border collie." *Tippy was my favourite goat catching dog.*

"Two Spot" *"Two Spot"* was *"Ribbons'* first colt and was a clear bay male horse with a white spot on either side of his belly." *I named Ribbons' first colt "Two Spot."*

"Two-Step" *"Two-Step"* was "one of Dad's tallest saddle horses and was a sway-backed, well-broken brown gelding that stood about seventeen hands tall at the shoulders." *We double-decked "Two-Step" to Gladstone Valley School.*

A billy goat *A billy goat* is "a male goat that has not been castrated." *A billy goat is used for breeding purposes.*

A man of honour *A man of honour* is "a person who is totally honest in all ways." Grandpa Tyson was a man of honour — when he signed a contract, he stuck to it.

A stranger *A stranger* refers to "a new goat." Henry was a stranger amongst my goat herd; he was a brown, horned goat which Dad had got from Henry Altermatt."

A talking to *A talking to* means "a mild scolding." *My dad gave me a talking to.*

GLOSSARY

Acid test The *acid test* means "the most crucial test." *We knew that this trip was the acid test of our invention; we were more than a little nervous as we started out.*

All dressed up *All dressed up* means "wearing our newest and best clothing ready to go some place special." *We got all dressed up to go to the Castle River Stampede.*

Along the grade *Along the grade* means "travelling on a straight, level, stretch of road that was about one-half mile long and about one mile from our ranch house on the way to Beaver Mines. 'The grade' was cut out of the west end of a short range of hills." *When Mom started along the grade on her saddle horse she thought she saw some movement at the far end of it.*

Baby of the family *Baby of the family* refers to the "youngest child in a family." *My sister, Marion, was the baby of the family.*

Baby sitter *Baby sitter* here means "the goat that stayed home and watched all the kids while the other goats grazed up on the high hill." *When the kids were younger than three months old, they were left at the home corrals with one of the nanny goats acting as a baby sitter."*

Baker's bread *Baker's bread* means "store-bought bread." *Occasionally, we bought a loaf of baker's bread.*

Bald prairie *Bald prairie* means "flat land with no natural trees on it." *Granny and Grandpa lived on what I thought of as the bald prairie.*

Barn manure pile The *barn manure pile* was "a heap of manure which accumulated over time as horse and cow manure was shovelled out of the barn each morning."

Barnyard The *barnyard*, in general, means "the U-shaped grassy area rimmed by the "little corral," the barn, the gate to the "big corral," the blacksmith shop, the carpenter shop and the north side of the house yard." *Mom took our pictures in the barnyard.*

Barnyard water trough *The barnyard water trough was located just outside the house yard fence and was filled by water from the little creek.*

Bay window A *bay window* is a colloquial expression meaning "a man's large stomach." *Billy Eddy had a bay window.*

Bear Mountain See The big hill.

Beaver Mines (AB) *Beaver Mines* is "a small hamlet southwest of Pincher Creek, Alberta that serves the ranch and farm families of that area." *I often rode to Beaver Mines.*

Beef ring The *beef ring* was "a cooperative whereby the farmers of the district took turns contributing a steer once a month. The meat was then divided amongst the contributors."
Often Granny bottled some of the meat that they got from the beef ring.

Bennett Buggies *Bennett Buggies* were "conveyances which were an ingenious adaptation by prairie farmers who could not afford gasoline for their Model T or Model A Ford cars." *Many farmers took the motors out of their cars, renamed them Bennett Buggies and hitched farm teams to them, and drove along in style.*

Big game hunting *Big game hunting* means "the shooting of elk, deer, bears, or other large wild animals for sport." *In the 1930s, big game hunting was not allowed in the Castle River Forest Reserveand is still not allowed there.*

Bill Bremner *Bill Bremner* was "a neighbour who lived about one mile west of our ranch at Beaver Mines." *We learned to take a shortcut past Bill Bremner's place.*

Bit A *bit* is "a metal bar, which is put in a horse's mouth." *A bit enables a rider or driver to steer and stop the horse(s).* (See also Bridle bit)

Blaze A *blaze* is "a stripe of white hair." *Smokey had a blaze down his face.*

Blinders *Blinders* are "heavy flaps of leather which prevent a harness horse from looking backwards and being frightened by whatever contraption it is pulling." *First, the ponies had to get used to the harness with its blinders and croup strap.*

Blindfold *Blindfold,* used as a verb, means "to put a covering over an animal's, or person's, eyes. *Pete LaGrandeur blindfolded my horse with a strip of cloth torn off his saddle blanket.*

Bottling the meat *Bottling the meat* means "preserving meat for later use by cutting the meat into small pieces, then putting it into jars and boiling the jars for three hours on the cook stove in an oblong boiler full of water." *Granny preserved chicken by bottling the meat.*

Box stall *Box stall* means "a closed-in area of the barn used to confine animals without tying them up with a halter shank." *Sometimes a goat or sheep was in the box stall.*

Brain wave A *brain wave* is "a bright idea." *On my way to meet Don at Coalfields School, I got of the brain wave of stopping to visit Mrs. Holmes.*

Break our horses To break our horses meant "to train them to be quiet saddle horses." *Usually, Dad did not break our horses the horses to ride, until they were three years old.*

Bridle bit A *bridle bit* is "a metal bar that is put in a horse's mouth." *A bit enables a rider or driver to steer and stop the horse(s).*

Bridle lines *Lines, or bridle lines,* are "part of a horse's tack, and are long, narrow, leather straps that are attached to either side of a horse's bridle bit and used to control and guide the horse. We generally used the word 'lines' when talking about the reins on the bridles of workhorses." *I held the lines firmly to make sure the team did not move forward.* See also bridle reins.

Bridle reins *Bridle reins* are "narrow, leather straps attached to either side of the bridle bit and used to control the horse. We generally used the word 'reins' to refer to the shorter straps used to control a saddle horse." *Mom held the bridle reins firmly, and spoke gently to her saddle horse, while Don and I helped get Bill up behind her.*

Bronc *Bronc* is "a bronco which means a wild, or partly tamed, horse. *Dad got in the habit of keeping a bronc in the house yard.*

Brood mare A *brood mare* is "a mature female horse used for breeding purposes." *"Babe" was Don's first brood mare.*

Brought down the house *Brought down the house* is a colloquial expression meaning "caused an assembled crowd of people to break into gales of laughter." *When I as a very young child admired Billy Eddy's bay window, it brought down the house.*

Bruce, Mrs. Ted (Edward) *Mrs. Ted (Edward) Bruce* was "an artist who lived near the Beaver Mines Store and Post Office." *Mrs. Bruce was a good friend of my mother's.*

Brush *Brush* can mean 1. "A tool for applying paint or varnish to a wall or ceiling." *The paintbrush left a hair on the ceiling.* 2. "To groom an animal." *We had to brush our ponies morning and night.* 3. "Scraggly trees and shrubs covering a certain area." *The brush had not been cut back very far from beside the trail.*

Bullwhip *Bullwhip* means "a quirt that had a short braided leather handle about six inches long and a lash about eight feet long, tipped with separate thongs of leather." *Dad offered to get Dickie started with the bullwhip.*

Bunny foot *A bunny foot* is "when an animal's leg ends at the ankle joint and has hair growing over the end of it instead of having a hoof." *My dad named this little kid "Bunny" because it had bunny foot.*

Bunt To *bunt* means "to run into a person from the side or from behind with enough force to knock one down." *The ram would bunt us children whenever he caught us unawares.*

Bushes *Bushes* are "small, scraggly shrubs." *All three of us scurried into the bushes beside the road, and waited for Mom to ride alongside.*

Cantle *A cantle* means "the raised back part of a saddle against which a rider's buttock rests." *Once her left foot was in the stirrup, Mom could lift her right leg over the cantle and sit squarely on her mount.*

Caraganas *Caraganas* are "hardy shrubs that grow well in dry climates like the Canadian prairies." *A row of tall caraganas formed a windbreak that protected the house from the worst blasts of the west wind; a smaller patch of caraganas protected the other side of the house from northeast winds.*

Castle River Forest Reserve The *Castle River Forest Reserve* means "an area in the extreme southwestern corner of Alberta, just north of Waterton Lakes National Park."

Castle River Stampede The *Castle River Stampede* was "an annual — mostly horseback riding — sports day. It was held in a flat open area half encircled by a big bend of the Castle River about eight miles south of Burmis, and about the same distance from our ranch." *The Castle River Stampede was usually held in July.*

Castrate To *castrate* means "to remove the testicles of a male animal." *Young male goats in a herd are castrated so that they cannot breed the nanny goats to which they are related, and thus cause inbreeding.*

Catch the mail stage *Catch the stage* means to "be at the post office before the mailman left and pay a small fare for the trip." *People could catch the mail stage and ride into Pincher Creek and back when they had a doctor's appointment.*

Chicken A *chicken* is "a person who is not brave. It is a term used to taunt a person into doing what they otherwise would not do." *Bill did not want to appear to be chicken in front of his big brother, so he swallowed the minnow Don handed him.*

Chinook A *Chinook* means "a flow of warm air from the Pacific Ocean which spills over the Rocky Mountains in South Alberta covering an area as far north as about Calgary and east to the Saskatchewan boundary." *A strong wind often accompanies a Chinook.*

Close call A close call means "a time when a person or animal is in danger of serious injury, yet escapes being injured through good luck, by making a wise last-minute decision, by being quick-witted and well prepared for any eventuality, or simply by the grace of God." *As a child, I had a number of close calls.*

Closer coupled *Closer coupled* means "shorter in the back." *Laddie was a little closer coupled than Rex was.*

Coalfields School *Coalfields School* was "a one-room country school located about 12 miles west of Pincher Creek, that Don and I attended for grades one and two." *I started school at Coalfields School, which was located about four miles away from our home, in January on my sixth birthday.*

Cow pies *Cow pies* are "heaps of fresh cow manure on the grass." *Once I stepped in a cow pie with my brand new shoes on.*

Cows came fresh The *cows came fresh* means "our milk cows had new calves and started producing milk again." *Goat milk provided much-needed nourishment for the family before the cows came fresh, after being dry all winter.*

Cream separator A *cream separator* means "a farm household machine designed to separate the cream from fresh whole milk." *A cream separator has a large metal bowl on top, into which Grandpa poured the fresh milk.* Cross-hobbled the animal on three legs

Cross-hobbled the animal on three legs means "tied three of the horse's legs together with a lariat-type rope so that the horse could not kick out nor jump around without falling down." *Dad cross-hobbled the horse on three legs so that he could put shoes on it.*

Croup strap A *croup strap*, also called a *crupper* is "a part of a fancy buggy harness. It is a strap that is attached to the back strap, which is attached to the collar. The croup strap has a loop on the end that goes under the horse's tail." *The croup strap helps to hold the harness in place.*

Crow-hopping *Crow-hopping* describes "when a horse bucks by bouncing on straight legs and kicking its hind end up in the air." *My dad would have called Ribbons' bucking "crow-hopping."*

Curry comb and horse brush A *curry comb and horse brush* refers to "equipment for cleaning horses." *We cleaned the dust and dirt off our horses with a curry comb and horse brush.*

Cut out *Cut out* means "divide." *A knee-reined horse is a great advantage when a person wants to cut out a certain animal from a herd.*

Cutter A *cutter* is a "light sleigh which is pulled by one or two horses." *Aunt Marion's children drove to school in a cutter in the wintertime.*

Deadfall A deadfall is "a tree which the wind has blown over; a windfall." *Suddenly there was a deadfall across the trail in front of my pony and me.*

Depression Years The Depression Years means "the decade of the 1930s up until the beginning of the Second World War in 1939." *People had to live frugal lives during the Depression Years.*

Diamond hitch A *diamond hitch* is "a special knot used to keep a load securely fastened atop a pack animal." *Behind him Bill led another goat — Baby Darling — on which Dad had loaded a small pack bundle, complete with a diamond hitch.*

Dirty Thirties *Dirty Thirties* was "the decade of the 1930s — so called because of the many dust storms on the Canadian prairies and the terrible economic conditions during that stressful decade." *Bennett Buggies were named after the Rt. Hon. R.B. Bennett, who was Prime Minister of Canada during the infamous decade known as the Dirty Thirties.*

Double-deck *Double-deck,* verb, means "to ride on the same horse as another person, often sitting behind the saddle." *When he was little, Bill double-decked behind Mom.*

Double-jointed leg A *double-jointed leg* is "a limb having a joint that bends backwards as well as forwards." *Bunny had a double-jointed hind leg and a bunny foot.*

Doubletree A *doubletree* is "a crossbar made of wood, which swings in the middle, and to which singletrees are attached when a team is driven abreast." *We fastened a doubletree securely onto the tongue of the cart.*

Down at the spring *Down at the spring* refers to "a spring that was about one-quarter mile northwest of the barn along the road to Beaver Mines. *When the little creek dried up in mid-summer we had to water our horses down at the spring.*

Down on the river *Down on the river* means "along the Waterton River east of Granny and Granpa Tyson's farm." *Granny picked chokecherries down on the river.*

Dropping his teeth down *Dropping his teeth down* means "loosening his false teeth with his tongue, opening his mouth, and thrusting his upper plate out at us." *Uncle Tommy loved to scare us kids by dropping his teeth down.*

Dry *Dry* means "producing no milk." *In the spring the cows came fresh — after being dry all winter.*

Dry lightning storm A *dry lightning storm* is "a lightning storm during which no, or only very little, rain falls." *One dark night in early July in 1936 — during a dry lightning storm — a particularly powerful bolt of lightning hit dry spruce tree high on a mountainside setting it afire and starting a devastating forest fire.*

East Cardston Hutterite Colony School The *East Cardston Hutterite Colony School* is "a one-room country school near Cardston, Alberta." *My son Jim, who spoke English very well at age four, was a great help to me when I taught at the East Cardston Hutterite Colony School. (See also Hutterites & Hutterite colony school)*

East quarter *East quarter* means "the quarter section of land on the east side of the road, where our ranch house was located." *Our horse corrals were on the east quarter. (See also Home quarter.)*

Ekelunds, the The *Ekelunds* were neighbours of ours and who lived about fifteen miles southeast of our ranch in the Twin Butte district." *The Ekelunds always rode past our place a couple of days before the stampede leading a packhorse so that they could camp out during the stampede.*

Elk Lodge *Elk Lodge* was "a forest ranger station on the north end of the Castle River Forest Reserve south of Beaver Mines." *Grandpa Vroom lived beside the road to Elk Lodge.*

Engineer 1. On a train, the *engineer* is "the person who drives the train and watches the track ahead." 2. In our case, the *engineer* was "the one who held the reins and controlled the horse we were double-decking." *Don was the "engineer" — sitting in front in the saddle and controlling the horse with the bridle reins.*

Experiment An *experiment* is "a different than usual action taken to find out what will be the outcome." *About mid-June, I decided to try an experiment with my driving goats.*

Fairer *Fairer* means "more equal." *I thought it would be fairer for other goats, if I gave them a turn, too.*

Fall *Fall*, noun, "harvest time." *We picked potatoes in the fall.*

Fall off To *fall off* means to "inadvertently take a tumble." *Don walked on the other side of Smokey to make sure I didn't fall off.*

Farrier A *farrier* means "a blacksmith" or "a man who can shoe horses." *Since Dad was a farrier, he could shoe his own horses and save costly trips to town to get the job done.*

Fast rides *Fast rides* were "a kind of game that Don and I played where we hung onto the hair at the top of the sheep's or goat's hips, then ran fast along behind the animal as it tried to get rid of us." *We had fun taking fast rides over at the stack yards.*

Filly *Filly* means "a young female horse." *"Ribbons" was a brown filly.*

Fire had its way The *fire had its way* means that the "forest fire burned furiously." *Needless to say, the fire had its way until heavy rains in late August finally drenched the tinder dry forest and undergrowth.*

Fireman 1. On a train, the *fireman* is "the person who adds fuel to the engine." 2. In the case of Don and me, the *fireman* was "the one who controlled the speed of the horse we were double-decking." *I was the fireman — sitting behind the saddle and nudging Two-Step with my heels to make him go faster.*

Fishburn District The *Fishburn District* is "a farming area east of Pincher Creek, Alberta." *My mother's parents lived in the Fishburn, Alberta District of Alberta.*

Fizzy dope *Fizzy dope* was "my name for the cool drink mixture that Granny always made in the summertime—a mixture of egg whites, sugar and cream of tartar, water and baking soda." *Granny laughed when I called the cool drink that she made "fizzy dope."*

Fly in the ointment A *fly in the ointment* means "an unexpected problem that had to be solved." *There was another fly in the ointment, so to speak.*

Forge A *forge* is "a specially-built fire where metal can be heated to white hot so it can be pounded on an anvil into another shape." *Dad's forge was in one corner of the blacksmith shop.*

Freak accident *Freak accident* means "an incident where someone is hurt in a situation that is extremely unlikely to occur." *My starting school in early January came about as the result of a seemingly freak accident.*

210

Gable roof A *gable roof* is "a roof that has a single ridge pole and two sloping sides, looking somewhat like an inverted V." *Our first root cellar had a gable roof.*

Genovese, Miss Ida *Miss Ida Genovese* was "my grade two teacher at Coalfields School *Miss Genovese was an energetic young schoolteacher.*

Gilmore Ridge The *Gilmore Ridge* refers to "a range of high hills about two miles west of our ranch. It was located on land owned by a Mr. Gilmore. *The panoramic picture that I have of the Ralph and Mollie Vroom ranch was taken from atop the Gilmore Ridge.*

Gladstone Valley *Gladstone Valley* means "a ranching area southeast of Beaver Mines, AB." *Bill stayed with the Truitts up Gladstone Valley for the summer.*

Gladstone Valley School *Gladstone Valley School* was "a one-room country school, located about seven miles south of my ranch home, and was the school I attended for grades three through seven." *We rode horseback four miles to Gladstone Valley School.*

Go down East *Go down East* means "go to Ontario in eastern Canada." *"I think I'll go down East this summer," Mom remarked one day.*

Going out to play *Going out to play* was "a loose term which could mean almost any kind of adventure, ranging from very safe to very risky." *Mom never really knew what we were going to do when we said that we were going out to play.*

Gone soft *Gone soft* means "no longer suitable for its original use." *The coal in the mines at Beaver Mines had gone soft.*

Good breakfast A good breakfast was "usually a bowl of home cooked porridge and milk." Sometimes we had toast, which was toasted on the hot lids of our wood-burning cook stove, as an addition to our usual good breakfast.

Good brood mare A good brood mare means "a mare which is used for breeding purposes that has many desirable qualities." *"Rainbow," being part Morgan and having a gentle nature, was a good brood mare.*

Got hung up in the stirrup *Got hung up in the stirrup* means "he was being dragged along the ground by the bronco, while his foot was still in the stirrup." *When the pick-up man dropped him, Dad was hung up in the stirrup.*

Grade, a; the grade 1. A *grade* is "a flat stretch of road or railroad, slightly raised above the surrounding land to let water drain off it." *As we drove along what we called "the grade," Mom had Dad stop the team and pick a bouquet of wild roses.* 2. The *grade* was "what our family called a straight, level, stretch of road about one and one half miles from our house." *The grade was along the west end of a short range of hills, and just south of Number One Coal Mine.*

Graded *Graded* is an adjective meaning "made smooth by pulling a piece of road-building equipment over it." *We followed the graded dirt road as far as Elk Lodge, which was located at the entrance to the Forest Reserve.*

Grizzly bear *Grizzly bear.* "a very large, very fierce North American bear." *Grizzly bear colours range from cream to dark brown.*

Gus's gate *Gus's gate* means "the gate into a quarter section of land owned by Gus Gamache that was located just across the road north of our west quarter." *A spring supplied water for the water trough that was near Gus's gate.*

Had me buffaloed *Had me buffaloed* means "had the better of me." *One day Paddy really had me buffaloed.*

Had natural, or situational, constraints *Had natural, or situational, constraints* means "we always suffered one way or another for not obeying any given rule." *Having natural, or situational, constraints taught us, as young children, to use our own judgement with regard to our behaviour in various situations.*

Halter A *halter* means "a piece of tack specially designed for leading or tying up a horse." *A halter is different from a bridle in that a halter does not have a bit that goes in a horse's mouth.*

Halter shank *Halter shank* means "the lead rope from a horse's halter." *Dad rode up, leading Paddy by the halter shank.*

Hand A *hand* is "a measurement that equals about four inches, which is used in determining the height of a horse." *Some of Dad's horses were seventeen hands tall.*

Harness A *harness* is "an arrangement of leather straps and metal buckles, rings, and snaps, which is put on an animal so that it can be attached to a vehicle to pull a load." *Dad could turn his hand to harness making and many other skilful tasks.*

Hayloft A *hayloft* is "the top part of the barn where sufficient hay to last the animals all winter was stored." *We climbed up into the hayloft and threw some hay down into the mangers.*

Haystack A *haystack* is "a large pile of loose hay." *A haystack is waterproof when built in an orderly manner and topped off correctly.*

Helping Dad *Helping Dad* meant "being with Dad while he was working." *I felt I was helping Dad even if all I had to do was hold the lines of the team's harnesses.*

Henry Altermatt *Henry Altermatt* was "a neighbour who lived up Gladstone Valley about six miles from our place." *Henry Altermatt owned a large herd of goats.*

High-tailed it *High-tailed it*, verb, "to run fast." *Bill high-tailed it as far as he could, and often got out of sight.*

Hitching rail A *hitching rail* means "a horizontal pole on top of two posts to which saddle horses and teams are tied temporarily." *We tied our horses to the hitching rail.*

Holmes, Mr. Frank and Mrs. Louise *Mr. and Mrs. Frank Holmes* were "good friends of my parents who lived at Beaver Mines." *Mrs. Holmes often gave us a cup of hot chocolate, when we stopped to warm up on the way home from Coalfields School.*

Home free *Home free* means "all our troubles were over." *Thing were going along so well that we began to think we were home free.*

Home quarter Our *home quarter* was "the quarter section of my parents' land where our ranch house was located." *The west quarter was in Coalfields School District; the east quarter was in the Gladstone Valley School District.* (See also East quarter)

Hoof rot *Hoof rot* is "a disease which strikes hoofed animals causing the hoof to shrivel up; then the horny covering loosens and falls off." *Jackie got hoof rot in his right hind foot and had to be destroyed.*

Horse will get spoiled *Horse will get spoiled* means "the horse will develop bad habits if the rider lets it get away with disobedient or bad mannered behaviour. *"Dad did not want us to spoil our saddle horses."*

Horses in training *Horses in training* means "horses that were not yet tame and reliable enough to sell or trade to novice riders." *Don and I often rode horses in training to school.*

Horseshoes *Horseshoes* are "flat pieces of metal shaped like a horse's hoof and put on horses' hooves for protection." *Dad put horseshoes on our school ponies in the spring.*

Household well The *household well* was "a well — located just inside the house yard fence about 100 feet from the kitchen door — where we got all the water for use in every day living." *We got water from our household well by vigorously pumping the handle of an iron water pump up and down and catching the water in a bucket.*

House yard dam The *house yard dam* was "a small dam which Dad had made in the little creek where it cut through one corner of the house yard." *We swam in the house yard dam in the summertime.* (See also little dam**.)**

Hutterite colonies *Hutterite colonies* are "communal farms having large tracts of land and a cluster of farm buildings — apartments, barns, machine sheds, and a cookhouse and dining room — where 150 to 300 Hutterites live and work co-operatively. They also have their own schoolhouse." *Our usual stopover place on the way to and from Granny and Grandpa Tyson's was at the Pincher Creek Hutterite Colony.* (See also Hutterites *&* East Cardston Colony School)

Hutterite colony school A *Hutterite colony school* is "a one-room school with a multi-graded classroom where one teacher teaches grades one to eight and where English is a second language for the children, who speak German at home." *One time, when we stopped overnight at the Pincher Creek Hutterite Colony on the way home after visiting Granny and Grandpa, the school was in session, and I attended class next morning while Mom and Dad were getting ready for the drive home.*

Hutterites *Hutterites* are a "religious sect whose members live communally in what are called 'Hutterite colonies." *We often stayed overnight with the Hutterites on our way to visit Granny and Grandpa Tyson.*

In foal *In foal* means "pregnant." *To get our herd started faster, Dad gave each of us a mare that was in foal.*

In tandem *Drive in tandem* means "to drive two or more animals one behind the other in front of a machine or conveyance, instead of side by side. *Dad suggested that I should drive Smokey and Baby Darling in tandem.*

Inbreeding *Inbreeding* occurs "when closely related animals are bred with each other." *Dad castrated the male goats so that there would not be inbreeding in our herd.*

Jackpot A *jackpot* is "an undesirable predicament." *We sometimes acted carelessly and got ourselves into a jackpot.*

John Babin's corner *John Babin's corner* referred to "the point where Dad's west quarter met John Babin's home quarter." *John Babin's corner was about one-half mile from home.*

Just my size *Just my size* means "a horse small enough that I could mount it in the regular fashion of horseback riders — standing on its left side with my left foot on the ground and reaching up to the stirrup with my right foot." *Dickie was just my size.*

Just to help make a show *Just to help make a show* means "to add to the entertainment." *Dad had entered the contest just to help make a show at the local stampede.*

Kelly, Jack *Jack Kelly* "was one of our hired men during the 1930s." *Jack Kelly was one of the 1000s of young men who travelled across Canada looking for work during the Great Depression.*

Kid, us kids 1. A *kid* is "a baby goat." *The summer I first learned to walk, I played in the house yard with of a couple of kids.* 2. *Us kids* is "a slang expression meaning 'children.'" *Community events were lots of fun for us kids.*

Knee rein *Knee rein* means "to guide a horse simply by leaning slightly to the side of the saddle in the direction the rider wants to turn and exerting pressure with the opposite knee." *Many of our saddle horses were taught to knee rein.*

Lady's saddle A *lady's saddle* means "an adult-sized saddle which is smaller than a man's saddle and has a padded seat." *My mother rode a lady's saddle.*

Lariat A *lariat* is "a rope about 15 to 20 feet long which is usually used by cowboys when handling horses or cattle." *Don would use Dad's lariat to tie up the ornery ram.*

Lazy *Lazy* means "not an energetic worker." *I did not notice that Smokey was lazy until Baby Darling came on the scene.*

Lead goat the *lead goat* means "the front goat in my tandem team and the goat that was steered with the reins." *Smokey was a good choice for lead goat because he was used to being steered.*

Learned the hard way *Learned the hard way* means "remembered what I was told after being punished several times." *I finally learned the hard way to obey the no-racing rule.*

Light hand A *light hand* means "holding the bridle reins with a light, gentle touch so that the horse's mouth is not bruised by the bit. *Dad taught us to ride with a light hand.*

Light team A *light team* is "team that was used for pulling only light loads, such as, buggies and small wagons." *Dad had the regular light team away on a fishing trip where they were doubling as packhorses.*

Lines The *lines (on a horse's tack)* are "long, narrow straps of leather that are attached to either side of a horse's bridle bit, and used to control and guide the horse. We generally used the word 'lines' when talking about the reins on the bridles of workhorses." *I felt I was helping Dad when I held the lines of the team that was hitched to the hayrack, or some other conveyance.* (See also Bridle reins)

Little corral The *little corral* was "a pole enclosure large enough to hold a small herd of horses, and small enough that a cowboy, or cowgirl, could lasso a bronco." *The little corral was located near the barn.*

Little halter A *little halter* means "a small-sized head harness with a band around the animal's nose." *Smokey had a little halter that Dad had made for him.*

Little harness A *little harness* means "a small-sized arrangement of leather straps and metal buckles, rings, and snaps that just fit Smokey." *I fastened Smokey to my sleigh or wagon using the traces of the little harness that Dad made for Smokey.*

Little singletree The *little singletree* was "a piece of kindling wood about 12 inches long." *Dad used a piece of baling wire to make a loop at each end of the little singletree to hook the goat harness traces onto.*

Loose hay *Loose hay* is "unbaled hay." *Dad used a pitchfork to throw the loose hay off the hayrack and arrange it on a haystack in a certain way.*

Loosened up for the pickup *Loosened up for the pickup* means "relaxed his leg-muscle grip on the saddle to get ready to swing into the pickup man's arms." *In the split second before the horses shied away from each other Dad had loosened up for the pickup.*

Low down *Low down* means "very small." *Don and I felt low down after our soaring flight.*

Lower gate The *lower gate* means "a gate located straight down the hill from Mrs. Bruce's house — not the gate by the store and post office." *When I left Mrs. Bruce's, I went out the lower gate.*

Loyalists (UEL) *United Empire Loyalists* were "people who remained loyal to the British king, George III, after the American Revolution which lasted from 1763 until after the Revolutionary War (1775–83)." *Many United Empire Loyalists moved to Canada.*

Madorski, Mr. *Mr. Madorski* was "a wool and hide buyer from Calgary, and a long time friend of our family." *Mr. Madorski drove my mother into Pincher Creek when I was due to give birth to me.*

Manure boat The *manure boat* was "a conveyance which was built like the stone boat, but had board sides about three feet high." *During the winter, Dad shovelled the manure from the barn manure pile into the manure boat and took the manure out to spread on the fields as fertilizer.* (See also Stone boat)

Mare A *mare* is "a female horse." *My mother liked to ride a half-Shetland mare called "Babe."*

Martial law *Martial law* is a "law imposed in an emergency situation, such as when a forest fire breaks out." *When martial law is imposed, for example during a forest fire, men and/or equipment can be commandeered to fight the fire — no if's, but's or maybe's.*

McDowall, Mrs. W. D. (Emma Mary Price) was "a farm woman who played the piano for the Coalfields School Christmas concerts." *Miss Genovese walked all forty of us about one and one-half miles to Mrs. W. D. McDowall's to practice singing with a piano.*

Mile A *mile* is "a measure of distance which equals 1.6 kilometres." *It was 2 ½ miles, or about four kilometres from our ranch house to the Beaver Mines Store and Post Office.*

Milk tea *Milk tea* means "regular tea with lots of milk in it." *I poured myself a cup of tea and made milk tea.*

Morgan A *Morgan*, according to *Webster's New World Dictionary*, 1970, is "any of a breed of strong, light harness or saddle horses, named after Justin Morgan, the New England breeder who developed the breed in the eighteenth century." *Most of Dad's part Morgan horses stood 14 or 15 hands tall, but some were as tall as 17 hands, depending on the cross.*

Mounting platform *Mounting platform* means "a stand made of boards with a top about a metre square and with three steps up one side." *The mounting platform was just the height of Mom's saddle stirrup when her saddle was on a medium-sized saddle horse.*

Nanny goat A nanny goat is "a female goat." Each spring most of the nanny goats had *kids.*

Near-outlaw horse A *near-outlaw horse* is a "very wild and/or mean horse." *Handling a near-outlaw horse requires skill and courage.*

Neck reining *Neck reining* means "putting light pressure on either side of a horse's neck to turn it whatever direction the rider wants to go." *A horse that responds quickly to gentle neck reining is a well-reined horse.*

Neck yoke A *neck yoke* is "a short wooden pole that is suspended between the two horses of a team driven abreast. It is held in place by straps on the horses' harnesses and holds the tongue of a wagon or cart up off the ground." *The neck yoke enables a team to steer a cart or wagon and to keep the cart from running up onto the horses' heels and precipitating a runaway.*

Neophyte kid *Neophyte kid* means "a kid that had no experience at sailing in the washtub." *One day I caught a neophyte kid and put it in with Bunny.*

No trouble *No trouble* means "did not complain about anything." *I had been allowed to go only if I was no trouble.*

Noose A *noose* is "a large loop in a lariat." *We held a noose over a wide space between the poles of the fence, and caught the ram when he put his head through for some oats.*

Nothing to do *Nothing to do* means "not able to do any of my usual activities." *There were no other children to play with, and no animals, either, so I had nothing to do.*

Nuisance birds *Nuisance birds* are "birds which are unwelcome around farmers' buildings as no use can be seen for them. *We considered magpies to be nuisance birds.*

Nuisance grizzly bear A *nuisance grizzly bear* means "a bear that is no longer afraid of humans and forages for food in the midst of human habitation." *The grizzly bear that Dad trapped and killed had become a nuisance grizzly bear.*

Number One Coal Mine hill The *Number One Coal Mine hill* was "a hill on the road to Beaver Mines that was about one and one-half miles from home. *Just as we were about to start down the Number One Coal Mine hill, a never-before-or-after incident occurred.*

Number One Coal Mine *Number One Coal Mine* means "a coal mine located about a mile from Beaver Mines, or one and one-half miles from Dad's ranch." *The Number One Coal Mine was the first coal mine we came to on the way to Beaver Mines.*

Off the hook *Off the hook* means "free and not liable to punishment." *I knew I was off the hook for that day.*

Old Studebaker Our *old Studebaker* was "1920-something model of car. *We owned our old Studebaker in the 1930s.*

On the fly *On the fly* means "on the run." *When the goat we were running behind charged into the middle of the herd, we would change to another goat on the fly.*

On the trail *On the trail* means "away from the house." *I would take a drink of goat's milk if I were on the trail.*

Out of nowhere *Out of nowhere* means "unseen by me." *The ram suddenly appeared out of nowhere.*

Out on the trail *Out on the trail* means "in an unsettled area where there was no barn or corral." *Dad used his lariat or for tethering his saddle horse over night if he was out on the trail.*

Outgrowing the goats *Outgrowing the goats* means that "I was getting too old to enjoy playing with them." *I took my frustration with Smokey and Baby Darling as a sign that I was outgrowing the goats.*

Outhouse An *outhouse* is "an outdoor toilet, situated over a deep pit." *Bunny became my special pet and followed me everywhere, even to the outhouse.*

Over at the stack yards The expression *over at the stack yards* means "at the fenced-in area south of the house where hay was stored in stacks during the summer time so that it could be fed to the animals in the winter time." *One daily wintertime task was feeding the cattle, sheep and goats over at the stack yards.* (See also Haystacks**.)**

Pack train A *pack train* is "a number of packhorses travelling together, one behind the other." *The pack train was carrying camping equipment, food, and fire-fighting equipment.*

Package of 'baccy A *package of 'baccy* means "some pipe tobacco." *Dad had ridden up to the Beaver Mines Store and Post Office to get a package of 'baccy.*

Packhorse A *packhorse* is "a sturdy horse that is used to carry heavy loads of supplies needed to survive in the back country where conventional vehicles cannot go." *The packhorses were loaded with camping equipment, food and fire-fighting equipment.*

Page wire fence *Page* wire is "wire that is divided into rectangles to keep animals like sheep and goats from crawling through the fence." *The little pasture was enclosed with a page wire fence.*

Palomino *Palomino* is the word used to describe the colour of a horse and means "silvery-gold coloured." *"Silver," a palomino, was as gentle as a lamb.*

Paris green *Paris green* means "a green powder that was mixed with water and sprinkled by hand on the leaves of the potato plants to kill the potato bugs." *We sprinkled Paris green on the potato plant leaves by hand.*

Parked To be *parked* means "left standing." *Don found the front axle and wheels of an old Model T or Model A car, up where the old cars were parked.*

Pete LaGrandeur: *Pete LaGrandeur* was "the stock rider for the Castle River Forest Reserve who was with Dad and me when Dad shot a nuisance grizzly bear up the Castle River." *Pete, the stock rider for the Castle River Forest Reserve, let Dad know when the grizzly bear was in the trap that Dad had set.*

Pick-up men at the rodeo *Pick-up men at the rodeo* are "cowboys, who firmly lift a bronc rider off a bucking bronco after the rider has completed his 10-second ride in the saddle bronc-riding event in a rodeo." *Pick-up men at the rodeo usually ride range-breed horses to do their task.*

Piled *Piled* is a verb meaning "bucked or thrown off a horse." *Ribbons piled me more than once.*

Pincher Creek, Alberta *Pincher Creek, Alberta,* is "a town east of the Crows Nest Pass, in southwestern Alberta." *My parents' ranch was southwest of Pincher Creek, Alberta.*

Pinto *Pinto* means "having patches of white on a different coloured background." *"Rainbow" was a bay and white pinto.*

Planks *Planks* are "boards about two inches thick and eight inches wide." *The floor of the stone boat was made of planks.*

Play work *Play work* is "playing with toy articles or small animals pretending to do grown-up tasks." *As a child, I would do play work for hours upon hours, gradually learning many skills.*

Ponies *Ponies* means "smaller-sized saddle horses." *When I was little, I liked riding ponies.*

Pull that stunt *Pull that stunt* means "do an unusual action which has an unexpected outcome." *I did not, as my Dad would say, pull that stunt again.*

Quarter section. A *quarter section* is "an area of land that is ½- by ½-mile." *The quarter section owned by Gus Gamache was next to my parents' land.*

Quick The *quick* refers to the "soft part underneath the hard shell of a horse's hoof." *Dad took care to rasp just the right amount off the horse's hoof so as not to cut into the quick.*

Quilting *Quilting* was "the process of hand stitching a patchwork quilt top to the bottom two layers of a new quilt using small running stitches." *Granny Tyson went to a daylong work bee to help with the quilting of a new quilt top.*

Ram A *ram* is "a male sheep used for breeding purposes." *We had a vicious black-faced ram that Dad got from Uncle Dominic Cyr.*

Range-horse breed *Range-horse breed* refers to "horses which are of no particular breed, but which are intelligent, mild-mannered animals". *Range horses are beautiful animals, both physically and by nature.*

Readin' and writin' and 'rithmetic *Readin' and writin' and 'rithmetic* means "all the school subjects." *Miss Clements taught readin' and writin' and 'rithmetic.*

Real work *Real work* is "work one has the responsibility to do to enable a family or a community to function smoothly and live together peacefully." *The skills that I learned from doing play work as a child came in useful for real work later in life.*

GLOSSARY

Re-break To *re-break* means "to rid a horse of bad habits." *Dad helped me to re-break Dickie.*

Red-letter day *A red-letter day* is "a very happy occasion." *It was a red-letter day for us children whenever we visited Aunt Marion or she came to visit us.*

Rheumatoid arthritis *Rheumatoid arthritis* means "a disease of the joints in which a person's joints become inflamed and swollen." *Rheumatoid arthritis makes joints very painful and sensitive to the lightest touch, particularly during the initial swelling stage.*

Riding the Goats *Riding the Goats* was *"a favourite winter game in which we hung onto the hair on a goat's rump and ran behind it, and then let go and grabbed another goat whenever we got close to one."* (See also Fast rides**)**

Rocked-up *Rocked up* means "lined with rocks to make retaining walls along the sides of a creek. *The little creek was rocked-up as it ran under the root cellar.*

Root cellar (See Root house)

Root house The *root house* was "a specially constructed building with controlled-temperature year round to keep vegetables from decaying during storage." *The root house was made of large logs and straddled the little creek in the northeast corner of the house yard.*

Rough *Rough* is a ranch expression meaning "barely halter broken when first ridden." *Some of our fresh horses were pretty rough.*

Roundhouse *Roundhouse* means "a circular building with a huge turntable in it which is used to turn train locomotives around at the end of a railway spur line ready for the return trip to the main railway line." *The roundhouse at Beaver Mines had at one time been the terminus of the Kootenay and Alberta Railway, which ran out to the coalmines at Beaver Mines from the main line of the Canadian Pacific Railway. The junction with the CPR was about 10 miles west of Pincher Station, near Cowley, en route to the Crows Nest Pass.*

Rump *Rump* means "the top of an animal's hips". *We would give the hair on the goat's rump a little jerk to make the goat start running.*

Run on all fours Run on all fours means "to move along on one's hands and feet." *When I was little I liked to run on all fours along the ground — not on my hands and knees.*

Running up *Running up* means "coming forward." *The pine tree wagon tongue rested in a strap in the centre of the neck yoke suspended between the two ponies. It kept the cart from running up onto the ponies' heels and precipitating a runaway with the cart.*

Saddle horses *Saddle horses* means "horses which stand about fourteen or fifteen hands tall and are used mainly for riding." *Until I was about eight years old, we rode tall saddle horses to school.*

Sail in the wash tub *Sail in the wash tub* means "stand or sit in a wash tub and float around." *Bunny stood still with his legs braced, and sailed around in a wash tub.*
Saplings *Saplings* are "small poplar, or any deciduous, trees." *The Cyrs planted saplings around the edge of their lawn.*

Saucered his tea *Saucered his tea* means "poured tea from his teacup into his saucer to cool and then drank from his saucer." *Grandpa Vroom saucered his tea. When I got home I mimicked him. My mother was not impressed.*

School ponies *School ponies* means "smaller-sized horses which we rode to school every day." *We had to feed and water our school ponies before we ate our own supper.*

Section A *section* is "an area of land which has four ¼-sections for a total of 640 acres per section. *Alberta was divided into parcels of land called "sections."*

Separate *Separate* means "divided off." *The long lash of the bullwhip had separate thongs of leather.*

Shack A *shack* is 1. "a small enclosure made of boards." *The mailman had a little shack built to fit on his sleigh to protect him during the coldest weather.* 2. "a building once used as a house, but now used for storage." *The shack by our house had once been a summer kitchen, so was connected to the house with a short boardwalk.*

Shoeing *Shoeing* a horse means "the act of putting specially shaped, thin, semi-circular iron plates on the hooves of a of a horse." *Dad was shoeing a near-outlaw horse.*

Shortcut A *shortcut* means "a trail that is used to cut distance off of a regular route." *The shortcut made it quicker to ride to Grandpa Vroom's.*

Silvertip grizzly A *silvertip grizzly* is "a dark brown grizzly bear with light-coloured tips on its hair." *The grizzly bear that my dad trapped and shot in the fall of 1936 was a silvertip grizzly that stood six feet tall at the shoulders and had claws six inches long.*

Single-foot *Single-foot* means "a horse's gait where the horse moves its front leg and hind leg on the same side at the same time, giving the rider a sensation of rocking back and forth sideways." *Imitating my horse, I would single-foot along the floor.*

Singletrees *Singletrees* are "pieces of wood which swing in the middle and to which the traces of a horse's harness are fastened to pull a wagon, or other conveyance. A set of two singletrees is attached to a doubletree." *We hitched the ponies' traces up to the singletrees.*

Sleeping sickness Sleeping sickness means "a disease fatal to horses in those days." *Unfortunately, Rainbow contracted sleeping sickness and died before having a second colt.*

Smoky buckskin *Smoky buckskin* is "a yellowish colour with a tinge of grey-blue in it." *Smokey was a smoky buckskin goat, hence his name.*

Snake tracks *Snake tracks* "a series of S curves." *Our old Studebaker car made snake tracks up the muddy hill.*

Snow angels *Snow angels* were "patterns in the snow made by lying on our backs and flapping our outstretched arms to make wing patterns in the fluffy snow." *Once we were covered with snow we would often lie in the snow making snow angels.*

Snubbed *Snubbed* means "securely tied up with a short piece of strong rope." *He snubbed the bronc to a sturdy post at the corner of the box stall.*

Something useful *Something useful* means "some work." *When Baby Darling was two or three years old he was tall and strong; I decided it was time he was taught to do something useful.*

Spread Eagle Stampede Day *Spread Eagle Stampede Day* refers to "a show put on by the local cowboys at the Spread Eagle District fair grounds west of Twin Butte, and about 15 miles south of Dad's place." *Stampede events at the Spread Eagle Stampede included saddle bronc riding, bareback riding, steer riding and calf roping.*

Spring, the, a 1. The s*pring* means "the growing season of the year." *In Alberta, spring is considered to be from the end of March until the end of June.* 2. A *spring* is "a place where water flows naturally out of the ground from an underground water supply." *We watered our ponies by letting them drink from a trough filled with water from a spring down by Gus's gate.*

Squared away *Squared away* means "had got hold of both bridle lines and was seated firmly and upright in the saddle." *About the time I got myself squared away again, Dad flicked Dickie with the whip another time.*
Stack yards The *stack yards* was "a fenced-in area south of the house with several haystacks in it." *Haystacks were arranged in the stack yards in an orderly manner.*

Stage, mail stage The *stage* means "the vehicle that the mailman drove." *In spring, summer, and early fall the stage was a team and buggy; in the depths of winter it was a team and sleigh with a sort of shack built on top of the sleigh for protection.*

Stampede grounds The stampede grounds refers to "the area where the Castle River Stampede was held." *The hustle and bustle of getting all of us ready to go to the stampede grounds helped to take my mind off my disappointment.* (See also Castle River Stampede & Spread Eagle Stampede)

Stampede pick-up man A s*tampede pick-up man* is "a cowboy designated to lift bucking horse riders to safety at the end of their 10-second rides." *The stampede pick-up man's saddle horse was not well trained and shied away from the bucking bronco.*

Stillman, Mr. and Mrs. Bob *Mr. and Mrs. Bob Stillman* were "neighbours who lived one-half mile south of us." *We sometimes called on Mr. and Mrs. Stillman on the way home from school.*

Stone boat The *stone boat* was "a conveyance which Dad made by nailing several four-foot-long planks across two runners made of small logs which were peeled of bark, then flattened on the bottom and chopped slanted at one end." *Dad used the stone boat to haul rocks off newly cultivated land and to do various other chores around the ranch.*

Swing, big The *big swing* was "a two and one-half-foot-long plank that hung on two thick ropes that were tied to a branch of a large tree in our house yard." *Two children could sit side by side on the big swing.*

Swing, little The *little swing* was "a board about 16 inches long that hung on two ropes tied to a branch of a large tree in our house yard." *I often stood up on the seat of the little swing and pumped as high as I dared.*

Tack *Tack* is a noun meaning "horseback riding equipment, such as saddles and bridles." *Dad kept our tack well oiled and in good repair.*

Tagging along *Tagging along* means "going with someone else when you are really not wanted very much." *When Bill could walk better he started tagging along with Don and me on our various adventures.*

Tail pulled down *Tail pulled down* means "had the tailbone broken." *One mare had her tail pulled down, and never again could she raise her tail in the normal manner of horses.*

Tailed together *Tailed together* means "tied together nose to tail using the horses' halter shanks." *The smell of the bear spooked the packhorses, which were tailed together.*

Tell the truth *Tell the truth* in this case actually meant tell an untruth. *The trial dragged on and my mother was threatened if she did not tell the truth, which was actually not the truth.*

Temper To *temper* means "to harden hot metal by sudden cooling." *Dad plunged each fiery-hot horseshoe into a bucket of cold water to temper the iron.*

The big corral *The big corral* was "a large-sized pole enclosure located outside the house yard." *The goat house was located inside the big corral.*

The big garden *The big garden* was "a plot of land fenced off from the little pasture. It was located directly north of the corrals behind the barn." *We grew larger vegetables for winter storage, like turnips, parsnips, carrots, beets and horseradish, in the big garden, and also vegetables for summer use, like green peas, green beans, broad beans, spinach, Swiss chard, and other vegetables. We also had a rhubarb patch in one corner of the big garden.*

The big hill *The big hill* was "a high hill that was about one-half mile north of our ranch buildings. It was located in a fenced-in area of about a half section of pastureland that was fairly rocky and about half covered with small poplar trees with a few fir trees here and there." *Our horses and goats often ranged on the big hill.* (See also Bear Mountain.)

The big potato patch The *big potato patch* was "the largest of our three potato patches. *The big potato patch was located in the west quarter about one-quarter mile south of our house beside the road leading past one of our neighbours to the south — the Stillmans — and into Gladstone Valley.*

The island *The island* was "what we kids called a small, semi-circle patch of grass between the house yard fence and the water of the little dam. *We children sometimes had a picnic lunch on the island, pretending to be at some faraway place.*

The lane *The lane* was "a narrow strip of land about 400 yards long that had a wire fence on either side and ran along the west side of the big garden. The trail which ran down the lane connected the big hill area with the corrals by the barn on Mom and Dad's 'home quarter.'" *Getting a herd of horses headed down the lane required daring horsemanship.*

The little creek *The little creek* was "an unnamed stream which started from a fresh water spring that gurgled to the surface in the northeast corner of the little pasture." *The little creek ran west along the bottom of the side hill, which was located just northeast of the barn, then under a culvert and through a rocked-up channel underneath the root cellar.*

The little dam *The little dam* was "a small pond, formed behind an obstruction of boards, rocks and soil in the little creek." *We watered plants in the little garden with water from the little dam.* (See also House yard dam.)

The little garden *The little garden* was "a garden patch located right beside the house and ringed by a row of low red currant bushes." *We grew lettuce, radishes, green peas and a few early potatoes in the little garden.*

GLOSSARY

The little pasture *The little pasture* was "an eighty-acre parcel of land located on the north side of the east quarter of my parents' ranch." *The little pasture had a couple of open side hills, but was mostly covered with brush.*

The shack *The shack* was "a small building that was attached to the house by a short boardwalk and once was used for a summer kitchen." *We stored a lot of household furnishings that were not in everyday use in the shack when I was a child.*

The side hill *The side hill* was "a south-sloping, rock-strewn, grassy hillside located in the little pasture, just north of our main corrals and adjacent to and east of the big garden." *We often played or chased the goats on the side hill.*

The Sleeping Beauty *The Sleeping Beauty* was "an operetta produced by Miss Grace Genovese at Coalfields School." *Miss Genovese's production of the operetta "The Sleeping Beauty" was the Christmas concert that I remember most vividly.*

The stampede *The stampede* was "our usual way of referring to the Castle River Stampede." *Getting ready for the stampede was the most exciting time of the summer for Don and me.* (See Castle River Stampede)

The truth would out *The truth would out* means that "we would have to tell Mom sooner or later just what we were doing." *Mom judiciously accepted our evasive answers, confident that eventually the truth would out.*

The Valley *The Valley* is "the local name for Gladstone Valley which is a wide, bowl-shaped area which was formed by glaciers during the last Ice Age and through which Gladstone Creek runs." *Gladstone Valley is bound by ridges of hills on the north, west, and east sides, and by the main range of the Canadian Rocky Mountains on the south side.* (See also Gladstone Valley)

The wrong side The *wrong side* here means "the right-hand side instead of the left-hand side as in getting on a horse." *I had to mount the bicycle from the wrong side when I got on it from the barn door step.*

Thorn in my side A *thorn in my side* refers to "something that was a nuisance to me." *Henry was a thorn in my side.*

To boot *To boot* means "to get a little something extra over the price the person was willing/able to pay in a trade or sale." *Dad got some surly, mean tempered horses as a "to boot" in a trade or sale.*

To harness, verb. *To harness* means "to put an arrangement of leather straps and metal buckles, rings and snaps on an animal so that it can pull a load." *Our team had to be harnessed and hitched to our buggy for the eight-mile trek to the stampede grounds.*
(See also Harness, noun,)

To ripen, verb. *To ripen* means "to store a fruit cake in a cool dark place for about two months so that the flavours of the various fruits permeate the cake and blend with each other." *Granny Tyson always made her fruitcakes in early October and stored them in the cellar to ripen so that they were ready to use by Christmas.*

Toggle The *toggle* was "a heavy log about 16 feet long." *Dad assumed that the bear was exhausted and chained to the toggle.*

223

Tongue A *tongue* is "a wagon, or cart, pole. It is affixed to the axle of the cart and is used to steer and stop the vehicle when suspended from the team's neck yoke." *When the tongue slipped out of my team's neck yoke, we were in a dangerous predicament.*

Tongue for our cart A *tongue for our cart* means "a pole to affix to the axle of the cart we were building." *My team and I were ready when it came time to get the tongue for our cart.*

Topped off *Topped off* means 1. "riding a horse very warily for a few days when the horse is first brought in off the range until it remembers what being a saddle horse means and is gentled down again." *Horses like Babe never had to be topped off.* 2. "to finish a haystack in a special way." *The haystacks had to be topped off, in order to stay waterproof.*

Topped *Topped* means: 1. "came over the top of." *As Dickie and I topped the small hill, a strong gust of wind blew us down the other side.* 2. "exploded into a shower of red hot embers." *As each succeeding tree topped, the flames, helped by a brisk wind, jumped from tree to tree, spreading literally like wild fire.*

Town kids *Town kids* were "children who lived in Pincher Creek, the nearest town to our ranch." *Some town kids had spoiled Dickie.*

Traces *Traces* are "the heavier straps of the harness used to attach the work animal to the vehicle being hauled." *The goat harness traces were attached to a loop of baling wire at either end of the singletree on our toy wagon or toy sleigh.*

Trails over the big hill *Trails over the big hill* means "paths that the horses followed that ran either around the east or the west end of the highest part of the big hill. The big hill was in the half section of pasture land located to the north of my parents' east quarter section." *We often chased horses on trails over the big hill.*

Turn a somersault *Turn a somersault* means "make a flip in the air." *When we eventually slipped on a frosty, unstable pole we deliberately turned a somersault to land on our backs in a snow bank.*

Turn on a dime To *turn on a dime* means "to whirl 180 degrees standing almost on one spot." *Many saddle horses of the range-horse breed are strong and agile, and can "turn on a dime," as the cowboys say.*

Twin Butte, Alberta *Twin Butte, Alberta* is "small hamlet about eighteen miles south of Pincher Creek, and about fifteen miles southeast of our ranch." *Alfie and Alice Primeau lived in the Spread Eagle District west of Twin Butte, Alberta.*

Up the (Gladstone) Valley *Further up the (Gladstone) Valley* means "south of Dad's ranch, closer to the mountains than we lived, in the general area through which Gladstone Creek flows." *Henry Altermatt lived up the (Gladstone) Valley*

Up the Castle River *Up the Castle River* means "in the Castle River Forest Reserve." *At home we always referred to the area encompassed by the Castle River Forest Reserve as "up the Castle River."* (See Castle River Forest Reserve.)

Us kids *Us kids* refers to "us children." *Community events were great fun for us kids.*

Used our heads *Used our head* means "we considered what the consequences of any given action might be before we did the action." *We sometimes got ourselves into a jackpot because we had not used our heads.*

Utopia School *Utopia School* was "a one-roomed country school in the Fishburn, Alberta, district that my mother attended." *My mother attended Utopia School when she first came to Canada.*

Walk the corral rails *Walk the corral rails* means "to climb to the top rail of a pole corral and walk upright along it." *Don and I tried to see who could walk the farthest along the corral rails without falling off.*

Water trough A *water trough* on our ranch was "a large log that Dad had hollowed out using an axe and an adz." *Dad made two water troughs for us to water our livestock in — one was in the barnyard and the other was at the spring near Gus's gate.*

We big kids *We big kids* means "Don and I." *By then Bill was old enough to want to be where we big kids were.*

Well-reined A *well-reined* horse is "a horse that responds quickly to neck reining." *My well-reined saddle horse could turn on a dime.* (See also Neck reining and Turn on a dime.)

Well-trained saddle horse A *well-trained saddle horse* means "a very gentle, easy to handle horse for riding." *My dad always had a well-trained saddle horse ready for my mother to ride.*

West quarter The *west quarter* was "the quarter section of my parents' land located across the road from our house." *My parents owned two quarter sections of land — the "west quarter" and the "east quarter."*

Wethers *Wethers* are "castrated male goats." *Smokey and Baby Darling were big wethers.*

What they should know *What they should know* is "essential knowledge, in the opinion of the older siblings." *Older siblings try to teach younger siblings what they should know.*

Wheedler A *wheedler* means "a person, often a child, who persuades by repeating the same request over and over using different phraseology and/or body language." *I wheedled my parents into letting me do rather adventurous things that may have involved some danger.*

Wheeler The *wheeler* means "the animal which is hitched directly to a vehicle, such as a sleigh or wagon, when two or more animals are being driven in tandem." *Dad thought Baby Darling should be the wheeler because he was younger than Smokey.*

Whipped him on both sides *Whipped him on both sides* means "swung the ends of my bridle lines from side to side so that the tips of the reins would flick Dickie under the belly." *When Dickie finally started running, I whipped him on both sides to keep him going.*

Wild with fear *Wild with fear* means "terrorized." *Wild with fear, the horses plunged through any trees that were still standing, and over deadfalls which had accumulated on the forest floor over the years.*

Windfall (See Deadfall*)*

Women's Institute The *Women's Institute* is "a farm women's organization." *The Beaver Mines Women's Institute, to which my mother belonged, met once a month.*

Woodland *Woodland* is "land that is covered with willows and small poplar trees, with some saskatoon and chokecherry bushes." *There were animal trails throughout the woodland in the little pasture.*

Work bees *Work bees* were "social get-togethers of women held for a specific purpose." *Grandpa drove Granny to Canadian Red Cross monthly meetings and work bees, which were held in various homes in the Fishburn, Alberta district.*

Workhorse *Workhorses* is "a term which generally referred to horses which were used to pull a wagon or a farm implement. *When the little creek dried up, we had to water the workhorses at the spring by Gus's gate.*

Working horses *Working horses* means "horses which were used every day, generally for a specific task." *The horses that we rode to school were working horses.*

Would run away with his rider *Would run away with his rider* means that "he would get out of the control of his rider, who could not stop him no matter where he was heading." *Jackie would run away with his rider.*

Appendix II

INDEX

"Cush! Cush, Bess!", 133

"*Dickie*", 40

"*Pioneer Adventurers*", volume 2, 113, 166

1930s, 1, 3, 22, 97, 156, 160, 161, 166, 178, 209, 214, 217

Adamson, Patrick N., 135

airplane, 120, 121

airplane, forestry, 120

Akamina Highway, 159

Alberta, 46, 51, 55, 60, 107, 128, 136, 149, 161, 201, 207, 218, 220, 221

Alberta guide, licensed, a, 161, 162

Aldridge, Oliver and Rachel Anderson, 126

Aldridge, William "Bill" and Annie Rolph, 126

Altermatt, Henry, 59, 65, 86, 87, 204, 212, 224

Ambleside, England, 2, 127, 135

American Revolution, 2

amphi-theatre, a, natural, 98

angels, 5

Ankill, Mrs. Beatrice, 122

Annand, Betty. *See* **Baker, George and Betty Annand**

Annand, David, iv, 70

Annand, George and Betsy Penny, 143, 145

Annand, Jim, iv, 29

Annapolis Royal, Nova Scotia, 2

Annapolis Valley, Nova Scotia, 2

Annie Oakley, 24

Arrow Lakes, BC, 113

arthritis, 32, 82, 102, 137, *See* also rheumatoid arthritis

attitude, positive, a, 6, 47

Aunt Marion. *See* Cyr, Dominic and Marion Vroom

Avion Ridge, 145, 184

Babe, 22, 33, 40, 92, 96, 97, 203, 204, 206, 215, 224

Babin, John and Mrs. G., 31, 59, 87, 88, 214

Babin's, John, corner, 77, 214

Baby Darling, 75, 76, 77, 78, 79, 80, 87, 203, 209, 213, 214, 217, 221, 225

baby sitter, 80, 205

Baker, George and Betty Annand, iv, 143

Baker, William J. and Elsie, 116

Ballantyne, Alma, iv, 15, 20, 25, 44, 139

Ballantyne, Elva (McClelland), iv, 15, 20, 25, 59, 139

Ballantyne, George and Sarah McJanet, 15, 16, 25, 31, 114, 174

Ballantyne's Store and Post Office. *See* Beaver Mines Store and Post Office

bandage, figure-eight, 82

Barclay, Alex and Margaret Martin, 59

Barclay, C.J. and Mrs., 59

Barclay, Charlie and Sonia Chiesa, 59, 162

Barclay, William and Jane Rae, 25, 77

bareback, 37, 98, 115, 221

barefoot, 145

barn doorstep, 41, 158, 159

barnyard, 8, 9, 12, 13, 17, 21, 24, 28, 41, 54, 71, 76, 77, 80, 98, 99, 102, 109, 113, 115, 120, 123, 125, 132, 151, 155, 157, 158, 161, 163, 172, 205, 225

Bauerman Brook, 184

bay window, 16, 205, 207

BC boundary, the, 184

beadwork, 101, 155

bear grease, 192

Bear Mountain. See hill, the big

Beattie, Jack, 111

Beauvais Lake, *Alberta*, 140, 145

Beaver. *See* Beaver Mines, Alberta

beaver dam, 46

Beaver Mines. *See* **Beaver Mines, Alberta**

Beaver Mines Creek, 8, 31, 33, 36, 84, 87, 91, 110, 145, *167*, 177, 184

Beaver Mines Creek Valley, 25, 36, 59, 87, 109, 110, 112, 117, 166, 184, 186, 187

Beaver Mines dances, 16

Beaver Mines General Store. *See* Beaver Mines Store and Post Office
Beaver Mines Lake, 184
Beaver Mines livery stable, 174
Beaver Mines Store and Post Office, 17, 20, 22, 25, 56, 77, 103, 167, 174, 176, 177, 183, 207, 215, 217
Beaver Mines Tennis Club, 114
Beaver Mines Women's Institute, 16, 19, 21, 24, 145, 148, 225
Beaver Mines Women's Institute Hall, 22, 43
Beaver Mines, Alberta, 1, 4, 5, 10, 13, 14, 15, 16, 17, 18, 19, 20, 21, 22, 24, 28, 31, 34, 39, 42, 51, 52, 59, 75, 77, 79, 89, 91, 100, 101, 107, 108, 110, 114, 115, 118, 119, 120, 122, 125, 131, 137, 140, 141, 145, 146, 148, 155, 171, 172, 173, 174, 176, 178, 182, 183, 184, 186, 205, 206, 209, 210, 211, 212, 216, 219, 225
Bechtal family, 140
Becker, Eugene and Vivian Slater, 135
beef ring, 130, 205
Bennett Buggies, 168, 178, 205, 209
Bertha Creek, Waterton Park, 171
bicycle, 155, 156, 157, 158, 159, 160, 223
big garden, the. *See* garden, the big
biplane, 120, 121
Biron, George and Antoinette Babin, 31, 114
bit. *See* **bridle bit**
Blackburn, Cecil, 135
Blackburn, Clara V., 135
Blackburn, Laurie, 131
blacksmith, 9, 12, 19, 21, 34, 35, 39, 63, 151, 205, 210
blacksmith shop, 9, 10, 12, 19, 24, 34, 35, 39, 63, 97, 150, 151, 205, 210
Blairmore, AB, 161, 162
blinders, 169, 178, 206
blindfold, 110, 111, 206
Blondie, 101
Blood Indian Reservation, Cardston, AB, 106
blubber, 192, 195
boat, the, manure. *See* boat, the, stone
boat, the, stone, 168, 215, 218, 221
Bosley, "Kokie", 94, 96, 203
Bouthier, Mr. and Mrs., 114
box stall, 51, 66, 206, 220

brain wave, 28, 84, 206
Brand, Mollie Tson Vroom (horse), 156
Brands, Alberta Registrar of, 156
bread, baker's, 13, 52, 205
break our horses, 53, 206
breakfast, a, good, 72, 88, 146, 211
Bremner, Bill, 31, 59, 110, 206
bridle, 90, 109, 115, 136, 166, 195, 212, 221
bridle bit, 66, 206
bridle lines, 41, 53, 54, 119, 206, 221, 225
bridle rein(s), 24, 34, 38, 42, 43, 55, 57, 61, 93, 206, 210, 214, *See* bridle lines
Brocket, Alberta, 69, 127
bronc, 35, 48, 50, 51, 93, 98, 115, 140, 206, 220
bronc rider, 218
Brown, Isabella "Nichemoos", "Kookem" (Kootenai), 3, 66, 141, 143, 145
Brown, Kootenai, 3, 143, 180
Bruce, Anthony, 116, 184
Bruce, Katherine, iv, 26
Bruce, Major Edward (Ted) and Mabel, 17, 26, 31, 66, 79, 116, 184
Bruce, Michael, 26, 184
Bruce, Mrs. Ted (Edward), 17, 18, 19, 21, 38, 91, 107, 153, 156, 207, 215
Bruder family, 140
brush, 139, 223
Bucar, Betty, Stanley, Helen, 112
Bucar, John and Mrs., 31, 59
Buckhorn, the. *See* Ranch, Buckhorn
bucking bronco, 113, 218
buffaloed, 66, 110, 212
bullwhip, 41, 46, 207, 220
Bunny, 80, 82, 83, 84, 85, 207
bunny foot, 81, 82, 83, 88, 207, 209
bunt, 61, 63, 207
Burmis, Alberta, 31, 98, 120, 207
Burns, Jean McEwen, 121
bush. *See* bushes
bushes, 9, 148, 151, 159, 207, 222, 225
Cain, Melvin, 16, 25
Calgary Stampede, 102, 105, 188
Calgary, Alberta, 43, 215
Cameron, Miss, 114
Canadian Bucking Horse Champion, 105, 188

Canadian Expeditionary Force (CEF), 45

Canadian Pacific Railway (CPR), 31, 114, 219

Canadian Pacific Railway (CPR) settler's train, 112, 166

Canadian prairies, 128, 161, 207, 209

Canadian Rodeo Hall of Fame, 105

cantle, 21, 26, 207

caragana bushes, 207

Cardston Power House, 126

Cardston, Alberta, 29, 209

carpenter shop, 9, 10, 12, 24, 97, 148, 205

cart, the, building, 170

cart,a, our, the, 48, 117, 167, 168, 170, 171, 172, 173, 174, 178, 204, 216, 219, 224

Castle Mountain, 70, 145, 162, 164, 184

Castle Mountain, North. *See* North Castle Mountain

Castle Peak. *See* Castle Mountain

Castle River, 8, 70, 94, 95, 98, 101, 103, 107, 110, 116, 120, 125, 145, 156, 162, 163, 164, 165, 171, 179, 182, 184, 186, 192, 203, 205, 206, 207, 218, 221, 223, 224

Castle River Forest Reserve, 4, 107, 110, 112, 120, 162, 165, 167, 169, 171, 179, 182, 184, 187, 206, 207, 210, 218, 224

Castle River Forest Reserve, stock riders' (cow) camp, 186

Castle River Ranger Station, 161, 167, 169, 186

Castle River Stampede Grounds, 31, 98, 101, 103, 106, 221, 223

Castle River Stampede parade, the, 102, 203

Castle River Stampede, the, 94, 95, 98, 99, 101, 102, 103, 104, 105, 140, 156, 203, 205, 207, 209, 221, 223

Castle River Valley, 188, 193

Castle River, up the, 107, 162, 218, 224, *See* also Castle River Forest Reserve

Castle River, West. *See* West Castle River

catalogue, 155, 156, 157

chaps, angora, 26

chaps, buckskin, 101

chaps, goatskin, 160

chicken, 129, 147, 206, 207

Chicken Coop school. *See* School, Chicken Coop, Beaver Mines

Chief, 160

Chiesa, Noemi, 23

child, a, iv, 1, 9, 16, 29, 36, 47, 55, 76, 77, 103, 122, 139, 208, 218, 223, 225

childhood, iv, 1, 2, 3, 8, 47, 149

children, iv, 1, 2, 3, 7, 8, 16, 21, 28, 29, 32, 33, 39, 43, 47, 48, 54, 57, 61, 63, 71, 72, 84, 86, 89, 91, 93, 94, 99, 101, 102, 112, 113, 115, 117, 119, 120, 122, 127, 128, 131, 136, 137, 139, 142, 145, 146, 149, 152, 163, 177, 178, 203, 207, 208, 212, 213, 214, 216, 219, 221, 222, 224

Chinook, 33, 46, 154, 208

Chipman Creek, 145

chokecherries, 24, 128, 209

chokecherry jelly, 128

chokecherry syrup, 128

chokecherry wine, 128, 133

Christina Lake, BC, 169

Christmas, 17, 29, 42, 131, 156, 215, 223

Christmas concert, school, the, 42, 43, 156, 223

Christmas cooking, 131

Chuch, Ambleside Anglican, the, England, 44, 127

Church, St. John's Anglican, Pincher Creek, Alberta, 133

Churchill River, 8

Cisar, Frank, 59, 65

Cisar, W. and Mrs., 59

City Cafe, 119

Clarke Range, Rocky Mountains, 163

Clements, Miss Marjorie, 28

Clementsport, Nova Scotia, 2, 112

Clinic, Dr. Locke's. *See* Dr. Locke

close call, 48, 82, 160, 191, 208

closer coupled, 96, 208

coal, 115, 129, 211, 216

coal mine. *See* Number One Coal Mine

coal shed, 10

coal, lignite, 131

Coalfields school. *See* School, Coalfields

concert, school, Christmas, the, 156, 215

Condon, Milt, 161, 162

constraints, 47, 212

constraints, natural, or situational. See constraints

Corner Mountain, 65, 164

corral rails, 152, 154, 158, 225

corral, the, big, 9, 62, 63, 80, 205, 222

corral, the, little, 9, 205, 214

costume, fairy. *See* fairy costume

cow pies, 120, 158

cowboy, 3, 9, 12, 104, 112, 115, 201, 214, 221

cowboys, 93, 98, 102, 104, 105, 115, 140, 201, 214, 221, 224

cowgirl, 9, 214

Cowley, *Alberta*, 114, 147

cows came fresh, 70, 88, 208, 209

Cox, Orville and Essie McWhirter, 180

Crandell Mountain, Waterton Park, 171

cream separator, 132, 208

creek, the, little, 8, 10, 71, 72, 151, 154, 159, 205, 209, 213, 219, 222, 226

Crosbie place, the, 19, 31

croup strap, 169, 178, 206, 208

crow-hopping, 52, 208

Crown Brand horses, the, 108

Crows Nest Pass, 28, 112, 114, 120, 165, 166, 218, 219

crupper. *See* croup strap

culvert, 8, 96, 110, 133, 222

Currie, Gilles, 31

Currie, Grace, 44

curry comb and horsebrush, 98, 208

cut out, 9, 27, 93, 205, 208

cutter, 117, 208

Cyr, Dominic and Marion Vroom, 43, 60, 66, 112, 113, 114, 117, 119, 125, 140, 143, 145, 177, 208, 219

Cyr, Esther, 118

Cyr, Eugene and Dorothy Hahn, iv, 118, 119

Cyr, Marie Alberta, 118

Cyr, Rita. *See* D'Amico, Rita Cyr

Cyr, Vera. *See* **Gingras, Vera Cyr**

Dad, helping, 108, 212

Dad's pack and saddle horse outfit, 176

Dalager, Clara, Eileen, Marian, Neil, Tilman, Yvonne, 65

Dalager, Tom and Alice, 65

dam, house yard, 8, 84, 213

dam, the, little. *See* **dam, house yard**

D'Amico, Rita Cyr, 74, 118

Dandy, 97, 203, 204

Dartmoor pony, 60, 188, 203, *See* also *Jackie*

deadfall, 93, 106, 179, 189, 208, 225

Depression Years. *See* **1930s**

diamond hitch, a, 102, 192, 209

Dick, 128, 133

Dickie, 39, 40, 41, 42, 43, 56, 60, 96, 97, 203, 204, 207, 214, 219, 221, 224, 225

Dirty Thirties. *See* 1930s

double-deck, 5, 6, 23, 56, 57, 61, 115, 204, 209

double-jointed, 81, 82, 88, 209

doubletree, a, 169, 170, 176, 178, 209

Dowling, Dan, 59

down at the spring, 8, 209

down on the river, 128, 209

Dr. Brayton, 74

Dr. Locke, 66, 137, 138, 145, 160, 177

dropping his teeth down, 126, 209

dry, 36, 81, 85, 106, 127, 128, 129, 157, 159, 161, 165, 179, 195, 208, 209, 210

Drywood Creek, 66, 125, 145, 164

Drywood Creek, South. *See* South Drywood Creek

Drywood Mountain, 164

Drywood school. *See* School, Drywood

Dungarvan Creek, 145

eagle, golden, 184

Eastend, SK, 65

Eddy, Billy, 16, 31

Eddy, Jack and Mrs., 31, 114

Ekelund family, 98, 209

Elk Lodge, 25, 59, 107, 165, 167, 172, 173, 174, 184, 186, 187, 210

Elk Lodge Ranger Station. *See* **Elk Lodge**

elk, bugle, whistle, 193

emergency, 165, 167, 215

equipment, camping, 20, 217

equipment, horseback riding, 221

expedition, dangerous, 189

expedition, horse-chasing, 93

expedition, magpie-egg, 155

experiment, 79, 210

fairy costume, 42, 43, 156

fall, 5, 7, 9, 10, 33, 34, 57, 60, 69, 78, 90, 91, 92, 131, 145, 152, 158, 161, 182, 210, 220, 221

fall off, 10

families, ranch and farm, 5

family, the, baby of, 205
farmland, 28, 46
farrier, 34, 210
fast rides, 68, 210, 219
Fenton, Hughie, 59
filly, 95, 204, 210
fire, 34, 35, 46, 81, 131, 161, 162, 163, 165, 172, 182, 188, 210, 215
fire crew, 162
fire threat, 172
fire, forest, 162, 165, 166, 167, 172, 176, 179, 180, 181, 188, 209, 210, 215
fire, the, had its way, 165, 210
fire, wild, 161, 224
firefighter, 176, 178
firefighters, 120, 165, 166, 172, 176, 179, 181
fire-fighting equipment, 20, 165, 217
fire-fighting operation, 179
fireman, 57, 210
fire-ravaged, 172
fires, 120
fires, quick, 131
firewood, 81
Fishburn district, 2, 210
Fishburn Post Office, 135
Fishburn Townsite (Proposed), 135
Fishburn United Church, 135
Fishburn, Alberta, 1, 3, 5, 23, 122, 126, 127, 128, 130, 131, 133, 136, 210, 225, 226
Fitzpatrick, Glenn, 135
fizzy dope, 125, 210
flowers, cultivated, 136
flowers, houseplants, 174
flowers, wild, 86, 126, 133, 150
Fly, 101, 177
fly in the ointment, 39, 210
fly, the, on, 85, 217
foals, half-Shetland, 39
Foothills Creek, 125, 135, 145
foothills, Alberta, 23, 47
forge, 34, 35, 39, 46, 210
Fort Benton, Montana, 46
Fort Macleod, Alberta, 46
Foster, Gladys, Robert, 112
Frankish, Jack and Alice Jenkins, 25, 165, 173, 174, 182, 187
freak accident, 51, 210
Froese Bros., 135

fruit cake(s), 131, 223
gable roof, 151, 211
Gamache, Ed and Mrs., 31, 114
Gamache, Gus, 8, 31, 59, 115, 121, 178, 212, 218
Gamache's gate, Gus. *See* Gus's gate
Gamble, Archie, 176
gambrel roof, 53, 97, 150
games, 140
garden, the big, 9, 72, 222, 223
garden, the little, 9, 151, 222
Genovese, Miss Ida, 42, 211, 215, 223
get tired of it, 29
Gilmore Ridge, 78, 211
Gilmore, Mr., 87
Ginger, 53, 54, 55, 93, 203
Gingras, Vera Cyr, iv, 118, 164
Glacier National Park, Montana, 171
Gladstone Creek, 55, 65, 86, 125, 145, 164, 223, 224
Gladstone Valley, 4, 25, 55, 56, 65, 75, 77, 86, 99, 116, 137, 161, 162, 166, 169, 211, 212, 222, 223
Gladstone Valley School. *See* School, Gladstone Valley
Gladstone Valley, up the, 25, 59, 137, 224
Gladstone, Billy, 143
Gladstone, George, 66, 142
Gladstone, Mount, 109, 164
goat house, 10, 62, 75, 80, 85, 86, 87, 168, 203, 222
goat team, 77, 78
goat, lead, 77, 79, 80, 214
goat's milk, 72, 74, 75, 217
goats, the, nanny, 74, 75, 80, 88, 205, 207, 216
Goble, Frank, 171
going out to play, 146, 211
Gold, Glen "Rusty", 117
golden eagle. *See* eagle, golden
gone soft, 115, 211
Grace, Heather Bruce, iv
grade ones, the, 28
grade, the, 133, 148, 174, 205
grade, the same, 51
graded, the, dirt road, 172, 211
grades, the old, 115
Great Depression. *See* 1930s

Great Divide, Rocky Mountains, the, 163
Great West Saddlery Co. Ltd., 40
Great-Aunt Bessie. *See* Vroom, Ralph Voorhees and Bessie Newcombe
Grechman, Marion Vroom, iv, 3, 19, 34, 44, 94, 101, 104, 106, 115, 146, 205
Grechman, Mike, iv
grizzly bear, 4, 41, 179, 181, 186, 189, 192, 194, 216, 218, 220
grizzly bear, carcass, 187
grizzly bear, grease, 195
grizzly bear, head, 196
grizzly bear, jugular vein, 190
grizzly bear, nuisance, 181, 182, 183, 196, 216, 220
grizzly bear, pain-maddened, 190
grizzly bear, rearing, 191
grizzly bear, silvertip. *See* grizzly bear, nuisance
grizzly bear, skin, 192, 195, 196
grizzly bear, the, wanted a snapshot of, 189
grizzly bear, trap, 181
grizzly bear, trap, diagram, 188
grizzly bear, trapped, 187
Grunty, 26
gunnysack, 111
Gus's gate, 115, 159, 212, 221, 225, 226
Hagglund, Eric and Olga, 59, 64
Hagglund, George and Kay Kettles, 64, 66
Hagglund, Otto and Anna, 59
halter, 35, 51, 66, 77, 94, 115, 179, 206, 212, 215, 219, 222
halter shank, 113, 136, 179, 212, See also halter
halter, little, 215
Halton, Mrs., 5
Hamilton, Gordon, 31, 59, 64
Hamilton, Mrs. Jessie Wilger (Rev. Gavin), 31, 59, 64, 66
Hamilton, Rev. Gavin and Mrs. Jessie, 159
hand, 66
harassing, 119
Harder, Dave, 184
harness, 66, 69, 76, 77, 88, 94, 169, 170, 178, 206, 208, 212, 215, 216, 220, 223, 224
harness making, 21
harnesses, 68, 80, 167, 169, 170, 195, 212, 216

harnesses, buggy-horse, 168
Harwood, Arthur H. "Pop", 180
Harwood, Steve, 180
Hawk's Nest (Lodge), 163, 182
hay, loose, 212
hayloft, 105, 121, 131, 136, 212
hayrack, 62, 159, 215
haystack, 62, 68, 94, 212, 215, 217, 221
Henes, Edith, 112
Henry, 85, 86, 87, 203, 204
Hepler, George and Mrs., 59
Hepler, Josephine, 59
Heppner, Val, 135
high-tailed it, 7, 212
highway, Number Six, Alberta, 160
Hill, Gordon, Vada, 112
hill, the big, 9, 10, 13, 15, 26, 31, 43, 78, 89, 99, 159, 222
hill, the big, trails over, 9, 224
Hillier family, 140
Hillspring, Alberta, 129, 130, 132
hitching rail, 15, 21, 25, 26, 212
Hodgkins place, 116
Hollenbeck, Earl, 31
Holmes Grocery Store, 20, 22
Holmes, Betty (Mrs. J. Raffin), 20, 22, 112, 139
Holmes, Frank and Louise Riley, 3, 19, 20, 22, 28, 29, 31, 43, 56, 114, 118, 137, 139, 145, 206, 212
Holroyd family, 140
home free, 174, 212
home, my, 77, 115, 122, 211
hoof rot, 61, 213
hornets, 148, 149
horse stall, 51
horse, 17-hand tall, a, 66
horse, an outlaw, 49, 101, 203, 216, 220
horse, well-reined, 93, 216, 225
horse/pony, spoiled, 14, 39, 41, 66, 213, 224
horseback, on, 3, 5, 14, 33, 34, 39, 48, 52, 54, 55, 57, 93, 98, 102, 107, 117, 119, 136, 165, 187, 207, 211, 214
horses in training, 94, 213
horses, chasing, 13, 52, 53, 70, 99, 113
horses, hunting, 13, 20, 21, 37
horses, Morgan, 40, 216
horses, range, 93, 98, 218

horses, saddle. *See* saddle horse
horses, work. *See* **workhorses**
horseshoe, 35, 36, 213, 222
horseshoes, corked, 35
horsewoman, 5, 115
Hoskins, Grace, 31
hospital, 5
house yard, 7, 8, 9, 10, 21, 24, 48, 50, 61, 62,
    95, 96, 115, 125, 132, 150, 151, 152, 205,
    206, 213, 214, 219, 222
house yard fence, 8, 21, 151, 152
house yard garden. *See* **garden, little, the**
household well, 8, 213
Hudson Bay, 8, 55
Hughes, Tommy, 59
Hutterite colony school, a, the, 123, 136,
    209, 213
Hutterite Colony, East Cardston, Alberta,
    209
Hutterite Colony, Pincher Creek, Alberta,
    122, 125, 209, 213
Hutterites, 122, 123, 136, 209, 213
Ice Age, 55, 223
ice cream, 103
ice, glare, 33, 36
icehouse, *103*, 139
icy, 33, 35, 36, 90
if's, but's or maybe's, 165, 215
immigrants, 2, *16*
in foal, 94, 213
in tandem, drive, 77, 213, 225
Indianfarm Creek, 125, 145
island, the, 8, 222
Jack, Edith "Toots" (Hochstein), 129
Jack, Emil and Annie Hescott, 129
Jack, Harvey "Buck", 129
Jack, Irene (Slater, Marcinko), 129
Jack, Pearl (Hochstein), 129
Jackie, 60, 61, 188, 193, 203, 213, 226
jackpot, 47, 213, 224
Jaggernath, Ruby Peters, iv, 22
Jenkins, H.H., estate, 135
Jenkins, John E., 135
Jenks, Mr. and Mrs., 115
Joyce, Edward and Elsie Crosbie, 19, 31,
    114
Joyce, Jack, 22, 31
just my size, 39, 214

Kelly, Jack, 137, 160, 214
Kelly, Pat, 160
Kelly's Camp. *See* Castle River Ranger Station
Kemble, Vic, 178
Kerr, Jimmy, Betty, 112
kid, neophyte, 85
kids, 48, 76, 80, 81, 82, 85, 207, 214, 216
kids, we, 16, 20, 21, 24, 32, 34, 36, 62, 65, 84,
    87, 94, 126, 132, 138, 152, 161, 176, 183,
    209, 214, 222, 224, 225
Killarney of the Foothills, the, 151
Kimberley Airport, 135
Kimberley, BC, 135
Klazinsky, P. and E., 59
knee rein, 93, 214
knitter, 118, 130, 131
Kobza, John and Mrs., 31
Koermer, W., 59
Kookem Mrs. Brown. *See* Brown, Mrs.
    Isabella (Kootenai)
Kootenay and Alberta Railway, 22, 114,
    116
Kovatch, Joe, 97
Kyllo, Art and Christie Barr, 59, 65, 138
Kyllo, Gordie, 59
Kyllo, Peter and Petrena Aure, 114
Kyllo, Roy, 59
Laddie, 96, 177, 203, 208
LaGrandeur Crossing, 105
LaGrandeur, Esther, 112
LaGrandeur, Mary, 112
LaGrandeur, May "Chick", 112
LaGrandeur, Moise and Julia Livermore, 105
LaGrandeur, Pete, 39, 41, 110, 111, 190, 193,
    206, 218
LaGrandeur, Pete and Edith Vliet, 59, 105,
    112, 182, 184, 186, 187, 188, 191
LaGrandeur, Ramon, 112
LaGrandeur, Robin, iv, 112, 186, 188
Lailey, Evelyn Annand, iv
Lake District of England, 2
lane, the, 10, 222
lariat, 63, 83, 175, 208, 214, 216, 217
Larsen, Louie and Mrs., 59
law, martial, 165, 215
Leaf, 94, 96, 101, 203
learned the hard way, 92, 214
Lees Lake, 31, 120, 121, 151

leg, double-jointed, 82, 88, 209

lie down, 37, 38, 152, 204

light hand, 93, 214

lines. *See* bridle lines

lines, harness, 62, 66

Link, Fred and Anne Harley, 16, 31, 45

little creek, the. *See* creek, the, little

little pasture, the, 8, 9, 42, 72, 217, 222, 223, 225

Little, Joe, 135

loose hay, 62, 215, *See* hay, loose

Louise Bridge, Calgary, AB, 43

lower gate, 17, 215

Lowery, George, 31

MacFarlane, Winnifred, 2

Madorski, Mr., 5, 6, 215

magpie eggs, 154, 155

Main place, 116

man of honour, a, 132, 204

Map (1) House yard, barnyard and corrals, 1936, 10

Map (2) Beaver Mines – Castle River, ca 1935, 31

Map (3) Gladstone Valley and Beaver Mines Creek Valley, 1930s, 59

Map (4) Trails in the little pasture and over the big hill, 1936, 72

Map (5) Forty Miles on a Load of Poles, 125

Map (6) Fishburn District Neighbours, 1920s – 1950s, 135

Map (7) Vroom Ranch to Spread Eagle Stampede, 1934, 145

Map (8) Vroom Ranch to Killing the Grizzly Bear, 1936, 184

Marcellus, Claribel, 135

Marcellus, George, 135

mare, a brood, 22, 94, 95, 96, 97, 104, 106, 179, 203, 204, 206, 211, 213, 215, 222

mare, half-Shetland, 22, 92, 203, 215

Marr Lake, 125, 145

Marr school. *See* School, Marr

Martin, Floyd and Edith, 59

Martin, Howard, 59

Martin, Mary, 59

Matthews, Charlie and Mrs., 65

Matthews, Henry and Mrs., 59

Matthews, Wesley, 65

McAuley, Robert, 135

McClelland, Elva Ballantyne. *See* **Ballantyne, Elva (McClelland)**

McClelland, Sam and Elva Ballantyne, 59

McDonald, "Mickey" and Edna, 114

McDowall, Ken and Ina Kokkila, 20, 31

McDowall, W.D. and Emma Price, 26, 31, 43, 102, 114, 215

McFarlane, J.J., 135

McGlenning, Hector, 127

McGlynn, H.C., 135

McGlynn, H.E., 135

McLaughlin, Hugh, 186

McLeod, Mr. and Mrs., 114

McRoberts Store, Pincher Creek, 156

McVicar, Samuel and Gertrude, 114

McWhirter, Bill and Frances Riviere, iv, 66, 142, 180, 194

McWhirter, Logan and Ina Dyer, 180

Meade, Joe, iv

meat, bottling, 130, 206

Meridian, Idaho, 166

Metzler, J.W. (Bill), 135

Mike and Pearl, 62, *See* also workhorses

milk tea, 111, 215

Mill Creek, 65, 115, 116, 125, 145, 164

Mill Creek ranger station, 169

minnow, raw, a, swallowed, 147

minnows, 31, 147, 207

Missouri River, 46

Mitchell, Charlie V. and Sis (Buchanan), 45, 59

Mitchell, Washington and Belle, 116, 166

Model A, 125, 170, 178, 205, 217

Model T, 170, 178, 205, 217

Moodie, Mr. & Mrs., 114

Moonshine, 101, 203

Moose Jaw, SK, 45

Morgan, 26, 39, 40, 94, 95, 97, 203, 204, 211, 216

Mormon (LDS) Temple, Cardston, AB, 126

Morrison, Mr. & Mrs., 114

Moses with His Eyes Knocked Out, 203

mothers, little, 29

Motil, J., 31

Mount Gladstone, 55

Mountain Mill church, 43, 44, 114, 116

Mountain Mill railway trestle, 115, 116

Mountain Mill, Alberta, 31, 45, 115, 116, 145

Mrs. Nellie Gladstone Riviere. *See* **Riviere, Mrs. Henri Frenchy**
mushroom, giant. *See* puffball
my sister. *See* Grechman, Marion Vroom
mystery, the, was solved, 75
nanny, children's, 127, 131
neck reining, 93, 216, 225
New England, 2
Newman Peak, 145
Newton, George, 135
Newton, Thos. H., 135
Newton, W.P., 135
Nichemoos. See **Brown, Mrs. Isabella (Kootenai)**
Nickle. See Pickles
night sounds, eerie, 193
no trouble, 14, 189, 204, 216
noose, 63, 216
North Castle Mountain, 184
nothing to do, 39, 96, 139, 146, 216
Nova Scotia, 2, 13, 60, 118
nuisance birds, 154, 216
Number One Coal Mine, 19, 79, 139, 216
Number One Coal Mine hill, the, 174, 216
oatmeal porridge, 32, 130
oats, pan of,, 63
Oczkowski, J., 31
Old Moon. See Moonshine
Oldman River, 8, 55, 105
Oshawa, Ontario, 137
outhouse, 10, 82, 83, 84, 217
over the big hill, 72
ox train drivers, 46
ox trains, 41, 46
Pacific Coast, 114
pack train, 162, 165, 179, 181, 217
package of 'baccy, 176, 217
packhorse, 20, 98, 179, 180, 186, 192, 193, 209, 217
packhorses, 161, 165, 167, 179, 180, 181, 187, 188, 192, 193, 194, 195, 214, 217, 222
packhorses, heavily-laden, 193
Paddy, 12, 13, 14, 15, 17, 31, 107, 108, 109, 110, 111, 113, 115, 187, 203, 212
page wire fence, 9, 26, 217
palomino, 37, 76, 204, 217
panniers, 181, 184, 192, 195, 196
Paris green, 217

parked, 170, 217
parrot, 156
Pass Creek valley, Waterton Park, 171
Paulson, BC, 169
Peigan Indian Reservation, Brocket, AB, 69, 105, 106
Pelletier family, 123, 125
Perley and Rideau Veterans' Health Centre, Ottawa, Ontario, 19
Perley Rehabilitation Centre. *See* Perley and Rideau Veterans' Health Centre, Ottawa, Ontario
Peters, Miles and Mae Peters, 166
Peters, Miles and Mae Vroom, 22, 45, 165
Peterson, Chris, 135
Pickles, 54, 83, 97, 101, 146, 177, 203, 204
pick-up man. *See* pick-up men at the rodeo
pick-up men at the rodeo, 93, 104, 105, 106, 211, 218, 221
pickup, the, loosened up for, 104, 215
pictures, paint-by-number, *19*
pile, the, barn manure, 168, 205, 215
piled, 52, 93, 94, 115, 218
Pincher Creek, Alberta, iv, 2, 5, 15, 31, 39, 51, 55, 66, 105, 106, 117, 119, 122, 125, 127, 131, 133, 140, 145, 156, 160, 167, 201, 202, 203, 205, 207, 208, 210, 218, 224
Pincher Creek, the river, 66, 125, 194, 195
pinto, 67, 81, 95, 96, 204, 218
Planger, N., 135
planks, 168, 218
platform, a, the, mounting, 21, 37, 56, 96, 216
Pleasant Valley, 59
Pommier, Lorraine Riviere, iv
ponies, 48, 52, 53, 60, 84, 89, 90, 91, 92, 93, 95, 98, 99, 119, 121, 167, 168, 170, 171, 195, 204, 206, 213, 218, 219, 220, 221
ponies, half-Shetland, 40, 168
ponies, school, 52, 90, 91, 98, 220
ponies, Shetland, 39, 40, 41
ponies, the, trained, 168
ponies, the, training, 170
pony, half-Shetland, 96, 203, 204
pony, Shetland, 39, 40, 95, 203, *See* also Shetland
Pope, Mr. and Mrs., 114
porridge, 131, 132, 211

potato patch, the, big, 99, 222

prairie, 127, 178, 205

Prairie Bluff. *See* Corner Mountain

prairie, bald, 122, 205

. Prigge, Alan, Billie (Miss), Brian, Dennis, 169, 187

Prigge, Forest Ranger and Mrs., 59, 162, 169, 172, 187

Primeau, Alfie and Alice Riviere, 3, 66, 140, 141, 145, 194, 224

Primeau, Jimmy, 140

Prince of Wales Hotel, Waterton Park, 126

Prince of Wales, the, 113

Prozak, Mike, 8, 31

puffball, giant mushroom, 88

quarter section, 8, 55, 115, 128, 132, 136, 209, 212, 213, 218, 224, 225

quarter, our home. *See* **quarter, the east**

quarter, the east, 9, 10, 55, 77, 209, 213, 214, 222, 223, 224, 225

quarter, the west, 8, 55, 77, 99, 115, 155, 212, 213, 214, 222, 225

quick, 35, 48, 51, 208, 218

quick thinking, 175

quilting, 130, 218

Rackette, Adelle, 171

Rainbow, 60, 94, 95, 96, 97, 204, 211, 218, 220

raisins, 51

ram. *See* ram, the vicious

ram, the, 61, 62, 63, 85, 86, 216, 218

ram, the, to chase me, get, 63

ram, vicious, 62, 63, 90

ranch buildings, our, 91, 150

ranch economy, our, 94

ranch house, our, 10, 42, 82

ranch yard, our, 8, 78

ranch, a, the, 110, 111, 115, 118, 119, 120, 122, 139, 166, 168, 178, 182, 194, 195, 204, 205, 206, 207, 209, 213, 216, 218, 219, 221, 222, 223, 224, 225

Ranch, Buckhorn, 59, 183, 184, 186, 187, 193, 194

Ranch, EP, 113

Ranch, JO Guest (1950), 59

ranch, our, returned to, 34

Ranch, Ralph and Mollie Vroom, iv, 1, 3, 4, 5, 7, 8, 9, 10, 12, 17, 20, 21, 23, 26, 31, 39, 40, 41, 44, 45, 47, 48, 49, 51, 55, 67,

68, 70, 72, 78, 79, 86, 87, 89, 96, 97, 98, 101, 104, 106, 107, 140, 145, 149, 150, 162, 184

Ranch, Roodee, 116

Ranch, Victoria Peak, 66, 194, 195

ranch, work, 93

Ranche, Sunny Vale, 113, 186

range-horse breed, 93, 224

ranger station, forest, 107, 210

ranger, forest, 165, 181

ranger, forest, Mill Creek, 162

readin' and writin' and 'rithmetic, 29, 218

re-break, 40, 219

Red Cloud, 56

Red Cross, Canadian, 130

Red Rock Canyon, Waterton Park, 182

red-letter day, 117, 219

Remington, Glen, 60

Remington, Glen's Grandfather, 59, 61

Rex, 24, 33, 54, 95, 101, 146, 177, 204, 208

rheumatoid arthritis, 6, 13, 20, 51, 137, 142, 160, 167, 219

Ribbons, 24, 33, 52, 53, 60, 95, 97, 204, 208, 210, 218

Riding, 85, 86, 219

rifle, 190, 191, 192

rifle, Winchester, .30-06-calibre, a, 189

Riggall, Bert and Dora Williams, 163, 182, 192

rights, women's, 47

Riviere, Charlie "Chink", 65, 194

Riviere, Floyd and Evie Olson, iv, 143

Riviere, Frances. *See* McWhirter, Bill and Frances Riviere

Riviere, George and Maggie Clark, 66, 141, 142

Riviere, Henri "Frenchy", 66, 142, 145, 192, 194, 195

Riviere, Henry (son of George), 66, 142

Riviere, Inez (Rae), 66, 142, 194

Riviere, James and Gay DeMeester, 37, 66, 140, 141, 143, 155, 194

Riviere, Mrs. Nellie Gladstone (Frenchy), 3, 66, 142, 143, 145, 155, 194

Riviere, Nellie "Babe" (Murphy), 194

Riviere, Nellie (daughter of George), 66, 142

Robbins, Gerald and Adeline Cyr, iv, 118

Robert Kerr district, 129

Robertson, James, 135

rocked-up, 8, 151, 219, 222

rocking horse, wooden, 10, 14

Rocky Mountains, 4, 46, 55, 64, 70, 86, 149, 163, 189, 208, 223

root cellar, 8, 10, 53, 150, 151, 157, 211, 219, 222

root house. *See* **root cellar**

roses, wild. *See* flowers, wild

Rossland, British Columbia, 44, 127, 137, 162

rough, 7, 50, 54, 94, 151, 155, 159, 219

Round Mountain, 65, 70

roundhouse, 31, 114, 219

ruckus, a, heard, 75

rump, 193, 219

Rumsey, Clint and Mrs., 59

run on all fours, 50, 219

running up, 67, 170, 216, 219

rural mailboxes, 135

Russell, Andy, 66, 115

Russell, John, iv, 66

saddle, 5, 15, 21, 23, 24, 26, 37, 39, 41, 51, 52, 57, 60, 90, 94, 105, 109, 136, 147, 166, 167, 183, 195, 214, 215, 216, 221

saddle blanket, 109, 110, 206

saddle bronc, 218, 221

saddle cinch, 110

saddle horn, 6, 15, 21, 37, 57, 105

saddle horse, 5, 6, 7, 8, 12, 13, 14, 17, 20, 21, 23, 24, 26, 33, 34, 35, 36, 37, 40, 41, 47, 54, 56, 57, 63, 89, 90, 92, 93, 94, 97, 98, 99, 101, 104, 113, 117, 119, 141, 148, 187, 192, 195, 203, 204, 205, 206, 212, 214, 216, 217, 218, 219, 221, 224, 225

saddle horse, well-trained, 186, 225

saddle making, 15, 39

saddle stands, 90

saddle stirrup, 17, 21, 216

saddle up, 21, 118, 119, 120

saddle, adult-sized, 20, 56, 214

saddle, child-sized, 56

saddle, lady's, 20, 214

saddle, man's, 20

saddle, the little, 39, 40, 97

saddled, 7, 28, 41, 99, 101, 147, 195

saddle-pony race, kids', 102

Santa Claus, 29

saplings, 119, 219

Sarcee Army Camp, Calgary, AB, 45

Saskatchewan, 46

Saskatchewan River, 8, 64

saskatoons, 9, 24, 75, 128, 129, 225

saucered, 111, 220

school, 2, 3, 16, 27, 28, 29, 32, 33, 34, 35, 36, 37, 39, 41, 42, 43, 51, 52, 53, 54, 55, 56, 57, 60, 80, 89, 90, 91, 92, 94, 98, 117, 127, 141, 145, 156, 178, 187, 208, 209, 210, 211, 213, 218, 219, 220, 221, 225, 226

school divisions, large, 55

School game, Fox and Geese, 65

School game, Run Sheep Run, 65

School game, Two Batters Up, 64

School, "Chicken Coop", Beaver Mines, 112

School, Coalfields, 22, 25, 28, 31, 33, 36, 37, 42, 52, 55, 56, 64, 114, 155, 156, 206, 208, 211, 212, 215, 223

School, Coalfields, District, 55

School, Drywood, 145

School, Fishburn, the new, 135

School, Fishburn, the old, 135

School, Gladstone Valley, 53, 54, 55, 56, 59, 60, 64, 92, 156, 204, 211

School, Gladstone Valley, District, 55, 213

School, Gladstone Valley, route to, 56

School, Hutterite Colony, East Cardston, Alberta, 29, 209

School, Hutterite Colony, Pincher Creek, Alberta, 122

School, Marr, 125, 145

School, Spread Eagle, 145

School, St. Michael's, Pincher Creek, AB, 66, 118, 143, 177

School, Utopia, 125, 135

School, Yarrow, 125

Scobie, Mr. and Mrs., 114

Scout, 33

Screwdriver Creek, 25

Second World War, 1, 3, 135, 209

section, 9, 136, 218, 220, 222, 224

sewing machine, Singer, a, treadle, 130

sewing machine., Raymond, 156

shack, 10, 16, 76, 139, 156, 220, 221, 223

Sharp, Bob, 59, 65

shoeing, 21, 34, 35, 51, 220

short cut, 115

shortbread, Scottish, 131

shortcut, 28, 33, 36, 110, 136, 206, 220

show, a, just to help make, 104, 214

Sicotte, 31, 57

side hill, the, 8, 9, 10, 13, 15, 61, 71, 72, 80, 168, 222, 223

Silver, 37, 38, 155, 204, 217

Simpson, Will, 135

single-foot, 50, 220

singletree, the little, 76, 88, 215

singletrees, 170, 178, 209, 220

Slater, Cliff and Vi, 135

Sleeping Beauty, The, operetta, 42, *See* Genovese, Miss Ida

sleeping sickness, 95, 220

sleigh, 16, 62, 76, 77, 78, 79, 88, 89, 117, 131, 168, 178, 208, 215, 220, 221, 224, 225

sleigh runner, front, the, under, 62

sleigh, dog, 79, 174

sleigh, little, 69, 76

Smith, Dexter and Mrs., 114

Smith, Grant and Co., 116

Smith, Harry and Anna, 145

Smith, Jessie "Babe" and Iona (Truitt), 59

Smith, Max and Mrs., 59

Smith, Phyllis, 187, 194

Smithies, Edith Annand, iv

Smokey, 10, 12, 13, 75, 76, 77, 78, 79, 80, 87, 103, 203, 204, 206, 210, 213, 214, 215, 217, 220, 225

Smokey and Baby Darling, 75, 78, 79, 80, 102, 168

snake tracks, 125, 220

snapshot, 190

snow angels, 154, 220

snubbed, 51, 220

South Alberta, 208

South Drywood Creek, 164

South Saskatchewan River, 8, 55

Spellman Bros., 31

Spellman, Mr., 155

Spread Eagle District, 221

Spread Eagle school. *See* School, Spread Eagle

Spread Eagle Stampede, 140, 145, 221

Spread Eagle Stampede Grounds, 3

Spread Eagle-Drywood-Twin Butte area, 140

spring, 5, 6, 7, 8, 9, 14, 33, 35, 36, 37, 41, 50, 53, 56, 60, 68, 69, 70, 71, 72, 84, 90, 92,

115, 117, 121, 159, 195, 209, 212, 213, 216, 221, 222, 225, 226

spring thaw, 35

squared away, 41, 221

St. Henry's Roman Catholic Church, 125

St. Michael's Roman Catholic Church, 143

St. Michael's school. *See* School, St. Michael's, Pincher Creek, AB

St. Vincent's Hospital, Pincher Creek, Alberta, 5, 105, 106, 140

stack yards, 62, 68, 69, 77, 217, 221

stack yards, the, over at, 68, 210, 217

stage, 15, 16, 43, 75, 207, 219, 221

stampede pick-up man. *See* pick-up men at the rodeo

station, mounting, 15

Stevenson, Robert Louis, 153

Stiebertz, "Bear Grease\ John, 188

Stillman, Robert and Agnes Pope, 55, 57, 59, 99, 159, 221, 222

Stillman, Tom and Muriel, 59, 65

stirrup, the, got hung up in, 105

Stoney Indian woman, a, 101

storm, a, dry lightning, 161, 209

stranger, a, 86, 176, 204

straw hat, Mrs. Bruce's big, 92

Stuckey, Aylmer and Grace, 135

Studebaker, 125, 217, 220

stunt, that, pull, 19, 85, 218

success, 8, 15, 32, 38, 39, 47, 93, 117, 174

survival, 94, 128

sway-backed, 56, 204

swing, big, the, 152, 153

swing, little, the, 152

Swinney, Dave, Noreen, 112

Table Mountain, 55, 70, 109, 164, 183, 184, 187

tack, 40, 90, 136, 178, 195, 206, 212, 214

tagging along, 62, 221

tail pulled down, 179, 222

tailed together, 179, 222

tapederos, 40

Taylor, H.O. (Harry), 135

Taylor, J.E., 135

Taylor, Jas. E., 135

teacher, 28, 29, 42, 57, 59, 67, 122, 136, 211, 213, *See also* Clements, Miss Marjorie, *See also* Genovese, Miss Ida teaching, 28, 39, 48, 67, 106, 137

team and buggy, 16, 117, 221

team and wagon, 12, 39, 89, 122, 125, 129, 131, 133, 157

team, light, 167, 214

team, work, 89, 167, 168

Ted, 176

temper, 35

Terrill, William "Bill" and Dora, 180

test, the acid, 174, 205

Therriault family, 140

Thirties, the, Dirty. *See* Depression Years

Thomas, A.E. (Art), 135

Thomas, C.W. (Wes) and Dora Vance, 135

thorn in my side, a, 86, 223

threshing crew, 132

threshing machine, 132

Tippy, 67, 68, 204

to boot, 93, 223

to ripen, 131, 223

Toban, Bill, 116

toggle, 189, 223

tongue for our cart, 224

tongue, the, 126, 170, 174, 175, 209, 216, 219, 224

topped, 43, 161, 224

topped off, 62, 92, 203, 212, 224

town kids, 39, 40, 119, 224

traces, 88

trail, the, out on, 63, 74, 75, 217

trees, big fir, 45, 71, 97

trees, small poplar, 9, 119, 222, 225

trees, tall poplar, 151

triplets, 80

Truitt family, 138, 139, 211

Truitt, Adam "Dutch" and Hazel Anderson, iv, 162

Truitt, Cy and Phyllis, 3, 59, 137

Truitt, Harry and Bessie Mitchell, 25, 59, 64, 65, 184

Truitt, John and Melcina, 25, 59, 77

Truitt, Lawrence, 137

truth , the, would out, 168, 223

turn a somersault, 154

turn on a dime, 93, 224, 225

Turner Valley Oilfields, 126

Twin Butte*, Alberta*, 98, 140, 143, 145, 163, 182, 192, 194, 209, 221, 224

Two Spot, 96, 204

Two Step, 46, 56, 57, 204, 210

Tyson, George Wilson and E. Mary Brotherston, 1, 2, 5, 6, 23, 122, 123, 125, 126, 127, 128, 130, 131, 132, 133, 135, 136, 204, 209, 213, 218, 223

Tyson, Thomas Banks (T.B., Tom), 127, 133, 135, 204

Tyson, Tommy and Mary Laidlaw, 126, 127, 128

Ully, Chris, 135

United Empire Loyalists (UEL), 2, 215

United States, 2

Upton Lake, 125

used our heads, 47, 224

Utopia School, 3

valley, the. *See* Gladstone Valley

Varley, E.W., 135

Vent, Charlie, 59, 65

Victoria Peak, 65, 70, 145, 164

Victoria, BC, 86, 88

visors, green, see-through, 101

Vrom family, homestead, 2

Vroom, Alena Munro, 1, 2, 20, 59, 112

Vroom, Alena Munro, homestead, *1920s (NW ¼-29-5-2-W5)*, 59

Vroom, Alfred and Margaret Coulter, 43, 45, 169

Vroom, Archie, 45

Vroom, Bessie, snapshot of, 12, 13, 14, 15, 38, 49, 50, 54, 59, 60, 69, 86, 90, 153, 177

Vroom, Bill, iv, 3, 13, 23, 24, 31, 33, 40, 44, 53, 54, 61, 62, 67, 68, 74, 75, 76, 83, 84, 94, 96, 97, 101, 102, 103, 104, 106, 115, 125, 137, 147, 148, 164, 174, 184, 187, 191, 195, 196

Vroom, Claude, 34, 59

Vroom, Donald R., iv, 3, 4, 5, 6, 7, 12, 13, 14, 21, 22, 23, 24, 28, 31, 39, 43, 44, 48, 51, 53, 55, 56, 57, 59, 61, 63, 66, 67, 68, 81, 84, 94, 98, 99, 101, 113, 115, 119, 120, 122, 125, 127, 129, 133, 137, 141, 146, 148, 151, 152, 154, 157, 158, 161, 162, 164, 166, 168, 169, 174, 176, 177, 183, 195, 196, 203, 206, 208, 210, 213, 215, 221, 223, 225

Vroom, Doreen Lund, iv

Vroom, Great-aunt Bessie. *See* Vroom, Ralph Voorhees and Bessie Newcombe

Vroom, Harold and Ruby Mitchell, 6, 7, 31, 36, 43, 45, 59, 111, 112, 165, 166, 167, 186

Vroom, Jacquie Rusch (Mrs. Donald), iv, 135

Vroom, Joan White, iv

Vroom, Mae. *See* **Peters, Miles and Mae Vroom**

Vroom, Moe Swainger, iv

Vroom, Mollie Tyson, 1, 2, 3, 5, 6, 7, 10, 12, 13, 14, 16, 17, 19, 20, 22, 23, 24, 28, 29, 37, 42, 43, 44, 48, 51, 69, 71, 74, 80, 81, 82, 83, 87, 92, 95, 96, 101, 102, 104, 108, 109, 111, 118, 122, 125, 127, 128, 131, 133, 135, 137, 140, 141, 151, 156, 157, 162, 163, 183, 187, 188, 195, 207, 210, 214, 215, 220, 222, 225

Vroom, Oscar, 1, 2, 31, 59, 107, 108, 109, 110, 111, 112, 150, 167, 210, 220

Vroom, Oscar and Alena Munro, 43, 45, 113, 114, 116, 184, 187

Vroom, Oscar Jr., 45

Vroom, Peter and John, 2

Vroom, Ralph, 1, 2, 3, 4, 5, 7, 8, 10, 12, 14, 16, 19, 20, 21, 23, 24, 27, 29, 32, 33, 34, 35, 36, 37, 39, 40, 41, 43, 46, 47, 49, 50, 51, 52, 53, 56, 57, 60, 61, 62, 63, 66, 67, 68, 69, 71, 72, 74, 75, 76, 77, 80, 81, 82, 83, 85, 86, 87, 89, 90, 92, 93, 94, 95, 96, 97, 98, 99, 100, 101, 102, 104, 105, 106, 107, 108, 109, 110, 111, 112, 113, 115, 116, 117, 119, 120, 121, 125, 133, 137, 139, 140, 145, 148, 149, 152, 155, 157, 158, 161, 165, 166, 167, 168, 172, 176, 177, 178, 179, 181, 183, 187, 188, 189, 190, 191, 192, 193, 195, 196, 197, 204, 215, 220

Vroom, Ralph and Mollie Tyson, 1, 10, 13, 20, 29, 44, 45, 48, 51, 56, 61, 64, 87, 91, 94, 99, 104, 107, 108, 119, 122, 123, 139, 140, 141, 183, 195

Vroom, Ralph Voorhees and Bessie Newcombe, 60, 61, 118, 177

Vroom, Ralph, homestead, 1920s (SW ¼-28-5-2-W5th), 59

Vroom, Ralph, where he shot and killed the grizzly bear, 184

Vroom, Robert and Isabel, iv

wagon, 5, 26, 76, 77, 80, 88, 125, 157, 158, 159, 167, 168, 170, 183, 187, 195, 214, 215, 216, 219, 224, 225, 226

wagon box, 12, 157

wagon load, 129

wagon, little, 69, 76

walk the corral rails, 152

Walkey, Dr., 75

Wall Lake, 180

warden, national park, 181, 191

Warren, L., 31

wash tub, the, sail in, 84

water tank, 132

water trough, 8, 41, 121, 159, 205, 212, 225

Waterton Lake, Upper, 171

Waterton Lakes National Park, 34, 107, 126, 135, 142, 143, 145, 159, 171, 180, 182, 184, 207

Waterton River, 125, 128, 132, 135, 209

West Castle River, 186

West Castle Ski Resort, 186

wethers, 87, 88

Wheat Pool, 132, 133

wheedler, 12, 225

wheeler, 77, 79, 80, 225

whipped him on both sides, 41, 225

White Leghorn chickens, 112, 166

Whitney Creek, 65, 145

wild men, 177

wild roses. *See* flowers, wild

Winchester, .30-06-calibre, a. *See* rifle

windfall, 93, 106, 208

Windsor Mountain. *See* Castle Mountain

Windsor Peak. See Castle Mountain

Windsor Ridge. *See* Castle Mountain

Wojtyla, A, 8, 31

Women's Institute. *See* Beaver Mines Women's Institute

woodland, 9, 225

woodpile. *See* **firewood**

work bees, 130, 226

work, ranch, 89

workhorses, 8, 17, 35, 62, 70, 88, 89, 90, 123, 131, 226

World War I, 45, 116

World War II, 34, 45, 74, 104, 135, 196, 197,
 See also Second World War
would run away, 60, 226
wrong side, the, 158, 223

Yarrow Creek, 125, 140, 145
yoke, a, neck, 170, 174, 175, 216, 219, 224
Zurowski, Harry, 28, 31

ABOUT THE AUTHOR

Bessie Vroom Ellis published her first book, *THE VROOMS OF THE FOOTHILLS: Adventures of My Childhood* in 2003. It is the story of her happy, adventurous childhood on her parents' ranch in the foothills of southwestern Alberta.

Bessie attended one-room country schools for her elementary grades, riding on horseback for a round trip of nearly nine miles each day. She graduated from Pincher Creek High School and attended Calgary Normal School. Bessie taught in a country school near Drumheller, AB, and at Waterton Park School. In Waterton, she met and married a local resident, George Annand Jr. They raised a family of four children, Edith, Evelyn, David and James.

During her more than 20 years in Waterton Park, Bessie wrote feature articles and the column "Wonderful Waterton" for *The Lethbridge Herald*. She also contributed news items to CJOC Radio and CJLH-TV in Lethbridge, and to *The Calgary Herald, Calgary Albertan,* and the *Hungry Horse News* of Columbia Falls, Montana. She was active in the Girl Guides of Canada and the Anglican Church.

After 15 years at home, Bessie returned to her teaching career. She updated her qualifications, through night extension classes, Summer School and day classes. Bessie was awarded a Bachelor of Education degree by the University of Lethbridge and a Master of Education degree by University of Alberta. She then taught in Lethbridge.

After her remarriage in 1975, Bessie moved to Regina, SK, and taught there for another 15 years, for a total of over 29 years of service in the teaching profession. At the University of Regina, she earned a post-graduate Diploma in Educational Administration.

During her years in Regina, Bessie travelled extensively in Canada, Europe, Mexico, and the United States. She was active in politics, running for political office herself, and then working to promote the election of more women at the provincial and federal levels. In the early 1980s, the Saskatchewan New Democratic Women (SNDW) established the Bessie Ellis Fund, which assists women running for nomination.

In 1992 Bessie was awarded the Commemorative Medal for the 125th Anniversary of the Confederation Canada, 1867 – 1992, "in recognition of significant contribution to compatriots, community and to Canada." Upon retirement, Bessie returned to her writing. She is currently writing a second book in the series entitled *THE VROOMS OF THE FOOTHILLS: PIONEER ADVENTURERS.*